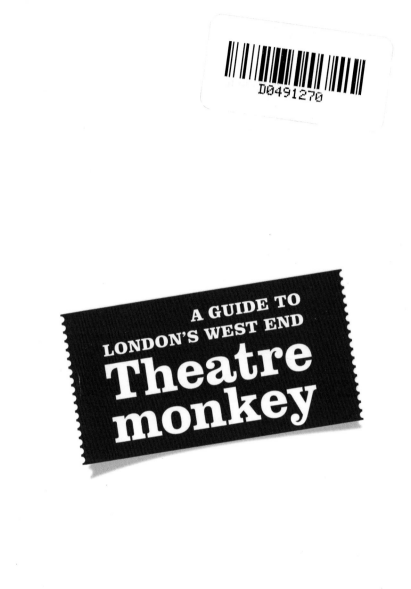

A GUIDE TO
LONDON'S WEST END
Theatre
monkey

For Mum and Dad

Published by Red Squirrel Publishing

Red Squirrel Publishing
Suite 235, 77 Beak Street
London W1F 9DB, United Kingdom
www.redsquirrelbooks.com
First Edition – First Impression
ISBN 9780955215988

Edited by Frances King

Proofreading by Robert Clark

Designed and typeset by Cox Design, Witney, Oxon

Printed and bound in Italy by LegoPrint

Contents

Section 5: Other London Concert and Performance Venues 133

Fringe Theatre Details 141

Further Reading 145

Acknowledgements 147

Map 148

Foreword by Mark Shenton

Of all the websites about the theatre – and I've contributed to a few in my time – none provides a more bespoke or remarkably candid and useful guide to negotiating the minefield of West End theatres, from the inside out, than Theatremonkey.com. It's a work of serious passion as well as diligent research. Like many web-based information sources, it has grown exponentially thanks to user comments, so it's no longer the work of just one man but an entire community of interested and passionate theatregoers.

There's now a sense of ownership, as well as serious authority, to its commentary. And while you can, of course, retrieve this treasure trove on your mobile phone web browser or PDA, it's a relief to finally be able to carry around this information in the form of the book that you're now reading, instead of downloading it first.

You'll find wonderful nuggets of quirky information in these pages, such as a story that the actor-manager of the Garrick Theatre likes to pat his actors on the back as they take the stairs to the stage … except that he died in 1927! But more than that, you'll also find out exactly where to sit in every part of each theatre – and any problems that might arise, row-by-row and sometimes even seat-by-seat. I love the discovery of front-row seats on a ledge in the balcony of Wyndham's, where "Theatremonkey considered permanent nesting residence, until management warned that any signs (banana skins, cable TV installation etc.) would result in its indefinite ban." There are also insiders' chapters on everything from how to get into sold-out shows to how to get discounts, the differences between agencies and touts and how to behave in the theatre. There's even a useful note to anyone who wants to impersonate being a critic: "Just look scruffy, old, bored, drunk, and show up on opening night or a performance very soon after. Actually, only the last is compulsory. Write furiously on a pad at the interval."

Joking aside – and there are plenty of good jokes in this book – theatreland is in a state of simultaneously unparalleled regeneration and degeneration. On the one hand, literally millions of mostly public (and some private) money has been spent on refurbishing the Royal Opera House, the Royal Court, the Almeida, Hackney Empire and the London Coliseum, while an entirely new building was expensively created for Hampstead Theatre to replace the temporary prefab construction that housed it for more than 40 years. The privately wealthy impresario and theatre owner Cameron Mackintosh made his vast fortune in the theatre. Now that he's ploughing some of those profits back into a wide-ranging scheme to regenerate the venues in his control – a scheme that's seen the Prince of Wales, Novello (formerly the Strand), Noel Coward (formerly the Albery), Wyndham's and Gielgud theatres join a refurbishment programme that his group initiated when it took over the management of the Prince Edward – the gauntlet has been thrown down for other theatre owners to follow suit.

Except that, by and large, they're not. Andrew Lloyd Webber, who presides over the theatres in the Really Useful Group, recently admitted to me: "You can't make a business case for owning theatres." Instead, he has gone public with an idea, voiced in a House of Lords debate, to suggest something more radical:

> "Most of them should be demolished and replaced. I love Victorian architecture, but you cannot alter the fact that a lot of these theatres were built at a time when people were literally and physically a different shape, let alone when there was a class system, with galleries that nobody wants to sit in any more. And nobody wants to sit in a theatre that has got pillars in it, and they don't want to sit in a theatre that isn't air-conditioned. But how do you air-condition a theatre which is Grade 1 listed? To restore the Theatre Royal, Drury Lane to the standard of the Royal Opera House today, you'd be talking of £200–£300m. So if we're going to keep buildings like this, I would have thought we will have to have a public subsidy, or they ain't going to survive. Or it may well be that there are a couple of rich Russians out there who would just like to own it in 20 years' time!"

Maybe so, but Mackintosh suggests a different possibility. When he talks about the transformation of the Prince Edward Theatre – the first privately owned commercial theatre to have had such an extensive face-lift – into one of London's most desirable musical houses, he says:

> "I hope that the money I'm spending will come back in my lifetime, but whatever happens, I will leave for my Foundation and indeed for the enjoyment of future theatregoers, buildings that are in a much better state than when I got them."

Such altruistic passion has rarely informed theatre ownership, the stock of which has been passed from pillar to post, literally, over the last century. Theatre buildings have famously high overheads. The costs of these, of course, are passed onto the theatre producers who hire them, if they're occupied, but borne by the owner if not, with the result that essential maintenance and refurbishment usually has to work around the shows, rather than in between them. But beyond those patch-up jobs, little is being done to stop the wholesale rot.

It's high time that something was done, or some of the 40 West End theatres that are commercially owned and managed – and between them account for some 5/6th of the total attendances in London – will eventually fall into a state of permanent disrepair, and that means they won't be able to function as working theatres any more. Of course, until the 1880s, theatres would routinely burn down within an average lifetime of around 18 years, so there'd be a natural process of renewal and refurbishment. Better fire protection and better buildings have created their own problems.

And in a world where the short-term gains of immediate profit are put ahead of the ambitions of long-term conservation and respect for what contributes to that cash cow, the situation can only get worse. This is a depressing spectacle to anticipate for any book that hopes to celebrate visiting these unique venues. But maybe, in pointing out the many pleasures alongside some of the penances of theatregoing, this book can also contribute to the debate that will ensure it lives on as one of London's defining features.

Mark Shenton is theatre critic of the Sunday Express, *writes a daily blog for The* Stage (www.thestage.co.uk/shenton) *and is London correspondent to Playbill.com.*

About this guide

A teenage theatregoer once found himself seated beside a noisy sound desk. Determined to avoid that happening again, he started asking questions and taking notes on every London theatre he visited.

In December 2000, his findings found their way online, as a private joke for friends. The unique colour-coded seating plans, special offers lists and humour attracted other surfers, many contacting "Theatremonkey" to share their own opinions. At their suggestion, advice on common problems like finding reliable ticket outlets and getting into "sold out" shows were added. And so Theatremonkey.com grew, with that teenager now writing as "the Monkey".

Theatremonkey's pages are always frank, independent and written from a paying customer's perspective. This is the founding concept to which it remains firmly attached. Now those practical tips, hints and seating plans are distilled here into this active guide to 21st-century London theatregoing.

How the guide is organised

With every adventurer seeking something different, each section of this book deals with a separate aspect of your theatre visit.

The first addresses those "Planning an Expedition" questions from first-time visitors. What's on, what's worth seeing, when to visit and theatre layouts.

The "Ticket Buying Jungle" explains how theatres capture your cash, sorts reliable seat sellers from rogue, and offers tactics for netting the most desirable seats.

"Native Wisdom" shares theatregoers' tips on saving cash, beating "sold out" signs, and things worth knowing before, during and after your visit.

Finally, Theatremonkey gives a "Theatre by Theatre Guide" to the main venues, sharing notes on seating, comfort and sightlines, distilled from thousands of readers' experiences.

SECTION 1: Planning an Expedition

End is centred around Sha...
...nt Garden and Piccadilly, w...
...ctoria and Waterloo. Most th...
...hed, usually housing shows...
...roducers hoping to profit by...
...e. Generally, lavish musical...
...eatres; classic or modern pl...
..."me" casts occupy the small...

... or subsidised venues, inclu...
...ouse, National Theatre and ...
...freer to experiment. Gover...
...allows them to present less...
...k in short seasons or fast-ch...
...hercial producers swoop on...
...nd lucrative) commercial tra...

...ne, throughout London are ...
...y funded fringe venues putt...
...new writing and innovative

What's on where?

Choosing a show is simple. Theatremonkey.com lists everything playing in the West End, and there are many other sources of information available. Below are a few of its favourites.

The Society of London Theatre's (SOLT's) officiallondontheatre.co.uk and the independently owned londontheatre.co.uk have comprehensive present and future listings for West End and fringe productions. SOLT's *Official London Theatre Guide* and glossy flyers for individual shows are found in all theatre foyers, plus many hotel, tourist attraction and restaurant leaflet racks. Many ticket agency booths also have their own guides available. SOLT also publishes a free weekly email news summary. For a fee, take SOLT's bi-monthly print *Theatre List* (020 7557 6771).

The full West End spread is published daily in newspapers, including *The Times*, *Daily Telegraph*, *Guardian*, *Evening Standard* and *Metro*. The *Daily Mail* newspaper's brilliant Baz Bamigboye column each Friday has a reputation for breaking the biggest West End stories. The weekly *Time Out* magazine covers practically every performance in the London area.

If you're a true hardcore fan, a glance through the auditions page of actors' newspaper *The Stage* can provide early clues about upcoming productions or shows that are extending their run. Whatsonstage.com and dresscircle.co.uk discussion boards are full of sometimes accurate rumours, though a good few are like chips – best taken with a pinch of salt.

What's to see?

On any given night, over 50 productions are performed in the West End alone. Feeling overwhelmed by choice? Theatremonkey's suggestion is to ask: "What do you enjoy reading or watching on television?"

Period costume drama? Try Ibsen, Chekhov, Goldsmith – the glories of centuries past – and don't forget longer musicals like *Les Misérables*. Staged Shakespeare is often more thrilling than any Hollywood film. Read the first few scenes, maybe catch a film adaptation or listen to a recording beforehand and you'll be fine.

Soap operas, easy stories and strong characters? Consider modern comedy and drama from Tom Stoppard, Alan Ayckbourn and Ray Cooney; or maybe classic musicals by Rogers and Hammerstein or Andrew Lloyd Webber could suit you. The broader-minded may also risk more experimental fare featuring stronger language and themes.

Talent shows and singing contests enjoyed with friends? Try musicals like *Mamma Mia!* combining popular songs with new stories, or stage adaptations of screen hits like *Dirty Dancing*. The communal atmosphere can be intoxicating.

With youngsters in the group, do remember that all theatre requires concentration (plus Zen-like ability to shut out uncomfortable seats and enthusiastic amplification). Can everybody sit still and silent for long enough? If a two-hour film won't hold a child's attention, thinking "maybe next year" could avoid an expensive mistake. Also be aware that theatres can't admit ticketholders with "babies in arms" and do not have baby-changing facilities or crèches. Some shows with strong language or adult content will post parental advice or impose age restrictions.

Which to choose?

Professional reviewers (or "critics", though they hate that term) usually attend a single press night rather than attend individually over a number of days as on Broadway. The *Evening Standard*, *The Times*, *Telegraph*, *Guardian* and *Independent* newspapers publish their opinions overnight. Whatsonstage.com usually provides a round-up of all these online.

The internet provides a space for mingling professional and public views. Theatreguidelondon.co.uk's professional reviewers regularly revisit productions to comment on changes, while Theatremonkey.com publishes public opinions throughout a show's run. Whatsonstage.com and Dresscircle.co.uk operate informative discussion boards. Infamous "Dress Circle Dave" is gone, but posters like "Theatresquirrel", "BoOverall", "Queenie", "Daniel K" and "Mr/Mrs Hugel" provide hours of fun, advice and commentary. The acclaimed blog westendwhingers.wordpress.com records the cynical yet truthful opinions of two ordinary theatregoing folk.

London theatre awards, presented annually by a number of organisations, may help you distinguish between shows. The Laurence Olivier Awards take place in March each year. Organised by SOLT, they're voted on by a panel of appointed professionals and ordinary theatregoers. The *Evening Standard* Theatre Awards (November) are bestowed by their experts, and the Critics' Circle (January) by their conclave of professional reviewers. Any interested internet user can vote in the Whatsonstage. com Awards (February), which produces a result reflecting public opinion.

When to go?

Major new productions usually open between March and May or during October and November, with fewer in the potentially non-air-conditioned heat of July and August. Season-specific entertainments, such as Christmas pantomime and summer holiday crowd pleasers, fill out the roster. Productions close when audiences dwindle, usually giving two weeks' notice before their demise.

Most productions play Monday to Saturday evenings with two extra afternoon (matinee) performances and extra shows during holiday periods. One matinee is usually on Saturdays, the second between Tuesday and Friday. Typically Tuesday, Wednesday and Thursday matinees begin between 2pm and 3pm. Friday and Saturday early shows start anywhere between 2pm and 5.30pm. Musicals usually start earlier than plays, as longer is needed to reset the stage and resuscitate the cast between performances.

Substituting Sunday for Monday performances is a recent development, with family-friendly and fringe shows most likely to experiment. If popular, this could eventually replace the Monday to Saturday timetable as the normal pattern everywhere.

Friday and Saturday evenings, particularly those early in the run of a big musical, can feel special with a more smartly dressed, sometimes celebrity-sprinkled, crowd. Matinees seem to attract mature audiences, plus children during weekends and school holidays. School parties favour examination syllabus productions like *Blood Brothers* and *The Woman In Black*. Early September and late May see fewest attending as their new school year or examination traumas take priority.

The Monkey likes midweek afternoons and evenings where actors are not worn out by performing an earlier matinee. The first Saturday afternoon after press night seems to test performers' reserves after a week of pressure and partying. During the closing week, a "muck-up matinee" may see actors take subtle liberties with their show, sometimes to the producers' irritation. Beyond heightened audience enthusiasm, the final performance is rarely specially marked.

The press/opening night is mostly for professional reviewers and invited guests. Occasionally, at the biggest new shows, press attend one evening and other VIPs attend another. Remaining tickets are sometimes made available to the public a day or two beforehand. Ask at the box office, but expect to be seated in the cheapest areas and safely out of stalking range.

Previews are the first chance to polish shows in front of paying audiences. They're not always cheaper, sometimes contain sketchily written material and may be cancelled at short notice or even abandoned mid-performance should scenery jam on stage. Sightline issues, particularly in front, rear or extreme side seats, may also emerge as staging is tested. Try for dates nearest to the press night, when the show is frozen (finally set at how it will be performed on opening night). Be careful if you're planning a special visit around early previews, and always confirm that performances are happening before travelling.

If seeing a particular performer is important to you, check for known absences when booking. Previews and the first two weeks following press night are usually the best bet, but theatres don't guarantee appearances. The Monkey's observation is that actors are most likely to appear on Fridays and Saturdays.

Which seat?

London theatres are usually rectangular, with tiers of seats facing a stage at one end. Each tier has a name and this is often unique to the particular venue. Unfortunately, things can get a bit confusing – the grand circle may not be all that grand if it's the top tier. To simplify this, on Theatremonkey.com and in this book, the Monkey uses the traditional tier names (ascending from the ground up): stalls, dress circle, upper circle and balcony. Any variations from these terms are highlighted as required.

For Broadway visitors, stalls translates to orchestra, dress circle to mezzanine, upper circle to second mezzanine and balcony to third. On British seating plans, the stage is shown at the bottom of the page, furthest balconies at the top. Beware of ticket touts ("scalpers" in Broadway speak) passing off balcony tickets as mezzanine to the unwary.

Seats are assigned by tier name (plus a block number in large pop venues), row letter and seat number. Unlike Broadway, London numbering is sequential, left to right and, say, 1 to 20 (rather than 101 for central seats with odd numbers for the left block and even ones for the right).

Stalls

Stalls lie in front of and just below the stage, on a slightly sloped (or raked) floor. The best rakes slightly raise audience heads above those in front, while allowing for circle overhangs. The worst slope downwards, entrenching baffled theatregoers below those in front.

Rows labelled AA, BB, AY, AZ or similar early letters of the alphabet first are found at the front of the auditorium, and may be added or removed as productions require. Rows designated XX, ZA or similar will be at the back of the theatre.

The very front row may be sold cheaply either out of generosity or to compensate for any neck ache from staring up at a high stage, scenery disrupting sightlines or the orchestra conductor bobbing into view. Otherwise, front stalls seats are the most expensive in the house.

Increasingly, producers designate seats they feel have the very best views as "premium" and charge around 30% more to occupy them. Some producers choose to designate only a few seats as premium, with box office staff mentioning them to customers only if specifically asked. Others openly promote whole centre sections as prime, and are then sometimes observed puzzling over the gaping hole in an otherwise full auditorium.

The back rows are cheaper, to compensate for distance or because views are restricted by balcony overhangs, pillars and so on. Beneath balcony overhangs, these rows can become unpleasantly stuffy without air-conditioning.

"View blocked by large people ahead" is a common stalls complaint. Shallow rake and poor offset (how seats are placed to view between the two in front) do little to ease this problem. Luckily, there is often "the slump". As Ms Tall relaxes, sinking into her seat, your view will clear wonderfully.

Dress circle

The dress circle is the first tier above the stalls, usually overhanging around two-thirds of all stalls rows. As in the stalls, the front rows are the most expensive in the house (auditorium), with perhaps some premium or restricted-view tickets sprinkled among them.

The circle's own front corners, the overhanging circle above, pillars, safety rails and lights clamped to the circle's front wall may intrude into sightlines. Shorter patrons often find prime views from front rows, though legroom may be tight for many others. As downstairs, rear rows can again become hot without air-conditioning.

Upper circle

Overhanging the dress circle, front upper circle rows cost around the same as rear stalls. The least expensive seats in the house are behind them, if there isn't a balcony.

Balcony

Above or behind the upper circle in larger theatres, here are the cheapest seats of all.

Both upper circle and balcony often suffer the same problems as the dress circle. Sound can be quieter up here, too. Some theatres have benches rather than individual seats in rear rows. Without balconies overhanging, patrons often have a better view of the whole stage compared to those occupying rear stalls (if vertigo isn't keeping their eyes shut). Pillars are not usually a problem in the top balcony, but extra safety rails may be.

It can be a long climb to your seats: pack crampons and Kendal Mint Cake. A few theatres still have separate entrances directly from the street to the balcony, bypassing the main foyer. Waiting outside in winter can be a chilly experience.

Other seating options

Boxes are small colonies of seats on jutting shelves in the side wall space between stage and balconies, or behind the stalls and dress circle. Most have sideways vertiginous views, losing the nearest corner of the stage. Retiring types might feel as if they're on display, although observing other audience members can be fun, particularly for "reality TV" fans.

Boxes generally have normal chairs rather than fixed seats, making them more comfortable. Note that some theatres insist you buy the whole box rather than just one seat. The positive side of this is that you share it only with your own choice of well-mannered companions.

Slips, formed in some theatres by extending a circle's front row alongside walls towards the stage, share similarly restricted views with less legroom.

For the truly desperate, some theatres will sell standing places behind or beside rear seats. These usually become available only after all other tickets are sold.

Some productions offer on-stage seats. This can allow close communion with actors; closer still if occupants are incorporated into proceedings. Not for the shy.

Overseas visitors should also allow for London's older theatres having uncomfortable differences in seat size. Boxes, outermost seats and gangway rows that do not have anything in front of them generally provide better legroom, though often at the expense of sightlines. A few venues, such as the Leicester Square and Prince of Wales theatres, have installed modern wide seating. Others, like the Donmar Warehouse which have armless benches, allow two seats to be purchased for single occupancy. Sometimes, armless standard chairs can be set in wheelchair spaces or boxes for larger patrons.

For parents of fractious youngsters, boxes or back row aisle seats near exits allow privacy and a quick escape. Limited supplies of booster seats are often made available for children (and small adults), particularly at child-orientated productions; arrive early to claim them. Stacking folded coats under young behinds is an alternative (but remember to remove your expensive BlackBerry® from the pocket).

Those sensitive to noise should choose seats furthest from potential speaker locations (upper circle, perhaps) rather than popular installation spots in the front stalls or boxes. Theatremonkey's experience is that the sound balance near the rear stalls mixing desk is often good.

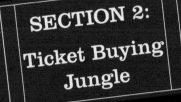

SECTION 2:

Ticket Buying Jungle

Having decided when to go,
what to see and where to sit, the
next step is to secure seats.

Tactics vary, depending on whether you're
seeking to book something specific in
advance or just fancy a cheap night out.

Just like buying an airline ticket, what
you pay and the seat you receive in return
often depend on where, when and how
you buy it. The Monkey shares "native
knowledge" on discounts and getting
into "sold out" shows in the next section.
First, it looks at how tickets are sold,
and potential pitfalls along the way.

Before buying

Genuine outlets will always make clear the ticket's face value (the original price set by the producer) and highlight any problems, like restricted views. Tickets are sold on a non-refundable and non-exchangeable basis. Specific performers' appearances are not guaranteed unless it's a solo show, of course, and refunds are only issued if the show is cancelled or less than half has taken place.

Allocations

Venues themselves hold the widest selection and largest number of tickets available. Often these are sold using an appointed "lead agent" (as the Monkey thinks of them). From a single office, perhaps in Nottingham, Manchester or even County Donegal, the lead agent provides all the necessary outsourced facilities for a chain of venues. It's no coincidence that some telephone operators are unfamiliar with the venue they're selling – they may never have visited it.

Remaining tickets are divided among official agents, usually members of the Society of Ticket Agents and Retailers (STAR), who charge higher booking fees. The final result is that each official outlet holds a different stock of seats at varying prices.

From around 24 hours before the show, agents' unsold seats are "marked back" (returned) to the theatre for sale, along with any "returns" (tickets that customers can't use), "house/production seats" (tickets that producers have kept for themselves but don't need) and "day seats" (tickets specifically reserved for sale on the day of the performance).

Booking fees

These are charged on all transactions. Only visitors buying tickets at the actual venue avoid them, unless the producer feels charitable. Uncharitably, some pop venues impose fees even on personal visitors who pay by credit card.

Lead agents charge the lowest fees. Around £1.50 to £8 is average, per seat or per transaction (regardless of how many seats you buy), or sometimes both. STAR ticket agencies usually limit service charges to around 28% above face value. Members of the Ticket Agents Association (another fine trade organisation) limit service charges to around 25%. Fees are usually minimal or waived on discounted tickets from all sources.

Increasingly, theatres add a mandatory restoration fee, too (revenue raised is assigned to a trust account for venue restoration). Theatres sometimes show this involuntary philanthropy as a separately billed item on website booking pages and receipts.

Payment

MasterCard and Visa, plus Maestro debit cards, are widely accepted; American Express, Solo, Delta and Electron less so.

The UK uses the Chip and PIN system. To ensure smooth transactions, overseas customers should seek advice from their issuer, and notify them that they're using their card abroad. One reader suggests overseas visitors do this before buying from a UK-based website, to ensure the card won't be declined at the crucial moment.

Personal cheques drawn on UK banks are welcome everywhere except Delfont Mackintosh venues. Ticketmaster only accepts cheques with written requests; most others will hold telephone reservations for a few days until your cheque arrives and clears.

Many box offices and agencies sell gift vouchers (gift certificates). Choose carefully. SOLT Theatre Tokens (see www.theatretokens.com or call 0870 164 8800) are accepted at many venues nationwide. Other issuers' vouchers make sense mostly if you regularly buy from their particular outlet. Theatremonkey readers occasionally report difficulties redeeming vouchers; issuers' helplines usually resolve problems efficiently.

For administrative reasons, some box offices may require a specific payment method, particularly immediately before the show. Always bring both credit cards and cash if possible. No venue, however, will accept Mother's favourite antique family silverware or other gifts in kind in exchange for that last hot ticket.

Ticket delivery

With enough time, and a UK address, tickets are posted – sometimes at extra charge. Otherwise the theatre or your STAR agent's outlet holds them for collection on the day. Make sure vendors have multiple contact details, including your home and hotel, just in case.

Arrive an hour or so before if possible (earlier if collecting meal vouchers before dining), preferably bringing your confirmation email or booking reference number. Remember that the actual card-holder and payment card used must be present. If your card is due to expire before your visit, hang on to it as renewal cards may have different numbers, which may make things awkward for you.

Occasionally, for administrative reasons, theatres will ask you to exchange your STAR agency-issued tickets for their own before entering the auditorium. Ushers will direct you to the appropriate counter.

Some companies allow online bookers to print tickets instantly, for a cheeky extra fee. Although not yet widely adopted, venues are also experimenting with sending virtual tickets to mobile phones.

Box office basics

Foyer counters

These are generally open Mondays to Saturdays from 10am until 8pm. They're closed on Sundays unless there's a performance, when they'll open for a few hours. If the theatre is dark (i.e. there are no performances), they may close at 6pm or display signs asking you to book at a nearby venue in the same chain.

Some venues accept bookings for others in their chain, as well as their own shows, which saves tourists' time and feet. Remember that lunchtimes see longer queues and advance bookings can't usually be made in the hour before the show.

Online booking

Computers constantly reserve and release tickets, so check back regularly. Some theatres allow you to select your own seats from the same selection that telephone operators have. You may need a Java plug-in for this (if so, the website will prompt you to download it).

If you're unable to choose seats directly, study seating plans before buying your tickets. A website fault once meant that a Theatremonkey.com reader was offered two seats split by an aisle. At quiet times, you may be able to work through entire allocations, using "back" buttons or holding tickets in multiple browser windows. Try this too often, though, and you could be kicked off the system. One reader ruefully remarked: "I didn't know when to stop, and lost what I wanted [while] seeking something better." With careful timing, it's also possible to compare online and telephone offerings simultaneously.

Mass releases for major events, particularly at 9am on Fridays, swamp some systems. Avoid such releases, unless specifically chasing these tickets.

Search engines like www.comparetheatretickets.com can scan multiple sources for online availability. Be aware that these miss seats from those outlets that keep their online and offline stocks separate, and that some search engines' results may include returns from unofficial sellers.

Telephone booking

The best clerks work hard to find good seats for polite customers but can't predict whether there'll be unsold tickets or discounts and can't conjure up extra seats from nowhere. If you're using a discount code, do avoid embarrassment by mentioning it immediately. Offers for "best available" tickets are often restricted to specific seats, and clerks need to know which tickets to look for.

You might find that box offices are quieter in the mid-afternoon, during popular soap operas or important football matches. When there is a rush for newly released seats, some people suggest dialling at odd intervals, for example every fourth not fifth minute, to beat "line busy" signals. Dialling numbers for other venues that share the same call centre as the one run by the lead agent sometimes works, if clerks haven't been instructed to refuse requests made via those lines.

Venues handling their own calls may still transfer you to a lead agent at busy times or outside working hours, and you may find there's a higher booking fee for this 24/7 service.

Specialist teams, with dedicated telephone numbers, exist to help people who have special access requirements or who wish to book for groups of ten or more.

Postal booking

You'll need to provide a list of dates and seat choices and give permission to charge your credit card up to a fixed amount. Do also enclose a stamped self-addressed envelope. You'll have to trust the theatre to allocate decent seats, but the Monkey has never been disappointed.

Other ticket outlets

STAR members

The 25 or so full members of the Society of Ticket Agents and Retailers (STAR) specialise in providing lead agency services or reaching particular markets like corporate clients, overseas visitors, groups or plutocrats (or the spontaneous but impecunious!). Committing themselves to selling a show, often paying for weekend tickets in advance, STAR members provide valued support to the industry and are an excellent option. Look for the STAR logo online and at booth outlets around London.

Buying from STAR members also provides consumer protection, thanks to a strict members' code of conduct. They even maintain evening duty desks to help theatre staff resolve clients' ticketing problems on the spot, which certainly isn't a service provided by touts.

Secondary sales websites

These allow ticket holders to resell seats; a very few of these websites are also given tickets by venues themselves.

The Monkey isn't keen on these sites, feeling that some offer easy opportunities for touting tickets that genuine customers could otherwise have bought at normal prices. Also, despite purchase guarantees, if venues refuse admission with fake tickets or those marked "resale prohibited", cash can't compensate for a ruined evening.

Ticket touts ("scalpers")

These vultures infest the internet, theatre doorways and booths around London. At best, you'll be overcharged; at worst, you'll be turned away at the theatre.

If you buy in person, genuine outlets confirm prices and seat numbers before expecting payment. Staff identify your seats on seating plans and hand over tickets immediately; they never say "pay now, collect later". They sell from computer screens, occasionally telephoning venues directly to obtain extra seats, and issue tickets bearing their company name. They don't use personal mobile phones (cellphones) to buy stock from friends, and don't hawk tickets from raincoat pockets to crowds outside venues.

Avoid dodgy desks in doorways and disused shops. Signs can occasionally look convincing but if they don't have the STAR logo, keep on walking. Scruffy notices promising seats to high-profile sold-out sports and pop events, and those claiming to offer "hottest tickets tonight" and unspecified "bargains" are always bad signals.

Never, ever, accept tickets with missing or blacked-out prices or tickets that are already sealed in an envelope. Check your tickets carefully before paying and, if in any doubt whatsoever, just walk away. One reader wishes he'd walked away:

> "We didn't know 'grand circle' meant 'upper circle' and the man in the booth certainly didn't tell us. He never told us either that we were paying a premium for the seats: the tickets were waved in front of us and then put into an envelope with the receipt and the envelope was sealed. We finished up in seats from which we were unable to hear or see. Stupid? Yes, we were. Gullible? Yes. But we are not regular theatregoers and, sadly, I still tend to trust people. It was bad enough being ripped off, but a very rare evening's enjoyment was totally spoiled."

Official newspaper advertisements use licensed show logos and contain the main box office number, and maybe details of other authorised outlets. Any that just list events and promise seats in the first few rows are worth ignoring.

Online searches may list tout-owned sites before official ones, as sharp operators buy show and theatre name variations. If the website doesn't have a STAR symbol, has high service charges, or is missing VAT or comprehensive contact details, click elsewhere.

A former box office manager writes:

"A group of five Greek people booked through a website that seemed fine. Charged £115 per seat, no tickets were left for them at my theatre and there was no way of contacting the company. I had to turn them away."

It really can be a jungle out there.

STAR members guide

NOTE: (£) indicates that a booking fee of 10% to 15% is usually added to full-price ticket sales; (££) indicates that around 22% to 28% is added.

Often Lead agents

KEITH PROWSE
www.keithprowse.com   0870 840 1111   (£)

SEE TICKETS*
www.seetickets.com   0870 830 0200   (£)

TICKETMASTER UK
www.ticketmaster.co.uk   0870 534 4444; 0161 385 3211   (£)

Ticket centres include

GREENWICH TOURIST INFORMATION CENTRE
2 Cutty Sark Gardens, Greenwich, London SE10 9LW

TKTS
Kiosk 4, Centre Court, Upper Ground Floor, Brent Cross Shopping Centre, Prince Charles Drive, Brent Cross, London NW4 3FP

Recommended by Theatremonkey.com readers

ABBEY BOX OFFICE
www.abbeyboxoffice.co.uk   020 7798 9200   (££)

Branches:
Victoria: 55 Wilton Road, London SW1V 1DE
Marble Arch: Bryanston Street, Marble Arch, London W1H 7EH
Covent Garden: 30 Jubilee Market, Covent Garden, London WC2E 8BE

Scrupulously honest about booking fees, and staff really know their shows. Good choice of seats, plus discount bargains and insightful help at their West End counters.

ALBEMARLE OF LONDON
www.albemarle-london.com   0871 240 2978   (££)

Hotel desks include
Claridges, The Dorchester, Grosvenor House

Known for immaculate service and a famously informative website. Experienced staff offer sensible advice along with some top seats.

ENCORE TICKETS
theatremonkey.eolts.co.uk   020 7492 1515   (££)

Branches
The Original London Sightseeing Visitor Centre, 17–19 Cockspur Street, Trafalgar Square, London SW1Y 5BL

Opposite M&S Simply Food, West One Shopping Centre, 381 Oxford Street, London W1C 2JS

Discounts on long-running musicals and "meal and show" packages are a speciality, with the occasional surprising price quoted nearer showtime.

LASHMARS
www.londontheatre.co.uk/lashmars   020 7494 1767; 020 7494 1739   (££)

Hotel desks include
Sheraton Park Tower, Chesterfield Mayfair, London Marriott Grosvenor Square, London Hilton Park Lane

The oldest ticket agency name in London, with the family still involved in its day-to-day operations. Wonderful seats and deep knowledge amassed over many years. The Bond Street of the industry. A stylish and classy West End institution.

LASTMINUTE.COM
www.lastminute.com   (£)

Internet favourite, particularly renowned for cheap lucky-dip deals. Pick a show, hand over as little as £10 and collect your ticket on the day. Seat numbers not confirmed in advance, but readers invariably report being delighted on arrival.

LEICESTER SQUARE BOX OFFICE
www.lsbo.co.uk   020 7494 2301   (££)

Branches
1 Leicester Square, London WC2H 7NA
42 and 48 Cranbourn Street, London WC2H 7AN

Rated highly by Theatremonkey.com readers for availability. Their Leicester Square shops (not to be confused with the tkts booth) offer good last-minute bargains.

LONDON THEATRE BOOKINGS
www.londontheatrebookings.com   020 7851 0300   (££)

Branches
The Hippodrome and Hippodrome Foyer, 1 Cranbourn Street, London WC2H 7JH
St Martins's Court, 23 St Martin's Court, London WC2N 4AL
The Crystal Rooms 7–8 Cranbourn St, London WC2H 7JH
10–14 Cranbourn Street, London WC2H 7JH
Coventry Street, 31 Coventry Street, London W1D 6AS
188 Shaftesbury Avenue, London WC2H 8JN
4 Irving Street, London WC2H 7AT

Absorbed many older ticket agencies, including Rakes. Now famous for selling cheap last-minute tickets from Leicester Square Hippodrome booths as well as online.

LOVETHEATRE.COM
www.lovetheatre.com/theatremonkey 020 7907 7000   (£)

Owner and operator of Theatremonkey.com's Ticketshop. Motivated by quality, service and value, ensuring Theatremonkey.com readers try it first. Plenty of outstanding special offers available. Meal and Show packages are famously good value, refusing to tie clients to using a single restaurant or pub (instead, vouchers come with a long list of dining choices).

PICCADILLY BOX OFFICE (LONDON)
www.piccadillybox.com   0800 018 3123   (£ to ££)

Branches
Booth on Piccadilly Circus, junction of Regent Street, London W1J 0TR
2 Villiers Street, London WC2N 6NQ

Specialist in half-price and discounted tickets from their booths. Free telephone number for on-the-day and advance bookings. Prices quoted include booking fees of between 5% and 25%.

WEST END THEATRE BOOKINGS LTD
www.uktickets.co.uk   0871 789 1004   (££)

Branches
Criterion Theatre, Piccadilly Circus, London W1V 9LB
Leicester Square Underground Station, Charing Cross Road, London

Prides itself on good advance availability, both full price and discounted. Centrally sited shops, featuring many offers for that day, are recommended.

Other STAR outlets

ETICKETS LONDON LTD
www.ticketsyouwant.com   020 7734 2088   (££)

LONDON THEATRE DIRECT
www.londontheatredirect.com   0871 733 1000   (££)

Mostly an online trader. Wide choice of prices and cheap packages.

THEATRE TICKETS DIRECT LTD
www.theatreticketsdirect.co.uk   020 8429 7456   (££)

A newer operator with a growing reputation.

TICKETWEB
www.ticketweb.co.uk   0844 477 1000   (£)

This is Ticketmaster's site for smaller venues. Online bookings often attract lower fees than telephone transactions with them.

Accommodation package operators

Superbreak Ltd	www.superbreak.com	0871 221 3344
Theatre Breaks	www.theatrebreaks.com	0800 458 3408
LondonBreaks.com	www.londonbreaks.com	020 7492 1600

Group specialists

Ambassador Theatre Groups	www.ambassadortickets.com	0844 871 7627
Applause Groups	www.applausegroups.com	020 7014 8444
Delfont Mackintosh Theatres	www.delfontmackintosh.co.uk	0844 482 5100
Encore Groups	www.encoretickets.co.uk/group	020 7492 1525
Group Line	www.groupline.com	020 7580 6793
See Tickets Groups*	www.seetickets.com	0844 412 4650
Ticketmaster Groups	www.ticketmaster.co.uk	0844 844 2121

* See Tickets is not currently STAR registered, but is the official outlet for The Really Useful Group Theatres, plus many other venues.

How do regular theatregoers
effortlessly afford frequent trips,
manage to see "sold out" shows and
have their complaints heard?

The Monkey shares a little
of their native wisdom.

Saving cash

For those prepared to visit personally, the most famous discount outlet of all is tkts – the Society of London Theatre's official half-price theatre ticket booths. You'll find tkts in front of the Odeon West End Cinema, Leicester Square, and on the upper mall at Brent Cross Shopping Centre, Hendon, London NW4 3FP.

tkts booth, Leicester Square

The industry's own outlets offer a choice of plays and musicals, plus the occasional ballet or opera. Tkts.co.uk (updated daily at 11am) lists a selection of performances that day, with actual availability confirmed at the booths on arrival.

Many tickets can be bought up to seven days ahead for half their face-value price, with a few extra choices available at a smaller discount. A booking fee of £3 per seat is added to keep the system going.

Saving visitors' time, and giving more-distant venues a central box office outlet, the booths also sell some full-price tickets without a booking fee. Ticketmaster provides further advance booking facilities for events not otherwise offered, adding their usual agency fee. From Leicester Square, it may be cheaper to walk to the actual theatre for these.

Booths are open Mondays to Saturdays 10 am to 7pm and Sundays 12 noon to 3pm (in Leicester Square) or 6pm (in Brent Cross). Lines move quickly, and choices are plentiful, whatever line-prowling touts would have you believe.

The Leicester Square tkts booth accepts cash (sterling and euros), SOLT Theatre Tokens, MasterCard, Visa and Maestro debit card, but no personal cheques, other foreign currency or travellers cheques. The Brent Cross tkts booth doesn't accept cash, but accepts Brent Cross Gift Cheques.

Other ways to save

Upper circle, balcony and any day seats are cheapest; dress circle and stalls are more expensive. Midweek matinees and previews are sometimes cheaper; Friday and Saturday evenings are perhaps a few pounds more (no, not so the cast can afford fish and chips between performances!).

Almost all West End productions discount, some regularly, others not. Good timing and the right password, website or coupon may help you make great savings. Theatremonkey.com summarises the best advance offers around (click on the Latest Special Offers tab). The widest choice of discounted productions is for Monday to Thursday performances, with far fewer on Friday and Saturday evenings.

Local and national newspapers like *Metro*, plus emails from lead agencies and venue owners See Tickets, Delfont Mackintosh Theatres, Ambassador Tickets and

Ticketmaster are also prime sources. After these, avoid an overflowing inbox by joining other lists only if they provide something original.

Remember that most offers are subject to availability, and can be withdrawn at any time. They are usually made on an allocation of best available seats, not always prime rows. If one deal's quota is filled, try another code or agency outlet (truly exclusive offers are rare and prices are usually identical). If an offer requires special vouchers, don't claim without actually having them to hand: theatres sometimes check and keep customer records. There can also be a delay between newspapers publishing and box offices being notified of deals, so do try again later if the deal you're expecting doesn't appear on the telephone clerk's screen.

Agencies
Many agencies specialise in deals sold from their booths or online. Online, they do sell directly to customers but most, like Theatremonkey.com's own Ticketshop (run by Lovetheatre.com), maximise their audience reach through affiliate partnerships with other websites. As a Theatremonkey.com reader observes, "all the deals on all the sites lead to the same place", making it unnecessary to trawl a vast number of them. Since smaller websites rely on affiliate commission, following links from your favourite site to agency partners is appreciated.

Even for overseas visitors, buying from agencies through UK-based websites is strongly advisable. You'll get the same deals while avoiding the pitfalls. Non-UK sites can't troubleshoot for you quickly from another time-zone (they rarely have local knowledge or London-based staff), are more prone to highlighting poor deals or standard preview price reductions as "special", add currency mark-ups or simply act as touts.

Become an awards judge
SOLT lay panellists for the Laurence Olivier Awards get two free seats to every opening that year. You have to be dedicated (and preferably sober) enough to attend the theatre as often as a professional critic does, but the reward is helping to ensure that your favourites receive the trophies they deserve.

Complimentary seats
Tourist industry and emergency services staff, group organisers, unhappy customers and friends of the cast may get lucky and get free tickets. Always be discreet, as producers don't want anybody thinking that their house is "papered" (i.e. full of guests who haven't paid).

Also worth trying are local newspaper competitions, as they often attract few entries unless giving away seats to a huge hit. One Theatremonkey.com reader responds to marketing company requests that appear in programmes or online, and fills out "appreciation" reports in return for his "comps".

Family tickets
These are rarely publicised, so ask your operator when you enquire about tickets. Some box offices offer deals on four seats for adults accompanying children to nominated performances of some shows. To help larger families, cheap tickets for extra siblings can usually be added when booking.

Groups
Parties of more than twelve (sometimes eight, ten or even six) can expect big discounts and several weeks to organise before paying. Frequently, the larger the group, the lower the price. Extra savings may apply for schools and senior citizens, especially at midweek matinees.

Reservations are available through theatres' group bookings departments, which, oddly, may also sell for rival chains' venues, or independent specialists. These latter include multiple award-winning Group Line (a venerable operator with excellent allocations), Encore Groups and Applause Groups.

Hit shows may have fewer group deals; long-running shows may have more flexibility. Watch for accelerator rates, which are used to launch a show or boost quiet weeks.

Compare sources, as deals and availability vary. Some theatres designate specific seats rather than offer groups the best available; others (notably Delfont Mackintosh Theatres) allocate a fixed number of best available tickets per performance.

If the venue allows you to choose your own seats online, make sure you have the web page in front of you when phoning. The venue's own group booking desk staff can often then reserve the exact tickets you prefer as you pinpoint them.

Allowing your party to be dispersed in small groups over several rows helps, and larger groups could even buy from more than one agency to amass the best seats possible. Don't accept single tickets that you can't use, though, and try to include aisle seats for people with access difficulties or for organisers to slip into at the last moment.

Regular group organisers loyal to a single company get the pick of seats in short supply, and are invited to client nights, seeing the latest shows free. Encore Groups' Loyal Circle scheme awards points towards gifts. One industry insider advises that, if you're a frequent group booker and you're thinking about switching to another supplier, you should immediately seek out the manager, outlining the benefits you'd like in return for your custom.

Hidden stuff
Turn detective or super-fan to find these. Using Google to search for the show's title or keywords, like "London theatre", can yield results within the sponsored advertisement list. Tie-in books, CDs, programmes and leaflets handed out at the theatre may contain coupons. Official websites for shows, actors and venues and social networking web pages may also reward readers' loyalty.

In-house schemes
In return for an annual fee, venue owner's clubs like Ambassador Theatre Group's Ambassador Friends (020 8544 7424) and Delfont Mackintosh Theatre Priority offer savings on tickets, plus maybe useful exchange privileges and drinks or programme discounts. Taking out LiveNation's Livecard or See's myWorld credit card may yield exclusive offers. The Whatsonstage.com Club and Ticketmaster Priority are similarly longstanding sources of savings.

www.myworld-card.co.uk/see1
www.livenationtheatres.co.uk/livecard

Newspaper theatre clubs
Publications including the *Evening Standard*, *The Times*, *Sunday Times* and *Telegraph* sometimes use this device to benefit their readers. The notion that readers constitute an exclusive group convinces show marketers to create exclusive deals. The *Telegraph*, for example, often does a neat line in free champagne and programme vouchers if tickets are bought via their partner agency-run website and dedicated hotline.

Other email lists

If you've already joined theatres' and ticket agents' lists, consider the other specialists who fit neither category but also have something to offer. Whatsonstage.com and ShowSavers circulate their own offers alongside their affiliated agency ones. London Live, from a major marketing agency, also emails original deals periodically.

www.showsavers.co.uk
www.londonlive.net

Packages

"Meal plus ticket" offers are good value if the ticket and suitable restaurant are provided for the same price (or less) than a seat alone. It's fine to pay extra for drinks and additional dishes, but restaurant service charges for the basic package should really be included in the price.

"Hotel plus ticket" deals can also save you money, but consider your hotel location when booking. Staying near the theatres is more expensive but saves touring time and transport fares. Also, you won't need to brave the London Underground to far-flung destinations late at night. Encore is known for its creatively priced offers in this field.

Public group nights

Whatsonstage.com and Dress Circle arrange cheap evenings, often incorporating cast meetings or shopping discounts. There's no pressure to join in but you share the vibe of like-minded people as you save. Also, Lastminute.com, via Facebook, registers visitor interests and organises trips once minimum numbers are reached.

http://apps.facebook.com/theatreclub

Registered disabled theatregoers

Disabled people, plus a companion, are regularly offered substantial discounts at all performances via the dedicated box office helpline. Stalls may be sold at balcony prices to those unable to manage stairs, or wheelchair users can bring a companion free of charge.

Secret society

Members of these organisations pay an annual joining fee to receive details of productions offering free tickets that night or coming week. Select a show, pay a small per-ticket handling fee and collect your ticket by discreetly producing your membership card at the box office.

The Audience Club offers a selection of fringe events (plus limited West End show and occasional concert choices) for a membership fee of less than £1 a week, plus a small per-seat fee.

Other clubs exist, but some don't appreciate publicity. Others have few shows available, so choose carefully.

www.theaudienceclub.com

Senior citizens, jobseekers, students and theatre union members

Card-carrying members of these groups may be able to buy discounted seats in advance via the box office for certain performances like midweek matinees. They can also usually buy unsold seats (standby tickets) for half price or less from the theatre an hour before curtain-up.

Unlike day seats, standby tickets are sold at box office discretion. You can politely ask for preferred locations and sometimes, on quiet days, they're sold early – so it's worth dropping by the theatre. Some, including the National Theatre, offer standby tickets to everybody. Others, unofficially, may accept sensible cash offers from discreet enquirers at the last moment on slow nights.

Shape Arts

This charity supports elderly and disabled theatregoers, providing help or just company. Volunteers meet interesting new people, with all expenses paid.

www.shapearts.org.uk

Show Pairs vouchers

These small paper coupons are found in hotels, shops and restaurants or mailed to any workplace with 20 or more employees. Offers include Two-for-one, Discount, and Meal and Show deals. These coupons are a similar idea to Twofers that are used in New York.

www.showpairs.co.uk

Social clubs

Entertaining London, for single professional 20- and 30-somethings (a sister organisation caters for those aged 40 or over), and London IVC Theatre Club, which has no age restrictions, charge members an annual subscription fee. In return, they organise regular, cheap, social theatre evenings for like-minded souls.

www.londonivc.com
www.entertaininglondon.com

Special events

Two annual industry-supported events promote London theatre by offering big discounts to nearly every show, often including those that otherwise wouldn't dream of cutting their prices. Move fast, and don't always expect prime seats. Get Into London Theatre (January to March) is open to all; Kids Week (August) is for 5- to 16-year-olds.

www.getintolondontheatre.co.uk
www.kidsweek.co.uk

Teaching

"Teachers get free seats on school trips", notes a Theatremonkey.com reader. Mousetrap Theatre Projects' Teachers Preview Club offers registered UK teachers free or discounted seats and travel packages. Learnaboutlondontheatre.co.uk helps teachers by listing education programmes and deals, and has a comprehensive search facility.

www.mousetrap.org.uk
www.learnaboutlondontheatre.co.uk

Younger generation

Mousetrap Theatre Projects targets schools and families, and their "145" scheme offers 16- to 18-year-olds one show for £5. Gr8tix serves 13s to 18s, the National Theatre's Entry Pass is for 15s to 25s and TheatreFix is dedicated to 16s to 26s. Hit The Theatre goes up to 28-year-olds, with cheap tickets and an ambassador scheme. A Night Less Ordinary offers under-26s free tickets at selected theatres. The Old Vic's Aditya Mittal scheme sets aside 100 seats there each night for those aged under 25.

www.theatrefix.co.uk
www.hitthetheatre.co.uk
www.gr8tix.co.uk
www.anightlessordinary.org.uk

Zero options

If nothing else works out, some theatregoers practise the balcony trick. They buy the cheapest balcony seat going, expecting that, for example, the balcony may be closed on quiet evenings, in which case customers are moved downstairs (i.e. upgraded free of charge to better seats that would otherwise have been more expensive). Watch out for the signals – which include theatres refusing to sell their cheapest seats by telephone or putting an early morning "Closed" sign on their balcony doors – then try your luck.

Another tactic is to buy a cheaper stalls or dress circle seat then move forwards as the show starts. Ask an usher before doing this as it's frowned on by many, and you could be told to move back, leave or pay the difference in ticket price. Gallingly, you could even end up surrounded by smug balcony trick folk who've been moved legitimately into your own pricier neighbourhood.

And finally, there's the downright dishonest. From mixing with the interval foyer crowd (tickets are rarely checked when customers go back to the show after the interval) to fake student identity cards and printing your own tickets, there's a whole alphabet of tricks from A to Prison. Don't do it. The Monkey won't get you out of gaol.

Beating "sold out" signs

Forget touts or stealing usher uniforms. There's always a gap between "sold out" hype and reality, especially for the determined. One megastar's production was reputedly sold out every night. In fact, returns were invariably available for the asking.

Be first in line

Anything with an international star, famous writer or cast-by-television-vote actor sells quickly. Events staged in the smallest venues, notably the Donmar Warehouse, Cottesloe and Pit, are also among London's toughest tickets to net.

Many people hit the telephone as soon as they spot a "Major new show on sale at 10am today" advertisement in the *Sunday Times* Culture section. Signing up at production and ticket outlet websites for automated email notifications of booking dates can provide even earlier advance warning, allowing you more time to prepare. Before booking opens, box offices and some agents happily take contact details from those calling too soon, but be aware that they may not always phone back. Postal enquiries may also be dealt with early if you provide clear requirement and payment details. Group sales companies likewise may sell tickets for larger parties prior to individual booking opening.

Pop concerts regularly sell out in the first few minutes. "Extra dates" (really already planned) may then appear online. Keep trying throughout "launch day", even hours after the originals sold out. The Monkey has also noticed that, once the initial fuss has died down, single seats trickle onto official websites for weeks afterwards.

Signing up at official production websites sometimes provides priority buying opportunities, as do certain newspapers for their readers or issuers for their credit card holders. Be wary: these sometimes offer a limited selection of very average seats. Producers may also "hold off sale" some prime seats when full public booking initially opens, releasing them closer to opening night to satisfy the hype.

Individual theatres' own priority booking subscription schemes, like those operated by the Donmar Warehouse, Royal Shakespeare Company, Royal Court, Delfont Mackintosh and Ambassador Theatre Group, are reliable. Members should act fast, though, because they are competing with fellow avid theatregoers. A Theatremonkey. com reader comments:

> "the National Theatre's scheme has provided me with some excellent seats to some sold-out shows."

Be flexible
Flexibility works wonders for those willing to accept any date, time, price and seat available. Clerks will also search harder if you're polite, too.

A Theatremonkey.com reader advises:

> "I was on my own, buying only one ticket (obviously!). I was offered several good options for seats. I have in the past bought three single tickets for my family, sometimes scattered all through the theatre, in order to get to see a show – after all, you are watching the show, not chatting, and you can always meet up in the interval. You get a better choice if you buy singles, as they fit you in the gaps, so the seats may be very, very good. It wouldn't necessarily work if you have young children though."

Those on a first date may also feel similarly. But if your companion picks single seats on a second date, read the signs.

Day seats (or "rush seats" to Broadway fans)
Alongside returns, some top shows keep front-row stalls or standing places, sometimes with slightly restricted views, for sale on the day of the performance exclusively to personal callers at the venue. This isn't exactly an altruistic gesture; producers would probably get complaints if they were to sell them at full price, and it generates a handy line of people to buy other leftovers once the day seats have gone. The practice helps impecunious and casual theatregoers, though, and also frustrates touts (by guaranteeing that at least some tickets will be available even at otherwise sold-out performances).

Day seats are generally good value – especially when the row behind is top price. Tickets go on sale around 10am, with lines forming around two hours before or even earlier for hot shows. To further thwart touts, the venue may require that you pay immediately by credit or debit card but collect your tickets just before the show, producing the same card used earlier. Younger people without cards should check, before travelling to the venue, whether other official ID is acceptable.

Death rattles and suntans
If plague or scheduled holidays befall a star performer, tickets to their sell-out hit often become available as fans avoid these performances.

Golden keys
Top hotel concierges with tiny "golden keys" on their lapels are well-connected members of Les Clefs d'Or. Their networking often produces tickets... but at a price. It's good etiquette to give them a decent tip in recognition of their substantial

effort. Credit card-linked concierge services may help their own clients, though some Theatremonkey.com readers report disappointment with the quality of tickets offered.

Hotel packages
Specialist companies combining tickets with rooms can be a great late-availability source as the last-minute late-getaway break remains fashionable.

Returns
Customers', agents' and producers' unwanted tickets trickle in from around 24 hours before the performance. Phoning sometimes works, but many sold-out shows demand a personal visit to their venue on the day; dress for waiting around.

One Theatremonkey.com reader's experience is typical:

> "You can usually get really good returns at the Donmar (and other venues) for a sold-out Saturday if you get there early and are prepared to wait. It's first come first served, but if there's two of you, one can wait and the other shop, fetch food etc."

Hang around as tickets are returned right up until the curtain rises. Don't pester box office staff, but if they know you're there, endurance may be rewarded. Some, like the Royal Court, list callers' names from an hour before the show, allocating them return times to try for tickets.

VIP packages and premium seats
These are top tickets that come with extras like programmes and refreshments. Cheaper than tout offerings, they may be available at short notice as they can be released closer to the performance date than other seats.

Working the days
Monday to Wednesday evenings are quieter; Saturday then Friday evenings busiest. Weekend matinees (especially for child-friendly shows) and Thursday evenings are next. Midweek afternoons are popular with senior audiences. Early December, the week before Christmas holidays, the days when everyone goes back to work following New Year, and the weeks following Easter before summer tourists arrive often sell slowly for even the top shows.

The Monkey has observed that London folk buy tickets around three weeks ahead. An unexpected smash may have tickets available for the first few days after opening, though not often for long. Musicals may sell tickets up to a year ahead, plays a few months. Extra performances during holiday weeks or held as fundraisers often have tickets at short notice. Charity galas may require a donation, usually modest for the cheapest seats, which is a good way to see the show and support a cause.

If your preview is cancelled and the show is otherwise sold out, tickets may become available once the opening night is confirmed. Some shows secretly schedule a second press night date, just in case they aren't ready. When they know for sure the show is on track, great seats (originally intended for guests) may be released. Later in the run, invited groups may cancel at short notice, again providing unexpected opportunities.

Should transport workers threaten a strike paralysing the Underground, the wary may return their tickets. If the strike happens, and you can get there, box offices will often be delighted to sell you these. Similarly, if England is doing well at televised events like Wimbledon or international football, shows can go quiet. The following week becomes busier, though, as the sports fans who've neglected their partners patch things up with show tickets.

Working the seats

The availability of boxes, restricted views and standing room isn't widely publicised but these options are occasionally sold over the telephone to those who specifically ask. A personal visit to the venue is more often required, as theatres may prefer to explain drawbacks properly (to prevent complaints).

Pillars, safety rails, poor legroom or an eccentric set all bring prices down in proportion to the level of restriction or inconvenience. The Monkey once sat with chin on stage and body under it for just £5. Generally, "50% problem equals 50% off". Occasionally, a clear-view seat beside the restricted-view one is priced identically to create a saleable pair, which may be enjoyed by single people, or couples who like seat swapping.

Sometimes, box offices deny all knowledge of cheap seats among the expensive ones until other cheap tickets (upper circle or balcony) have been sold. If, like the Monkey, you prefer to be close to the stage even if it means having a partial view, persist with your request politely.

New shows and pop concerts regularly hold back odd seats until sightlines and technical needs are confirmed. Start asking about seats from a few weeks before the first scheduled performance.

Other things to know – before, during and after the show

Before the show

Car parking

The Theatreland Parking Scheme offers discounts at designated car parks, in conjunction with participating theatres; details are available from City of Westminster Council (0800 243 348). Remember to get your ticket validated at the theatre if using this deal.

On-street parking may be free after 6.30pm and at weekends – check signs before leaving the area. *The Blue Badge Parking Guide for London* (PIE Guides) helps permit holders.

> www.westminster.gov.uk/carparks
> www.thepieguide.com

Disabled audience members

While this book contains a little information, theatres' helplines (downloadable from www.theatremonkey.com) for disabled people can offer more specific details about access, sound problems and any strobe lighting effects used in a show. Venue staff will be happy to help where possible, but can't usually lift or wheel visitors. Programmes may be available in large print or on CD.

SOLT's brilliant *Access London Theatre Guide* has photo-illustrated maps to venues from wheelchair-friendly stations, lists of assisted performances and more. Artsline visits venues regularly, recording online their experts' findings. VocalEyes operates audio-described performances, STAGETEXT operates captioned ones, Envision helps sight-impaired young people and Visitlondon.com details suitable hotels.

www.artsline.org.uk
www.stagetext.org/performance
www.vocaleyes.co.uk
www.visitlondon.com/accessible

Dress code

Unless stated for a special gala performance, there's no dress code at any event. To get the right dress level, think "dining in a favourite local restaurant" and "comfortable when confined for three hours".

Lounge suits, jackets, slacks, smart T-shirts, jeans and trainers are acceptable for male theatregoers at almost all times. Suits are only near-compulsory at opening nights.

Female theatregoers negotiate the usual sartorial minefield. Comfortable casual is usually fine – dresses, slacks, jeans and sweatshirts. For opening nights, think "smarter but not elaborate" unless you're a celebrity. Weekend evenings can be a bit dressier than weekdays. Lower heels are better for negotiating venue stairs. Consider skirt length carefully if seated anywhere but the stalls. In tiered circles, knees and thighs will often be at head height to the person in front.

London nights are generally cool even in summer and air-conditioning can be over-enthusiastic. Having something light but warm to put on can be useful here.

Most theatres have cloakrooms. The National Theatre and Barbican are vast and efficient, so the Monkey uses them; most West End ones are smaller, so the Monkey uses them only when prepared to queue.

For security, empty pockets before checking in your coats. If you're keeping everything with you, don't place items under seats or leave anything unattended during the interval.

Eating out in London

London-eating.co.uk brilliantly collates public opinions online. Lunch is usually cheaper than dinner in decent restaurants; snack food and soft drinks are always cheaper bought outside the venue.

Insurance

For the risk-averse, many theatres offer TicketPlan. If your companions fall ill, your car breaks down or public transport fails, you'll be able to claim the cost of your tickets from the insurer.

www.ticketplangroup.com

Know the territory

Theatremonkey.com readers rate highly the National Theatre and Theatre Royal Drury Lane tours; many other venues also offer tours. Generally, both auditorium and surprisingly squalid backstage areas are visited as long-serving staff members regale you with their tales. Pre- or post-show talks by casts and directors may provide another interesting insight.

Language barriers

Bi-lingual sales clerks are few. Ticket agencies based in major department stores and hotels may have interpreters available. Otherwise, book online using own-language versions of sites like Ticketmaster and theatremonkey.eolts.co.uk

On the night

Arriving

Check your tickets for the exact starting time. It can vary from those published, particularly around holiday periods. Try to arrive at least half an hour (earlier if collecting tickets) before the show starts. Order interval drinks and buy a programme, have a final smoke outside (it's banned anywhere inside public buildings in the UK) then take your seats at least 15 minutes before curtain-up to allow time to settle in.

Entering

Doors from the foyer to the auditorium have signs indicating the closest rows and seat numbers. Using the correct door avoids climbing over fellow audience members. For those theatres with separate outdoor balcony entrances, dress for the weather-exposed wait.

Opera glasses

These are found in holders between seat backs at most theatres. Push your 50p or £1 coin hard into the slot, then pull glasses upwards to free them. Replace at the end of the show by pushing them down firmly into the holder, or hand them to an usher. Remember, though: don't push the glasses hard into their holder before the end of the evening, or you'll have to pay again. Magnification isn't bad, so arrive early to nab a set.

Programmes ("playbills" or "programs" on Broadway)

These aren't free, unlike on Broadway. Around £3 to £6 usually buys a cast list and brief biographies, scenes, settings and sometimes plot synopsis, a couple of photographs, plus a few articles about the author, play and theatre history. Foyer and auditorium vendors really appreciate correct change, rather than £20 notes, if possible. Incidentally, this also applies when buying interval refreshments, often from the same person.

Big musicals additionally sell glossy souvenir brochures for around £7 to £10. Cunningly, these are often sold in the foyer, shifting stock before cheaper options are discovered inside the auditorium. Expect large colour pictures, not necessarily of the current cast, and a few articles about the show's creation. For anything more specific, you'll need a programme.

Some companies make free cast lists available. Look for dispenser racks just beside the auditorium entrance.

Souvenirs and cast recordings

Many productions have a foyer shop to satisfy those *Phantom Of The Opera*-themed acne gel cravings. Cast albums are usually cheaper online, so concentrate on the exclusive goods. Quality is usually high, though many gifts look rather obviously mass-produced. Sales of T-shirts, sweatshirts, badges, pins, trinket boxes, watches, mugs and so on are generally restricted to the theatre itself, and often also the showbiz shop Dress Circle (at 57–59 Monmouth Street, London WC2H 9DG). Dress Circle also stocks a limited selection of bygone show mementoes. They happily ship orders worldwide.

The Record Album (at 8 Terminus Road, Brighton, East Sussex BN1 3PD) has an extensive vinyl LP stock. Very few recordings and souvenirs are collectable; limited-edition items that are sold only by the theatre and Dress Circle are usually the ones to hoard.

www.dresscircle.co.uk
www.therecordalbum.com

Tipping
This isn't expected in London theatres unless something way beyond the call of duty is required – like retrieving a shoe from an orchestra pit (don't ask…).

During the performance

Annoying the cast
Resist the temptation to do this … (unless, perhaps, the performance is really terrible). You could try impersonating a critic: just look scruffy, old, bored, drunk and show up on opening night or a performance very soon after. Actually, only the last is compulsory. Write furiously on a pad at the interval – or during the show to unnerve the cast from the front row. Seriously, though, if you do anything too noticeable, you'll rightly be asked to leave.

Applause
Rather than applauding every song or scene, experienced British theatregoers generally wait for the end of the act, with the odd ripple on a first entrance or exit. A standing ovation is usually saved until the end of the performance, as the cast take their final bows. Feel free if you're really impressed. If you wait until the star of the show appears, then stand up and clap wildly, others in the audience invariably follow. Exsibilation, by the way, is frowned on except during pantomime season, as is throwing anything except flowers.

Other noise
Turn off mobile phones and digital watch alarms before the curtain rises. Don't rustle sweet wrappers and bags and, please, don't talk during the quiet passages of music or dialogue. Wait for the interval or the end to decide who really did check that the gas was off before you left home. Not eating and only laughing, crying or gasping at the action on stage will make you look like a true, inhibited British theatregoer and endear you to all.

Taking photographs and recordings
These are strictly forbidden inside theatres for both copyright and safety reasons. Flash photography could kill performers, blinding them when they need to concentrate on the positions of other actors and heavy moving scenery. Souvenir brochure photographs are always better; yours will often come out black, anyway. Likewise, the official cast album will have easily superior sound quality.

Watch the background
With attention focused on the leading performers, keep an eye on supporting actors building up their parts or doing things to relieve the monotony. Listen out for "click tracks" (recordings dropped into musicals to help stressed actors) and try to spot quirky scenic design jokes. All provide perfect "did you notice?" conversations for the trip home.

At the interval
Most shows have a 15- to 20-minute interval (or "intermission" to Broadway folk). Some shorter plays have none; some productions have long first halves. Perhaps you could make use of bathroom facilities before curtain-up?

Cubicle queues

Expect only one lavatory on each level for each gender – and insufficient cubicles for female theatregoers. Delfont Mackintosh theatres, the National and Barbican Centre are best equipped. In others, try upstairs for quieter restrooms. Good theatre managers normally make sure lines for facilities have cleared before allowing the second half to start, so don't worry too much if the time is ticking away with a long queue still ahead.

Drinks and snacks

Pick a less busy bar, not the bar near the stalls (fewer seats upstairs, for example, means fewer customers). You can place a drinks order before the show and they'll be waiting for you next to a number on the bar or nearby shelf at the interval.

Remember that bar prices are usually higher than in normal pubs and that you may have to buy double rather than single spirit measures.

Larger bars may also offer a small selection of other snacks, from wraps to canapés. In the auditorium itself, ushers usually sell a range of packaged sweets and ice-creams from trays. They appreciate exact change, but don't appreciate you moaning about the prices (they know, they hear this every night).

Ringing bells

These can be heard throughout the theatre from around five minutes before curtain-up, and also towards the end of the interval. They indicate that the performance is about to begin.

After the show

Leaving the theatre

It's human nature to use the door you came in by when leaving, but theatres have many others. Some bypass the crowded foyers for a quick direct exit to the street, though the alleys they empty into aren't always salubrious.

Stage door autographs

The stage door (actors' entrance) is usually in a side or back alleyway. The bigger the star, the less likely it is that (for their own safety and crowd security) they'll appear to sign autographs. Politely ask the stage door keeper about the policy. If told no, please accept this and leave.

If you're waiting, remember that the whole cast and crew leave through this exit, so please stand out of their way. Do have a working pen (felt or fibre tip is best), paper and a respectfully polite attitude. Always consider your personal safety, too: deserted London alleyways are risky late at night.

Alternatively, obtain autographs later by writing to the theatre (c/o The Stage Door) or to the actor's agent. Addresses are also available online at websites like Spotlight and IMDB. Always remember that "off stage" is actors' personal time, and that they may have to disappoint you simply due to the sheer number of requests they receive.

www.imdb.com
www.spotlight.com

Transport home

The last Underground services and trains leave central London at around 12.30am. Night buses cover the gaps from 11pm onwards, with most routes leaving from Trafalgar Square.

Text HOME to 60835 (there's a 35p charge plus the cost of your call) for numbers of one traditional London black taxi and two licensed minicab firms operating nearby. Before you get into a vehicle, look for the white plate on the back of traditional London taxis, the green sticker on minicab windscreens, and ID tags around all drivers' necks.

Feeling inspired?

Your theatre visits may inspire you to get creative or boost your performance career.

Angels
SOLT (020 7557 6700) keeps lists of "angels" – backers who're willing to help producers by investing money in commercial shows. Stage One provides advice to aspiring producers on how to spend the money that the angels lend to them.

> www.stageone.uk.com

Aspiring actors
If you're one of these, you may like to check out the Conference of Drama Schools, National Council for Drama Training and *The Stage* websites. Jennifer Reischel's book *So You Want to Tread The Boards* and Lisa Gee's *Stage Mum* may also be helpful. Backstage skills are covered by The Association of British Theatre Technicians and the National Theatre's Stagework websites.

> www.abtt.org.uk – Association of British Theatre Technicians
> www.drama.ac.uk – The Conference of Drama Schools
> www.ncdt.co.uk – National Council for Drama Training
> www.stagework.org – National Theatre's Stagework website

Work experience
If you're seeking this, you might try sending single-page CVs to companies listed in *Contacts*, a handbook listing entertainment companies, or *The Original British Theatre Directory*, a printed directory and subscription-based website. Chances are low, especially for under-16-year-olds, as theatres can't provide the requisite chaperones for night working.

Problem solving

Do everything possible to resolve issues the moment they arise. Examine tickets immediately they arrive, and contact the seller quickly if anything is incorrect.

If the show is cancelled, theatres and STAR agents refund both the face value and booking fees of tickets, but not your personal travel expenses. Regent's Park Open Air Theatre allows ticketholders to exchange seats for another performance if the show is rained off.

A star is off
Occasionally, if central to the show, producers allow ticket exchanges in these circumstances. Chances increase if the performer's name is above rather than below the title in advertisements. Otherwise, the rule "your ticket is to see the show, not a specific cast member" applies.

Box office or STAR agency problems
These are dealt with by their internal customer services teams. SOLT provides general advice and STAR can sometimes assist in resolving disputes with members. For tickets bought as a package, the operator's regulating authority may help. As a final resort,

and for those who purchased tickets from touts, trading standards officers and the small claims court are options for the persistent.

Can't use your tickets

Many box offices and STAR outlets will try to help if you have a good reason, offering a refund or exchange for a moderate fee – though sometimes only if they can resell the seats. Awkwardly, you may also have to return the ticket to them at least 24 hours before the show.

Ticketmaster allows its customers to list unwanted tickets on a TicketExchange page on its website. Online auction and secondary ticketing sites offer tempting alternative places to list unwanted seats. Be aware that selling for profit, sometimes even reselling tickets at all, may violate the terms and conditions of purchase. Some box offices monitor these types of sites, cancelling any tickets they find.

General theatre issues

Try dealing with problems at the time, and ask for a house manager if possible. Theatres log all issues and may have CCTV to refer to. Complaints should be put in writing to the theatre if things weren't immediately resolved.

If you're still unhappy, try the operations manager, then a director at the theatre's owners (names are often in the back of theatre programmes). SOLT may provide general advice on how to proceed in disputes, but can't arbitrate between disputing parties.

Late arrivals

Latecomers may be asked to watch the production on a silent TV monitor in the bar, or perhaps seated at the back of the venue. Major incidents, like London Underground network failure, will always delay the performance. In the absence of these, there's no refund for the tardy, so it's worth allowing plenty of time for your journey.

Lost tickets

These can usually be reissued (sometimes for a fee) and collected on the night at the theatre or STAR member's booth. The same applies if you forget to bring your tickets on the day. ID, for example the credit card used to book the tickets, may be required.

Show performance complaints

Address any disappointment about the quality of the show to the company manager at the theatre, or to producers' offices.

Someone already in your seats

First alert an usher, who can check who is actually entitled to the seats. If you're asked to move, do so. Mistakes happen and theatres usually keep a few decent alternative tickets just in case. A polite discussion with senior theatre staff at the interval should resolve any lingering issues.

Upset

If a fellow audience member's behaviour is bothering you, do tell the venue's staff. One worried Theatremonkey.com reader was escorted to her Underground station following an incident, and kindly given tickets for another visit.

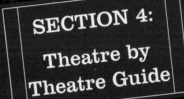

SECTION 4:

Theatre by Theatre Guide

Theatremonkey.com and its readers share their experiences of visiting the major West End Theatres.

Using the theatre information pages

Venue address: Following a venue's address, a letter and number – for example C31 – locates the venue as number 31 on map C at the back of this book.

Box office telephone numbers: These connect to the lead agent or theatre box office itself.

Online booking address: This is of the theatre's own website or appointed lead agent.

🚇 ⇄ 🅿

Nearest car park, tube and mainline stations: Most theatres are within walking distance of several. The Monkey gives those it finds most convenient.

A (T) symbol beside a car park name indicates that it participates in the Theatreland Parking Scheme (see "Other things to know – before, during and after the show"), provided customers are visiting a participating theatre and have obtained a validated ticket from the venue.

❄

Air-conditioning: Some theatres are "air-cooled" only – an older and far less efficient system.

🔭

Opera glasses: Locations of seat-back rental points where available.

Seating information: This covers the stalls, dress circle, upper circle and balcony as applicable. Tier names can vary between theatres; the grand circle in one may be the upper circle at another. For clarity, Theatremonkey uses the theatre's own circle name first, with a reminder of whether it's dress or upper in brackets. So, for example, "royal (dress) circle" is a first-level tier labelled "royal circle" by the theatre. Where there are only two levels, "(dress) circle" records that box office staff may refer to it only as "the circle" when speaking to customers.

Opinions, distilled and edited from the many collected from Theatremonkey.com readers and theatre staff, appear throughout the text.

Using Theatremonkey seating plans

Theatremonkey.com research and reader input combine to give each seat a colour rating. Factors including view, comfort, user expectation and value for money are used to compare each with all similarly priced seats available.

Green: Many feel that these seats may offer noticeable value or something to compensate for a problem, for example a reasonable price for a seat with a restricted view.

Beige: These usually provide about the promised fair value.

Pink: These are coloured to draw attention. They're not necessarily to be avoided; there may be nothing specifically wrong with the seats but there may be better ones at the same price. These seats won't usually ruin your evening; they're simply a third choice if others are available. At times, there may be something to consider before buying – perhaps overpricing, obstructed views or cramped legroom, for example.

Black: These seats are present, but never used… unless the box office manager is truly desperate.

 These are pillars.

The text with each plan gives more details to help you decide. Opinions are based on paying full price (plus any booking fee) for the seat. Cheaper seats often do not offer the same view or location quality as top-price ones, but can be worthwhile. A discounted top-price seat usually provides better than average value.

Do consider your own personal tastes and physical requirements. Front stalls or seats behind safety rails may be unsuitable for shorter folk. Likewise, cramped legroom may make some circle seats uncomfortable for those over 5ft 10in or so.

Even when planning carefully, you could still find Marge Simpson, Jack Pumpkinhead or the Incredible Hulk sitting in front or leaning into your view. Their presence being unpredictable, moving (or reviewing your medication) may still be required.

Typesetting seating plans is difficult: a seat, drawn with nothing in front, may have something in front in reality. Please assume that normal legroom and sightlines apply unless the text says otherwise.

Most theatres, old and new, have unexpected problems, like low circle overhangs or compulsory (always irritating) safety rails in view. Each new production may bring extra changes: sound control desks may replace rear stalls, intrusive lights and projectors may be hung from circle fronts, actors and scenery may be placed to block sightlines, and so on. Producers can also simply change prices, altering value for money. Do remember to allow for these factors and variations when choosing your seats.

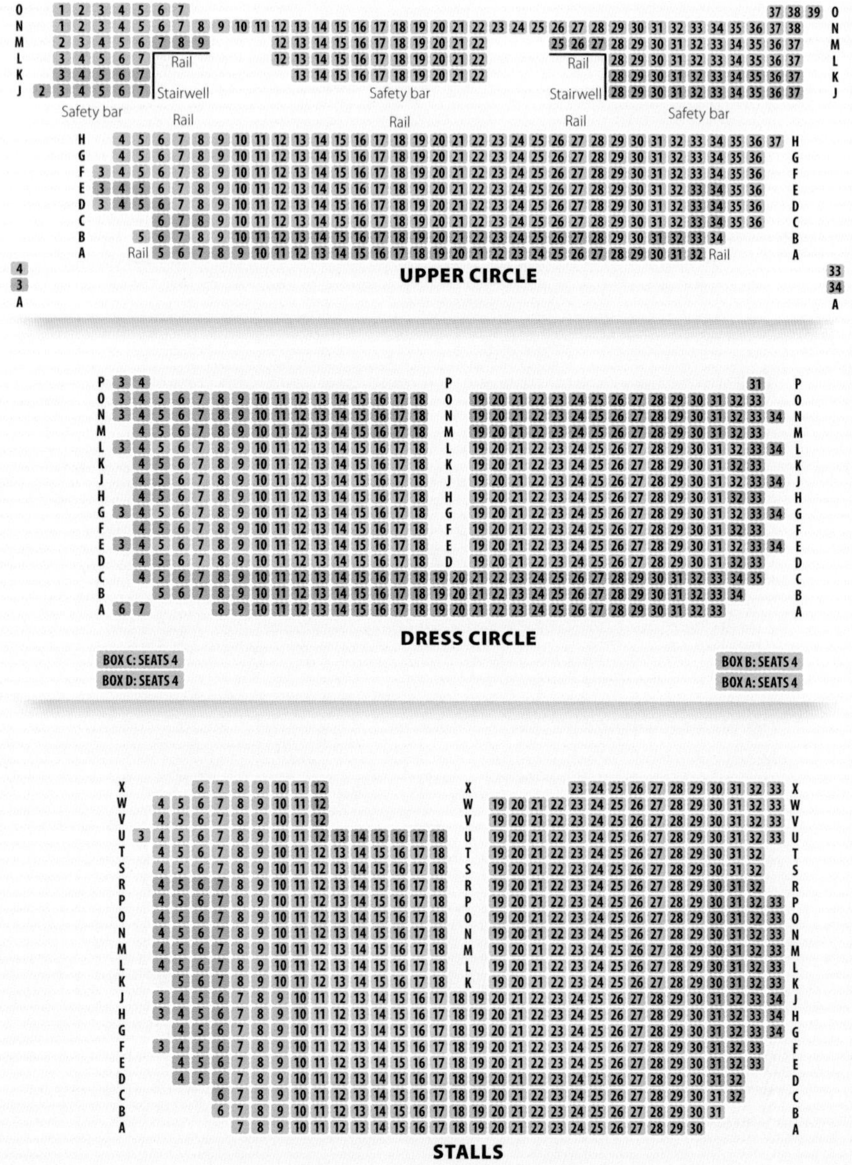

UPPER CIRCLE

Safety bar Rail Stairwell Safety bar Stairwell Safety bar

DRESS CIRCLE

BOX C: SEATS 4
BOX D: SEATS 4

BOX B: SEATS 4
BOX A: SEATS 4

STALLS

ADELPHI THEATRE

Adelphi Theatre

The Strand, London. WC2E 7NA   **C31**

With "How Do You Solve A Problem Like Maria?" 200 years away, impatient Jane Scott persuaded Daddy to build her a theatre in 1806. Retiring a star, she fared better than William Terris, murdered here at the height of his fame in 1897. Haunting the Adelphi still, he also (like most theatre workers) does a second job, spooking Covent Garden Underground station. The theatre was restored in 1993, revealing the façade's octagonal window.

BOX OFFICE:
0844 412 4651
0870 830 0200
020 7087 7500

ONLINE BOOKING:
www.seetickets.com

Charing Cross

Charing Cross

Spring Gardens (T)

1500

Air cooled only

stalls row L back and both circles

STALLS: Front stalls are popular, "A13 feels like being in the action", though some report neck ache and from "C15 to 18 sweat and spit can be clearly seen". Eww…

Rows extend beyond the stage's edges: C9 to 12 "are a little to the side", G30 to 34 "too off-centre for full price" and these expensive outermost seats potentially miss things. Views are better from seats further back: from K19 to 20 "I could see the whole stage without turning my head".

A shallow rake condemns some unlucky shorter folk to peering around heads, though in T21 to 24 "staggered seats let us see despite it". U13 to 18 may suffer restricted legroom if a sound desk is squeezed in behind them. The circle overhang is noticeable from row P and "V32, 33 missed stage top". Those in row X, including wheelchair spaces, really suffer. Discounts compensate, but some feel the upper circle is preferable for views if not comfort.

DRESS CIRCLE: Middle seats directly face centre stage; the outermost ten angle slightly towards it. Corner seats A6 and 7 peer around boxes, solitary row P perches on a plinth behind O. Many complain about comfort: "seat width feels narrow" and row C is particularly cramped. Sightlines divide opinion: "Do not pay full price anywhere here – heads in front block views." Balancing this, "F7, 8, 18 and 19 were perfect". Rear rows suffer from the overhang, but L25 to 29 "has plenty of legroom". At the sides of the circle, although cheaper and with restricted views, B33 and G34 can be "great, only missing action very far left".

Dress Circle Boxes: Not cheap, but C seat 1 offers "a very good view for the price; better than Box B opposite". "Highly pleased with legroom and sound. Would sit here again." Acceptable if willing to miss part of the stage.

UPPER CIRCLE: There are plenty of rails here. One runs across the front, another ends row B, two divide H from J, one fronts K13 to 22, and the rest protect stairwells before M8, 9, 25, 26 and 27.

Central front-section seats feel closer to the stage than rear stalls, with few drawbacks. In A15, 16: "Views are amazing. Only the very edge of the stage is obscured. Seats are slightly cramped, fine for us under 5' 6", tight if 6ft." "Typically, we couldn't see very front stage without leaning" (B15 to 18), which leads to a common complaint that "the view is obscured by leaners" (C12 and 36). Those further back report being happily above the problem. Restricted-view side seats are cheaper, and D3 has more legroom (just mind the sloping floor). In the corners, those in A4 and 33 must allow for companions leaning out even further than they do, to glimpse the stage.

In the rear section, row J, plus seats 9 to 11 and 23 to 25 in row N have the best of this block's legroom. "Steep stairs are not good for vertigo", however, and K may feel "outside the action". Rails cause problems: in K7 and 21 "leaning was the only way to see". Elsewhere (including N24 and 25), the rails go almost unnoticed. As ever, the rake is an issue: seats O5 to 7 "were amazing, until a big man sat in front", and in O37 to 39 "the height made us feel queasy". Vertigo sufferers should beware.

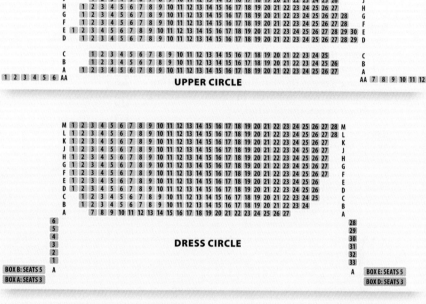

UPPER CIRCLE

DRESS CIRCLE

BOX B: SEATS 5
BOX A: SEATS 3

BOX E: SEATS 5
BOX D: SEATS 3

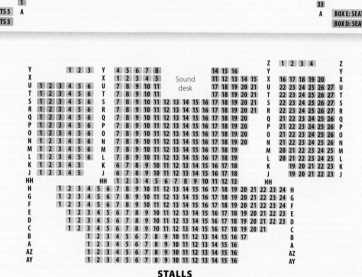

Sound desk

STALLS

ALDWYCH THEATRE

Aldwych Theatre

Aldwych, London. WC2B 4DF   **C39**

Remembered for the **Aldwych Farces** of the 1920s and 30s, and later as the pre-Barbican home of the Royal Shakespeare Company, this has become a musical theatre house for mid-sized crowd-pleasers. The foyer is splendiferous, housing box office staff doing their best to satisfy ticket demand. In the stalls, look out for the original fireplace alcoves – and imagine what it was like sitting further from them in a time before central heating.

BOX OFFICE:
0844 847 2330

ONLINE BOOKING:
www.ticketmaster.co.uk

 Covent Garden/Temple/ Holborn

 Charing Cross

 Parker Street

1176

Air conditioned

stalls from row K back, and both circles

STALLS: "The theatre is quite small so it did feel quite intimate and allowed the audience to feel part of the action." Allow for rows AY and AZ before A when counting rows back from the high stage. Central rows A to H are the best investment, and legroom disappoints few. C1, 2 and 21 and D1 have most legroom (as there's nothing in front of them). C7 and 8 may be "a little too close to the action" for some.

The notoriously low dress circle overhangs row H and views may be restricted. Reduced seat prices reflect how much is missed. Behind row H, seating splits into three blocks with aisles, giving J1 to 5 and 19 to 23 plentiful legroom. Rear corners feel like "satellite colonies" and miss the side action. Sound desk walls from the centre of row T and behind reduce views for four seats. Row Z comprises four flip-down perches, with audience backs resting against the wall (padding is planned). Z1 has unrestricted views down the aisle – a cheap bargain.

DRESS CIRCLE: The front six rows are intimately close to the stage, with a steep rake aiding sightlines. Aisle-end rails and lighting (with retaining clamps) hang from the circle front and disturb views. Shallow triangles of front stage aren't visible from A1 to 6 and 28 to 33 without leaning. Beyond row E, the upper circle overhang spoils stage views. Row M in particular seems expensive.

Sightlines from the narrow wheelchair positions next to C1 and 25 are fairly good (bar in view). D1 and 26 behind offer good views and legroom if wheelchairs aren't present. Elsewhere, legroom is average, with slightly more in the last two seats of rows B to M.

Dress circle boxes: Boxes A and D miss about half the stage (loudspeakers sited here don't help). Boxes B and E, on ledges at the corners of the dress circle, see two-thirds of the stage (though with a rail in view). Movable chairs assist comfort. Box D can house a wheelchair and a companion; dress circle spaces offer better views.

UPPER CIRCLE: This is high and steep; rows G and back feel a little remote. The bar across row A affects views; the outermost seats in B and C also suffer. Six slip seats, tacked onto the sides of row A, draw praise at low prices: AA1 and 2 "can be moved so that with a slight lean you can see everything but extreme left of stage; there's space to dance and stretch out too". The viewing angle isn't for everyone, legroom is less in seats 3 to 10, but the impecunious will be pleased.

In the back section, armrests vanish. Row D offers plentiful legroom and a decent view despite a rail and latecomers passing in front. Behind, extra seats have been squeezed in, with mixed reports. Rake and legroom are acceptable in rows F, H and K (tight elsewhere, particularly in row E with railings in front) and tickets are well priced. "F12, 13, 20 are fine for the money, didn't feel a long way from the stage, and could almost see all the action." Seat width is a problem, perhaps too cosy for some. At the very back, row L, on a shallow plinth, "has more view of the row in front than of the stage [and is] very cheap". K offers a preferable combination of price, comfort and view.

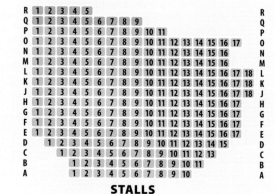

(DRESS) CIRCLE

STALLS

Ambassadors Theatre

West Street, London. WC2H 9ND   **B20**

"So good they named it twice…" Actually, only a "New" was added in 1999, only to be dropped again by a new owner in 2007 on the grounds that "everybody calls it the Ambassadors anyway".

Intended as a pair with St Martin's across the court, this is the elder sister by three years. While a tiny site compromised the final design, they did manage to squeeze in offices that have hosted many famous producing companies. A small foyer tribute recognises the Ambassadors as the original home of The Mousetrap from 1952 until 1974. Both theatres are now under the same ownership, and ever-friendly box office staff at the Ambassadors sell tickets for the 'whodunit' whenever the St Martin's box office is closed.

BOX OFFICE:
08448 112 334
ONLINE BOOKING:
theambassadorstheatre.co.uk

 Leicester Square/
Tottenham Court Road

 Charing Cross

P Newport Place,
Chinatown (T)

 400

❄ Air conditioned

STALLS: Uncomfortably snug for many, "the minimal rake cannot aid the view, and the circle overhangs the stalls by approximately two-thirds". The rear three rows also slope downwards behind those in front and most rows are cramped – but there are compensations.

A high stage ensures at least a fair view for everyone else, with the front row (A or B, depending on the production) discounted to compensate for potential neck ache. "A1 and 2 are very close to the stage. Price and loads of legroom make up for it." Some may prefer rows O and P.

Rows D to H offer fair value: seats E1 and 2 "were brilliant at a discount". At full price, tread a little more carefully if choosing row ends: some set designs render rear corners of the stage invisible, and Monkey instinct is "choose central if possible" – rows F to J are prime picks. Rows K, L and M feel "a little far back" for top-priced seats according to some. Also remember that row O may be cheaper than N, for similar views.

Rows P to R huddling at the back provide "the authentic trench experience" (bring your own periscopes), with the negative slope and overhanging circle. Fortunately, aware producers usually price these sensibly. Box office staff always takes great care, too, to explain sightline difficulties.

(DRESS) CIRCLE: Seats F7 to 15 are the ones to pick in this theatre, if budget and availability allow. Seats F12 and 13 "fall almost exactly centre stage and, as this row also provides the walkway across the circle, the legroom is fantastic… if quick, you can also be first in the ladies' loo queue".

Everywhere, "there is quite a steep rake and … seats felt very close to the stage, with a brilliant view". Front rows are fair value, but watch legroom: in A7 to A9 "legroom is not great. I'm 5' 9'', and would have found it uncomfortable for a longer performance". Row B has a "great view, but [as I'm] 6ft my knees uncomfortably dug into seats in front". Seats C9 to 12 are also reported to have a great view "but agree legroom is fairly limited, although the seat next to me was empty – so I was able to stretch out a bit".

Rows G to L are behind a low wall and rail at the back of the theatre. Sitting here feels a little far from the stage; try comparably priced stalls over wall-fronted G, in particular. Row K is usually cheaper than J, and happily shares similar views. Rows K and L offer a fuller but more distant view of the stage than equivalently priced stalls, without any circle overhang or backward rake to contend with. "L5: I would recommend as there are no seats in front of it, so view and legroom were fine."

Row A seats 1, 2, 21 and 22 are paired islands at the circle's front edges, give a sideways view and are cramped, but worth a thought if cheap enough.

Boxes: These have been converted to hold lighting, and are no longer sold to the public.

BALCONY

Row F: 1 2 3 4 5 6 7 | 8 9 10 11 12 13 14
Row E: 1 2 3 4 5 6 7 8 9 | 10 11 12 13 14 15 16 17 18
Row D: 1 2 3 4 5 6 7 8 | 9 10 11 12 13 14 15 16
Row C: 1 2 3 4 5 6 7 8 9 10 11 12 13 14 | 15 16 17 18 19 20 21 22 23 24 25 26 27 28
Row B: 1 2 3 4 5 6 7 8 9 10 11 12 13 14 15 | 16 17 18 19 20 21 22 23 24 25 26 27 28 29 30
Row A: 7 8 9 10 11 12 13 14 15 16 17 18 19 20 | 21 22 23 24 25 26 27 28 29 30 31 32 33 34

UPPER CIRCLE

Row F: 1 2 3 4 5 6 7 8 9 10 | 11 12 13 14 15 16 17 18 19 20
Row E: 1 2 3 4 5 6 7 8 9 10 11 | 12 13 14 15 16 17 18 19 20 21 22
Row D: 1 2 3 4 5 6 7 8 9 10 11 | 12 13 14 15 16 17 18 19 20 21 22 23
Row C: 1 2 3 4 5 6 7 8 9 10 11 | 12 13 14 15 16 17 18 19 20 21 22 23
Row B: 1 2 3 4 5 6 7 8 9 10 11 12 | 13 14 15 16 17 18 19 20 21 22 23 24 25
Row A: 6 7 8 9 10 11 12 13 14 15 16 17 18 | 19 20 21 22 23 24 25 26 27 28 29 30 31 32 33

BOX F: SEATS 2
BOX G: SEATS 2

DRESS CIRCLE

Row G: 1 2 3 4 5 6 7 8 9 10 11 |
Row F: 1 2 3 4 | 5 6 7 8 9 10 11 12 13 14 15 16 | 17 18 19 20 21 22
Row E: 1 2 3 4 5 | 6 7 8 9 10 11 12 13 14 15 16 17 | 18 19 20 21 22 23 24
Row D: 1 2 3 4 5 6 7 | 8 9 10 11 12 13 14 15 16 17 18 | 19 20 21 22 23 24 25
Row C: 1 2 3 4 5 6 7 8 | 9 10 11 12 13 14 15 16 17 18 | 19 20 21 22 23 24 25 26 27
Row B: 1 2 3 4 5 6 7 8 9 10 11 | 12 13 14 15 16 17 18 19 20 | 21 22 23 24 25 26 27 28 29 30 31 32
Row A: 2 3 4 5 6 7 8 9 10 11 12 | 13 14 15 16 17 18 19 20 | 21 22 23 24 25 26 27 28 29 30 31

BOX D: SEATS 3
BOX C: SEATS 4
BOX E: SEATS 3

STALLS

Row S: 1 2 3 4 5 6 7 8 9 10 11 12
Row R: 1 2 3 4 5 6 7 8 9 10 11
Row Q: 1 2 3 4 5 6 7 8 9 10 11
Row P: 1 2 3 4 5 6 7 8 9 10 11
Row O: 1 2 | 3 4 5 6 7 8 9 10 11 12 | 13 14

Row N: 1 2 3 4 5 6 7 8 9 10 | 11 12 13 14 15 16 17 18 19 20
Row M: 1 2 3 4 5 6 7 8 9 10 | 11 12 13 14 15 16 17 18 19 20
Row L: 1 2 3 4 5 6 7 8 9 10 | 11 12 13 14 15 16 17 18 19 20
Row K: 1 2 3 4 5 6 7 8 9 10 | 11 12 13 14 15 16 17 18 19 20
Row J: 1 2 3 4 5 6 7 8 9 10 | 11 12 13 14 15 16 17 18 19 20
Row H: 1 2 3 4 5 6 7 8 9 10 | 11 12 13 14 15 16 17 18 19 20
Row G: 1 2 3 4 5 6 7 8 9 10 | 11 12 13 14 15 16 17 18 19 20
Row F: 1 2 3 4 5 6 7 8 9 10 | 11 12 13 14 15 16 17 18 19 20
Row E: 1 2 3 4 5 6 7 8 9 10 | 11 12 13 14 15 16 17 18 19 20
Row D: 1 2 3 4 5 6 7 8 9 | 10 11 12 13 14 15 16 17 18
Row C: 1 2 3 4 5 6 7 8 | 9 10 11 12 13 14 15 16
Row B: 1 2 3 4 5 6 7 8 | 9 10 11 12 13 14 15 16
Row A: 1 2 3 4 5 6 7 8 | 9 10 11 12 13 14 15 16
Row AA: 1 2 3 4 5 6 7 | 8 9 10 11 12 13 14

BOX A: SEATS 3
BOX B: SEATS 3

Apollo Theatre

Shaftesbury Avenue, London. W1V 7HD   **B11**

Conceived in 1900 for operetta and light musicals, "star-vehicle" plays are now its most regular residents. Almost unaltered since opening, interestingly, the dress and upper circles retain their original 1904 seating layouts.

BOX OFFICE:
0844 412 4658
0844 579 1971
0870 830 0200
020 7087 7500

ONLINE BOOKING:
www.nimaxtheatres.com

 Piccadilly Circus

 Charing Cross

 Denman Street/Newport Place, China Town (T)

🚌 776

❄ Air conditioned

♿ stalls from row J back, dress circle, upper circle

STALLS: Many feel that stage height determines sightlines. Front rows suffer if it's high; low seats further back suffer if it's low. As the stage rises, row AA's price may fall, and best rows move further back.

With a low stage, "AA is fine" and "C is fine when discounted". Row F "feels involved in the action, with an unencumbered view," Its end also offers acceptable wheelchair spaces. Note that L11 and 12 "are not raked sufficiently to see around head in front".

With a raised stage: "F is too near, try H back", Seats K9 and 10 "have a great view thanks to the rake" and N7 "has a perfect view, reasonable legroom and comfortable chairs".

Row O has "luxurious leg space"; seats 7 and 8 look straight down the aisle ahead. With a decorous companion, isolated side seats O1, 2, 12 and 13 provide undisturbed viewing. Behind row O, circle overhang intrudes and the area's original use as the pit (a section of unreserved seats until the 1950s, second cheapest only to the balcony) becomes apparent. One Theatremonkey.com reader explains: "I'm only 5' 10.5" but was unbearably uncomfortable. The managers realise the limited legroom in those seats. Moved to P1, fantastic and central." Legroom elsewhere in the stalls is acceptable. Stalls boxes are either side of the stage. Nearside stage action is missed, but legroom is an improvement on some circle seats.

DRESS CIRCLE: This is shallow, with just five rows. Seats A2, 13, 20 and 21 have rails in front. Seats A2–4 and 27–31, B1–5 and 28–32, C1, 2, 25–27 and D1–3, 23, 24 and 26 are often designated "side view" and priced accordingly. Row A is cramped. Centrally, value and comfort improve further back, especially with discounts: "G1 and 2 had excellent views and plenty of legroom."

This circle curves noticeably, causing most side section seats to lose a little of the performance. Aisle seats suffer least and provide greater comfort. Some save by taking the closest cheaper seat adjacent to top-priced ones, maybe hoping for an obliging, wealthy seatmate to lean into. Dress circle boxes: Box D is best, half-way between stage and dress circle. All offer adequate views, missing nearside action. Again, an alternative to less comfortable circle seats.

UPPER CIRCLE: High up, with a shallow rake and balcony overhanging. A rail restricts outermost and central row A views and, doubling at the aisle, irritates those in A6, 18, 19 and 33 plus B12 and 13. From seat B13: "It was designed for a contortionist, though oddly had sufficient knee-room. A leaning head and the brass bar in front blocked my view." Many regular theatregoers prefer the cheaper balcony above. Upper circle boxes: Similar, higher angle, with views to boxes below. Worth considering for legroom. When cheap, this is a budget-priced upper circle/balcony alternative.

BALCONY: A notoriously high plane-spotters' paradise. Reassuringly, metal bars run between rows and aisle ends, though they might affect shorter folks' sightlines. A wall affects sightlines in row A: Theatremonkey.com readers in seats A12 to 15 report: "We had to move due to a high safety ledge … low seats meant leaning to see. Dreadful, and little legroom too."

Prices match the tight comfort and modest views offered. Rows A, E and F plus the outer ends of B and C are often cheapest in the house, with seats B5, 6, 25 and 26 and C5 and 24 (usually next to more expensive seats) average value (again, if you don't mind leaning into seatmates). Central row E is often cheaper than D, with similar views – helpful for the shallower pocket.

(DRESS) CIRCLE

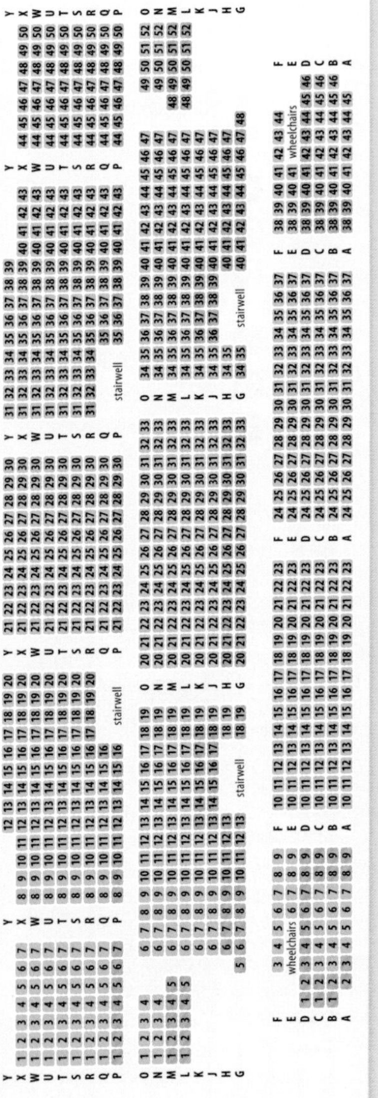

STALLS

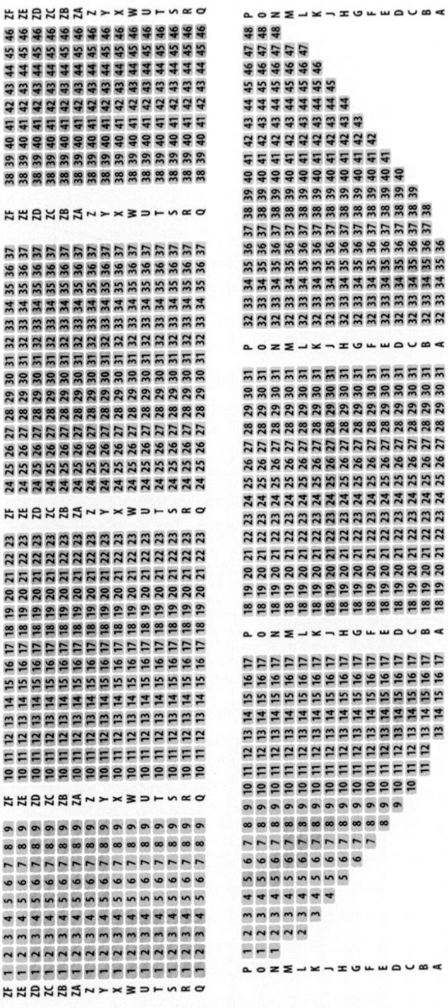

stairwell

stairwell

stairwell

wheelchairs

wheelchairs

wheelchairs

Apollo Victoria Theatre

17 Wilton Road, London SW1V 1LL

Originally a Super Cinema with an underwater theme (a few mermaids and shells are still present in the decor), and once home to Andrew Lloyd Webber's Starlight Express train set, this is now a vast musical house. The main foyer is unique, accessible from two parallel streets. The box office is at the Wilton Road entrance.

BOX OFFICE:
0844 826 8000
0161 385 3211

ONLINE BOOKING:
apollovictorialondon.org.uk

Victoria

Victoria

Semley Place

2313

No air conditioning

stalls from row R back, and in circle

STALLS: A low stage and discounts make row A popular for Wicked: "try to get A16 to 25". Behind, most are satisfied back to row G, though in B you may miss actors' footwork. Rows J and K disappoint some due to the shallow rake and in K24 to 27 "it would help if seats weren't directly behind each other". Things improve again with N19, 23, 24 and 25 "seeming higher than the row in front".

Side block seats nearest the central aisle share equally acceptable sightlines. From seats M15 to 17 "raking and aisle provide unrestricted viewing" and P36 to 39 are rated. Outermost seats may have problems: from B11, one Theatremonkey.com reader "could see dancers' pants in every scene" (a selling point for some?) and those in seats B35 and N1 to 4 "only saw half the show". Luckily, Wicked prices allow for this, with side section bargains to be had. Under less enlightened managements, these are worth skipping, except for comfort, and B17 "with nothing else in front, is effectively in the front row".

Row Q has exceptional legroom, and its resident ghost promises not to occupy your seat during performances. Behind, S21 to 33 are "close enough to take in detail". Circle overhang reduces views from row W but prices often remain high until ZD. The view from Z28 and 29 "wasn't brilliant" and a low ceiling may induce claustrophobia. When discounted, seats here become worth considering: from ZA "the steep rake allowed for an excellent view... children could see reasonably well with adults in front... binoculars weren't necessary". Fairly priced, ZE24 "is perfect, if a little far back".

To the sides, views are similar to central seats but there may be "nearby bar-stocking noise". One larger Theatremonkey.com reader finds all stalls seats comfortable with good legroom, and a parent advises using the booster seats available for children.

(DRESS) CIRCLE: Some note "slightly tight legroom" in its three deep sections . At the front, "rails intrude into views from aisle seats". Row A users "can peer through them like a frame." Unbalanced sound and forward-leaners in row B further cost the section its approval rating here. Otherwise, "D10, 11 were fantastic" and "E21 to 25 are well raked". Wheelchair plinths in row E allow users decent sightlines.

The middle section's front rail may cause problems for shorter theatregoers in rows G and H. All seats may lose some view and intimacy, and the theatre's cinematic origin is noticeable as actors contend with not being enlarged on a giant screen. Row K back may miss the front stage and some find the seats cramped. Seats J32 and 33 "feel far back". Seats behind high stairwell walls are avoidable unless heavily discounted: from K14 to 17, the stage may be "distant and cut off behind stairwell bars".

Beside the stairwells, two island pairs, H18 and 19 and H34 and 35, are popular with couples. Elsewhere, L37 "has a great view but poor legroom" and M18 and 19 "are a bit high up, but great for the price". Of the outermost seats O49 to 52 "49 and 50 are least affected by leaners".

In the back section, row P has a rail in front. Combined with stairwells, contortions seem almost obligatory: in R19 and 20 "you need to lean" and Theatremonkey.com readers in S27 to 30, despite a good rake, "constantly leaned to see". Many praise the sound in these remote rows, and rate both the distance and height compromises as fair, considering the budget price.

Sound Desk can take up F5–7
Wheelchairs can replace seats F1 and F2

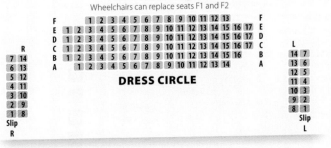

DRESS CIRCLE

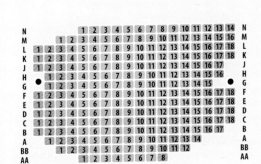

STALLS

Arts Theatre

6/7 Great Newport Street, London WC2H 7JB   **B22**

With the Lord Chamberlain censoring the British public's entertainment, a means to air more controversial material was required. Private "theatre clubs" were the answer, and the Arts Theatre was founded as one in 1927. Its most famous production was the original **Waiting For Godot** of 1955, directed by the unique Peter (later Sir Peter) Hall. Apocryphal stories abound: the Monkey favourite is the night they cancelled the show five minutes in, as a gentleman arrived waving an "I'm Godot" placard.

BOX OFFICE:
0845 017 5584
0870 830 0200
020 7087 7500

ONLINE BOOKING:
artstheatrewestend.com

 Leicester Square

 Charing Cross

 Newport Place, Chinatown

350

No air conditioning

The Lord Chamberlain discovered the internet in 1968 (allegedly), and stopped relying on playwrights for exotic reading matter. As a commercial venue, the Arts continued to flourish. Exciting work for grown-ups occupied the evenings; the amazing Unicorn Theatre For Children presented specially tailored performances by day.

The Unicorn spent its pocket money on a new building in 1999 and moved on. Since then, constant redevelopment plans have seen quality managements brought in to run things on short leases.

STALLS: Rows AA and BB can be substituted for an extended stage but, when they're not, some, including the Monkey, consider them worthwhile if identically priced to circle slips. Otherwise, rows further back are preferable for taking in the entire width of the stage without straining. Despite being a tiny place, rows AA to D can cause neck ache when the stage is high. From row E, distance, plus a reasonable rake, counteracts height variations sufficiently to create comfortable viewing. Only those in the very outermost seats may notice a temptation to lean in towards centre-stage action.

The circle overhang at row E is supported on pillars located at the ends of rows G and H. Connoisseurs particularly mourn the removal of J18, which once provided a commanding view of the left pillar instead of the stage. Elsewhere, for those in the mood, G and H1, 2, 15 and 16 are close enough to appreciate the pillars' finer points but keep them out of sightlines. Everybody else will probably prefer more central seats. Seats F5 and 6 "are as good as they get in this small venue". The overhang itself doesn't appear in views much before row L, with prices generally compensating if any aerial action is missed. At lower prices, the Monkey considers these rear stalls reasonable, offering fairly close views and acceptable legroom. M and N1, positioned more centrally than end seats in other rows, provide acceptable aisle seating.

(DRESS) CIRCLE: Six rows of seats cling to a narrow shelf. A further two rows of bench-style slip seats extend from the circle front down the sides of the theatre towards the stage. Ancient chintzy lights on the slips walls, which fascinated a tiny Monkey on its first visit, have sadly gone. Modern ceiling lights just aren't the same, though the plain walls do focus attention on the stage, which the actors probably prefer.

Views from central block seats in the circle are clear; only the low bar running across the front of row A provides a potential hazard for the shortest. Legroom tends towards tight, particularly in the slips. Wheelchair spaces are often created at the ends of adjustable row F, offering a good view. A potentially distracting sound desk may replace central seats here for musicals.

Circle slips R and L bring to mind jury boxes. Bars neatly enclose them, potentially intruding into sightlines. Again benches, heavy discounts can make them worthwhile for impecunious adventurers. Do check whether front-row stalls or rear circle are available at similar prices as legroom and seat width considerations generally make them a better choice, particularly for those preferring slightly less intimacy with unchosen seatmates

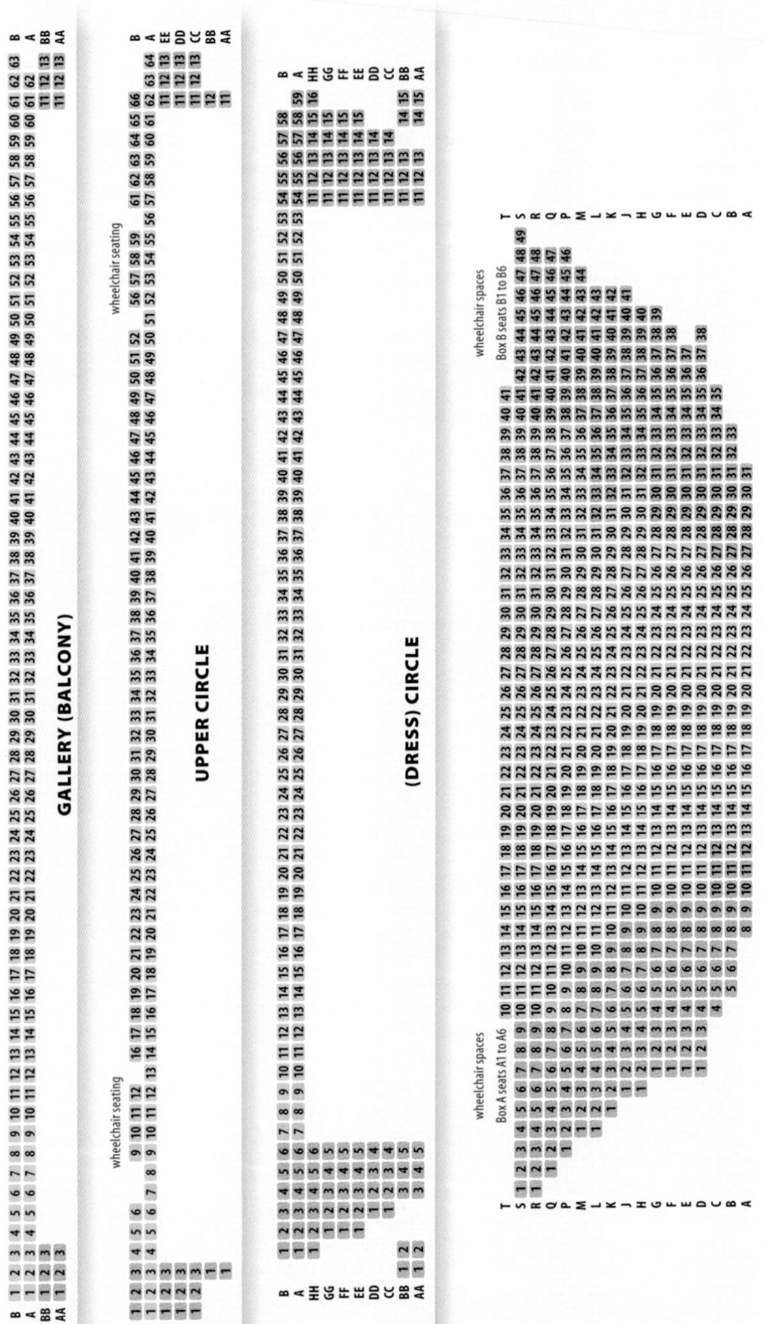

GALLERY (BALCONY)

UPPER CIRCLE

wheelchair seating

(DRESS) CIRCLE

STALLS

wheelchair spaces
Box B seats B1 to B6

wheelchair spaces
Box A seats A1 to A6

BARBICAN THEATRE

Barbican Theatre

Silk Street, London. EC2Y 8DS

Early press reports loved to mock the "confusing" location of this theatre, buried within a huge arts centre development. It isn't actually hard to find, or negotiate once inside, but allow for walking time from nearby stations.

BOX OFFICE:
0845 120 7500
020 7638 8891

ONLINE BOOKING:
www.barbican.org.uk

 Barbican/Moorgate

 Moorgate

P within building complex

1162 (main) 180+ (Pit)

❄ Air conditioned

The theatres were originally designed for the Royal Shakespeare Company (RSC). Modern architecture placed entrance doors at the ends of each row in the main house, eliminating aisles, with circles set back to overhang the stalls as little as possible. When the RSC left in May 2002, the centre created as a replacement their famous BITE (Barbican International Theatre Event) seasons. Regular theatregoers often select randomly from the monthly programme, knowing they're practically guaranteed something unusual and high quality every time.

STALLS: The ends of rows A to P are at an angle to the stage, with those in A to G sometimes feeling that the cast are constantly "sideways on" to them. Both these areas and central row A are often heavily discounted. In particular, central A can be a bargain if seeing the entire stage isn't an issue.

In other front rows, go central, avoiding angled seats. By row P, the overall view of the stage improves, though individual performances seem more remote. Wheelchair spaces in the rear stalls have sightlines on a par with seats around them, but upper circle positions may provide a greater overall view. Legroom meets modern expectations in all seats. Sometimes seating is boarded over to create a "traverse" central stage with grandstand seating facing it on two sides. In this case, views are generally fine from all seats, depending on production staging.

(DRESS) CIRCLE: The majority of seats are in a long-spanning section above and behind the stalls. The view is more distant than usually expected from a dress circle, with a bar also sneaking into shorter theatregoers' sightlines. Seats B9 to 51, followed at a pinch by A9 to 51, are worth considering if cheaper than stalls. To the sides of the theatre are two projecting balconies, sometimes named "the ashtrays", and designated rows AA to HH. Theatre architecture ensures that they miss the edges of the stage. Except in row AA, legroom is acceptable here.

UPPER CIRCLE: Quirky design makes it (and its "ashtrays") closer to the stage than the dress circle, and low prices make central seats an attractive choice. Shorter patrons should watch the safety rail, though. End seats A1 to 6 and 59 to 64 are reasonably priced, considering both their side views and comfort. Wheelchair spaces here provide a better overall view of the stage than dedicated stalls positions. Rows AA and BB have wide single seats with cramped legroom and side views – only worthwhile if exceptionally cheap. The extra wide seat was originally for two, but the one-and-a-half person width reveals why that idea was revised soon after opening – though it may make a comeback on "Singles' Night".

GALLERY (BALCONY): Seats here are slightly closer to the stage than the other circles, but also command a view of the lighting rig. Expect safety rails again, "ashtrays" with side views and also less legroom in row AA than elsewhere. Cheap end seats A1 to 8 and 55 to 62 and B1 to 8 and 56 to 63 are good value for the hard up.

The Pit

This is an infinitely adaptable basement space, usually a simple grandstand facing an open stage.

Central row A, when on stage level, is prime with good legroom. It also offers wheelchair users good views. Aisle seats on the rear row, with nothing in front but stairs, are also worth seeking. Legroom can be cramped elsewhere for the taller. When the playing area is the full width of the room, outermost seats may miss some action at the opposite end of the stage.

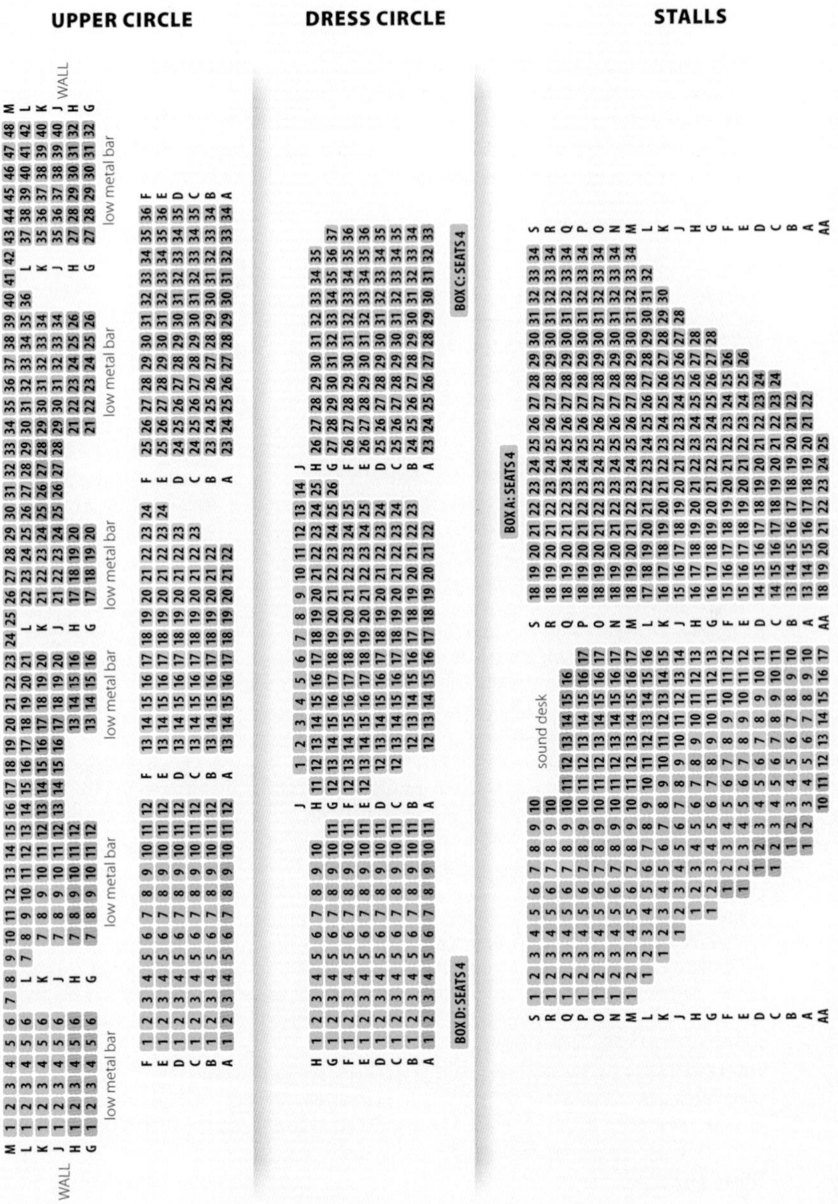

UPPER CIRCLE

DRESS CIRCLE

STALLS

WALL

low metal bar

low metal bar

low metal bar

low metal bar

low metal bar

BOX D: SEATS 4

BOX C: SEATS 4

BOX A: SEATS 4

sound desk

Cambridge Theatre

Earlham Street, London. WC2 9HU   **B7**

Relatively new by London standards, the 1930s style Cambridge is a friendly mid-scale theatre. Its quieter street location has led to wildly inventive programming, including Kenneth Williams paired with Ingrid Bergman for **Captain Brassbound's Conversion** in 1971; a short spell as **The Magic Castle** in 1986 and home of controversial **Jerry Springer – The Opera** in 2003.

BOX OFFICE:
0844 412 4652
0870 830 0200
020 7087 7500

ONLINE BOOKING:
www.seetickets.com

 Leicester Square
Tottenham Court Road

Charing Cross

P Newport Place, China Town (T), Shelton Street

1249

Air conditioned

stalls from row K back, and both circles

STALLS: "In this small theatre, you could see from anywhere, certainly in the stalls." Be aware of the shallow rake throughout, and watch outermost pairs of seats in the front seven rows for some productions as scenery can affect sightlines.

Row AA is popular: AA18, 22 and 23 "are pure luxury – stretch out… as if sitting on your own sofa". Behind, seats A5 and 6 have "great views, only missing the teeniest portion of the bottom of the stage". Central rows D to J are prime: seat G6 "combines a great view with good legroom for a 6ft man". Others favour centre aisle seats, for comfort and the need to compete for just one armrest. It's also easier to lean should the rake prove insufficient, as in seats O7 and 8 where the shallow rake may cause problems with heads in front: "We moved and were fine. Legroom was lacking for the exceptionally tall."

Stalls boxes: These are behind the main seating block. Little action is missed, despite the overhanging circle.

DRESS CIRCLE: A low rail may distract some in row A, while the upper circle overhang (and sometimes lighting equipment) cuts into the view from row G back. Otherwise, this shallow circle provides an acceptable view, with central B to G best. One Theatremoney.com reader, to whom the box office recommended C16 and 17, reports: "Raking adequate, legroom (I'm 6ft 1in) OK, view excellent. Back and extreme sides would have been less satisfactory." Seats C18 and 19 "are good seats, just as Theatremonkey describes them". Sound balance in row B was also considered excellent.

Seats furthest to the sides of the section may be less desirable (a projector used in one production irritated many Theatremonkey.com readers in rows F to H), but there's little to worry about if they're the only remaining option.

Dress circle boxes: From these, theatregoers may miss the sides of the stage, depending on staging. "Box C is fab – the view was great (though at an angle), with only a small part of the stage unviewable. Having a private area and great sound quality – speaker to side of box – was wonderful."

UPPER CIRCLE: The rail across the front of row A distracts. "Sitting up straight and leaning, you pretty much eliminate its effects. Felt far forward, didn't seem high, and could clearly see facial expressions." The Monkey likes central C to F seats and one contributor in E25 states: "I was perfectly happy with view and sound quality, and the legroom."

A rear section, behind a safety rail at row G, provides budget seating but may feel "out of the way". Skip the first two rows to avoid sightline problems, and avoid sitting beside or behind walls protecting stairwells in front of row J. Claustrophobics might wish to avoid outermost seats (rows G to M, seats 1 and 40), without aisles adjacent. Legroom is tight almost everywhere. Row M seats looking down stairway aisles provide most legroom, though loo-bound audience members may scuttle through your view mid-show. One Theatremonkey.com reader feels there's "no point paying much for these seats"; some feel they compare favourably with the cheapest in other London theatres.

```
     F  1  2  3  4  5  6  7  8  9  10 11 12 13 14 15 16 17 18 19 20 21 22 23 24   F
     E  1  2  3  4  5  6  7  8  9  10 11 12 13 14 15 16 17 18 19 20 21 22 23 24   E
     D  1  2  3  4  5  6  7  8  9  10 11 12 13 14 15 16 17 18 19 20 21 22 23      D
     C     1  2  3  4  5  6  7  8  9  10 11 12 13 14 15 16 17 18 19 20 21 22      C
     B     1  2  3  4  5  6  7  8  9  10 11 12 13 14 15 16 17 18 19 20 21         B
     A        1  2  3  4  5  6  7  8  9  10 11 12 13 14 15 16 17 18 19 20         A
```

BALCONY

```
     F  1  2  3  4  5  6  7  8  9              10 11 12 13 14 15 16 17 18 19      F
     E  1  2  3  4  5  6  7  8  9  10 11 12 13 14 15 16 17 18 19 20 21 22 23 24   E
     D  1  2  3  4  5  6  7  8  9  10 11 12 13 14 15 16 17 18 19 20 21 22 23      D
     C     1  2  3  4  5  6  7  8  9  10 11 12 13 14 15 16 17 18 19 20 21         C
     B        1  2  3  4  5  6  7  8  9  10 11 12 13 14 15 16 17 18 19 20         B
     A        1  2  3  4  5  6  7  8  9  10 11 12 13 14 15 16 17 18 19            A
```

ROYAL (UPPER) CIRCLE

```
                    F  1  2  3  4  5  6  7  8  9  10 11  F
     E  1  2  3  4  5    E  6  7  8  9  10 11 12 13 14 15 16  E         17 18 19 20 21  E
WALL D  1  2  3  4  5    D  6  7  8  9  10 11 12 13 14 15 16  D         17 18 19 20 21  D WALL
     C     1  2  3  4  5 C  6  7  8  9  10 11 12 13 14 15     C      16 17 18 19 20     C
     B        1  2  3  4  5 B  6  7  8  9  10 11 12 13 14     B   15 16 17 18 19        B
     A           1  2  3  4  5 A  6  7  8  9  10 11 12  A  13 14 15 16 17               A
```

DRESS CIRCLE

```
     U  1  2  3  4  5  6  7  8  9  10    11 12 13 14 15 16 17 18 19 20       U
     T  1  2  3  4  5  6  7  8  9  10    11 12 13 14 15 16 17 18 19 20       T
     S  1  2  3  4  5  6  7  8  9  10    11 12 13 14 15 16 17 18 19 20       S
     R  1  2  3  4  5  6  7  8  9  10 11 12 13 14 15 16 17 18 19 20 21       R
     Q  1  2  3  4  5  6  7  8  9  10 11 12 13 14 15 16 17 18 19 20 21 22    Q
     P  1  2  3  4  5  6  7  8  9  10 11 12 13 14 15 16 17 18 19 20 21       P
     O  1  2  3  4  5  6  7  8  9  10 11 12 13 14 15 16 17 18 19 20 21 22    O
     N  1  2  3  4  5  6  7  8  9  10 11 12 13 14 15 16 17 18 19 20 21       N
     M  1  2  3  4  5  6  7  8  9  10 11 12 13    14 15 16 17 18 19          M
     L  1  2  3  4  5  6  7  8  9  10 11 12 13 14 15 16 17 18 19 20          L
     K     1  2  3  4  5  6  7  8  9  10 11 12 13 14 15 16 17 18 19 20       K
     J        1  2  3  4  5  6  7  8  9  10 11 12 13 14 15 16 17 18 19       J
     H  1  2  3  4  5  6  7  8  9  10 11 12 13 14 15 16 17 18 19 20 21 22    H
     G  1  2  3  4  5  6  7  8  9  10 11 12 13 14 15 16 17 18 19 20 21       G
     F  1  2  3  4  5  6  7  8  9  10 11 12 13 14 15 16 17 18 19 20 21 22    F
     E  1  2  3  4  5  6  7  8  9  10 11 12 13 14 15 16 17 18 19 20 21       E
     D  1  2  3  4  5  6  7  8  9  10 11 12 13 14 15 16 17 18 19 20 21 22    D
     C  1  2  3  4  5  6  7  8  9  10 11 12 13 14 15 16 17 18 19 20 21       C
     B     1  2  3  4  5  6  7  8  9  10 11 12 13 14 15 16 17 18 19 20       B
     A     1  2  3  4  5  6  7  8  9  10 11 12 13 14 15 16 17 18 19          A
```

BOX D: SEATS 4   BOX C: SEATS 4

STALLS

Comedy Theatre

Panton Street, London. SW1 4DN   **B17**

Tucked away between Haymarket and Leicester Square, this theatre remains popular with producers. Comedy, drama and even the odd musical come across well on this smallish stage – as newly **Cats** wealthy Cameron Mackintosh found with **Little Shop Of Horrors** in 1983. The 1881 auditorium's crop of iron pillars is a visible link with architects past.

BOX OFFICE:
0870 060 6637
020 8544 7424

ONLINE BOOKING:
ambassadortickets.com

 Piccadilly Circus

Charing Cross

P Whitcomb Street (T)

796

Air conditioned

STALLS: Think: "Those in front of row M pillars and those behind." Happily, these pillars do keep the dress circle out of sightlines back to row R. The front rows may be problematic. One Theatremonkey.com reader reports "B7, 8: possibility of neck ache because it's so close"; others feel "you might as well be on stage". The outermost seats in row A may find scenery blocking sightlines. A1 (plus C1, C21, K1 and K20) are designated "restricted legroom".

Mid-stalls before the pillars are popular. Only the first and last few seats in C to H, situated almost outside the proscenium arch, may miss stage-edge action – a Theatremonkey.com reader highlights this for G1 to 3. Otherwise, most seats back to row K can be summed up in a comment echoing many: "Excellent position, legroom adequate, seat comfortable… shallow rake means a lot of head dodging… seat spacing allows you to see through gaps... person behind me asked me to slouch but the legroom would not allow it." Rows J to L also feel close to the action.

Behind these, safest bets are the seats between the pillars – expensive at top price, but views are not badly affected. Aisle seats are next choice when cheaper. Very back rows have only the advantage of legroom over seats elsewhere at similar prices.

DRESS CIRCLE: Central block aisle seats are behind pillars. To compensate, overhang intrusion is minimal. Double bars at aisle ends are a sightline hazard for adjacent seats, particularly A6 and 12.

Central row A "appeared to have more legroom than B" while row F "has even less legroom than elsewhere in the dress circle, and my 6' 4'' husband had to move". Between, one Theatremonkey.com reader felt "the shallow rake in row E made the stage seem far way". Pillars frame the views from rows C back. It's not worth sitting directly behind these, but some feel the adjacent seat worth a try when discounted.

Side block seats follow the curve of the circle, allowing centre stage views only for those willing to lean. Outermost seats, without adjacent aisles, may make claustrophobics miserable. Wheelchair users should find their E17 space acceptable.

ROYAL (UPPER) CIRCLE: Metal rails interrupt row A views, particularly with supports roughly every fourth seat. Further aisle rails make A1, 2, 16 and 17 notably worth missing. Shallow rake and lack of legroom may cause discomfort. Central row C has a tiny bit more legroom; B5, 6, 15 and 16 have least. Central seats have best sightlines. Tall pillars minimise circle overhang but create other problems; take only the most central seats behind them.

BALCONY: A shallow rake lessens vertigo slightly, as do rails fronting and ending each row. No pillars here, but row A's front rail has the same extra vertical bars as the upper circle, with further aisle bars beside A1 and 20.

Side seats are often "restricted view" but not discounted. The short-legged should pick central C or B, considering also D or E if cheaper than this pair.

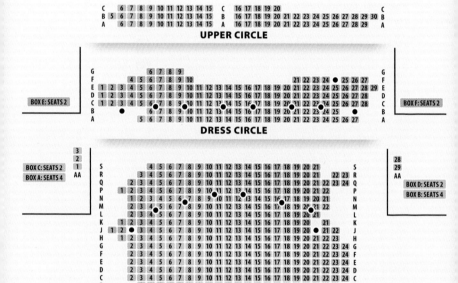

UPPER CIRCLE

DRESS CIRCLE

BOX E: SEATS 2

BOX F: SEATS 2

BOX C: SEATS 2
BOX A: SEATS 4

BOX D: SEATS 2
BOX B: SEATS 4

STALLS

Criterion Theatre

Piccadilly Circus, London. W1V 9LB   **B15**

The Victorian tiling in the entrance foyer is spectacular. Alas, much is now concealed behind an extended box office wall. Unusually, in this theatre you walk downstairs even to the upper circle. Rumour has it that the stalls could be given their own London Underground platform one day. Productions usually wish to stay a long time here. Partly because it's a beautifully decorated, well-managed, delightfully pink jewel in central Piccadilly; partly because the front of a box has to be removed before any scenery can be extracted.

BOX OFFICE:
0844 847 1778
0161 385 3211

ONLINE BOOKING:
www.ticketmaster.co.uk

 Piccadilly Circus

Charing Cross

P Denman Street

590

❄ Air conditioned

STALLS: "Marvellous theatre, but there are seats I wouldn't want to sit in." Check which ones have restricted views. The dress circle overhangs the stalls at row H, intruding into the view from row M back. Supporting pillars in rows J, K, N and P further complicate sightlines.

Those seated before the pillar forest are happiest: A16 "is very close to the action" with "notably good legroom". Some rate not just the seats creaky but their neck vertebrae, too, when viewing the high stage from front rows. Many find central seats from rows E to M acceptable, with good views and reasonable legroom. Very little rake, though, means "you could be unlucky if someone tall sits in front". With luck, and the "Huge Head of the Year Competition" taking place elsewhere, expect, "a perfect view of everything".

Outermost seats in rows A to E are often cheaper to compensate for missing nearside action, with many pleased at the saving. From row J, seats amid the pillars are cheaper, with P12, 15 and 16 normally combining a discount with a reasonable view. The following seats are designated "restricted view": K21, L 2 and 21, M2 and 21, N1, 3 and 20, P1 to 7 and 17 to 22, Q1 to 7, 11, 14, 15, 18 to 24, R1 to 7, 11, 12, 15, 16 and 19 to 23, S4 to 7, 10, 11, 14, 15 and 18 to 21. You'll benefit from legroom and price more than sightlines.

DRESS CIRCLE: Behind row B grows a Victorian pillar fan's dream. Users of row C back may become nostalgic for the cantilevered balconies installed elsewhere. Row A is better. For example, A22 and 23 have "adequate legroom (friend 5ft 8in) and an excellent view". Then consider central B perhaps: "in B6 to 8, the view was fantastic with no one in front", but "head in front of me in seat 9 blocked out centre stage". Behind, seats between pillars provide framed views of the stage.

Similarly priced front stalls are the better option, also providing more legroom for the taller. In the side corners, "Row AA has an odd viewing angle" and is labelled "restricted view" along with pillared friends C5, 9, 20 and 24, D1, 2, 4, 5, 8, 12, 16, 20, 24, 27 and 28, E1 to 5, 8, 9, 13, 17, 18, 21, 22, 25, 28 and 29, F4 to 7, 10, 21, 22, 25 to 27 and G6 to 9. These are attractive at low prices, though.

Dress circle boxes: Boxes A, B, C and D sit either side of the stage. A and B have the better viewing angle, though all miss nearside stage action. A fair alternative to pillar-blighted seats elsewhere.

UPPER CIRCLE: Fairly low and blessedly pillar-free, these seats are normally well priced but offer little legroom. "The front row may be cramped but I would try it… From B11, 12 and 13, row A heads would have blocked centre stage. Behind us, row C were complaining and asking, without success, to be moved." Row C wheelchair spaces have an adequate view.

Upper circle boxes: Boxes E and F, above the dress circle boxes, offer side views. "Box E is cheap, but you may have to lean forwards almost out of the box, legs pressed right up against the edge, to see anything."

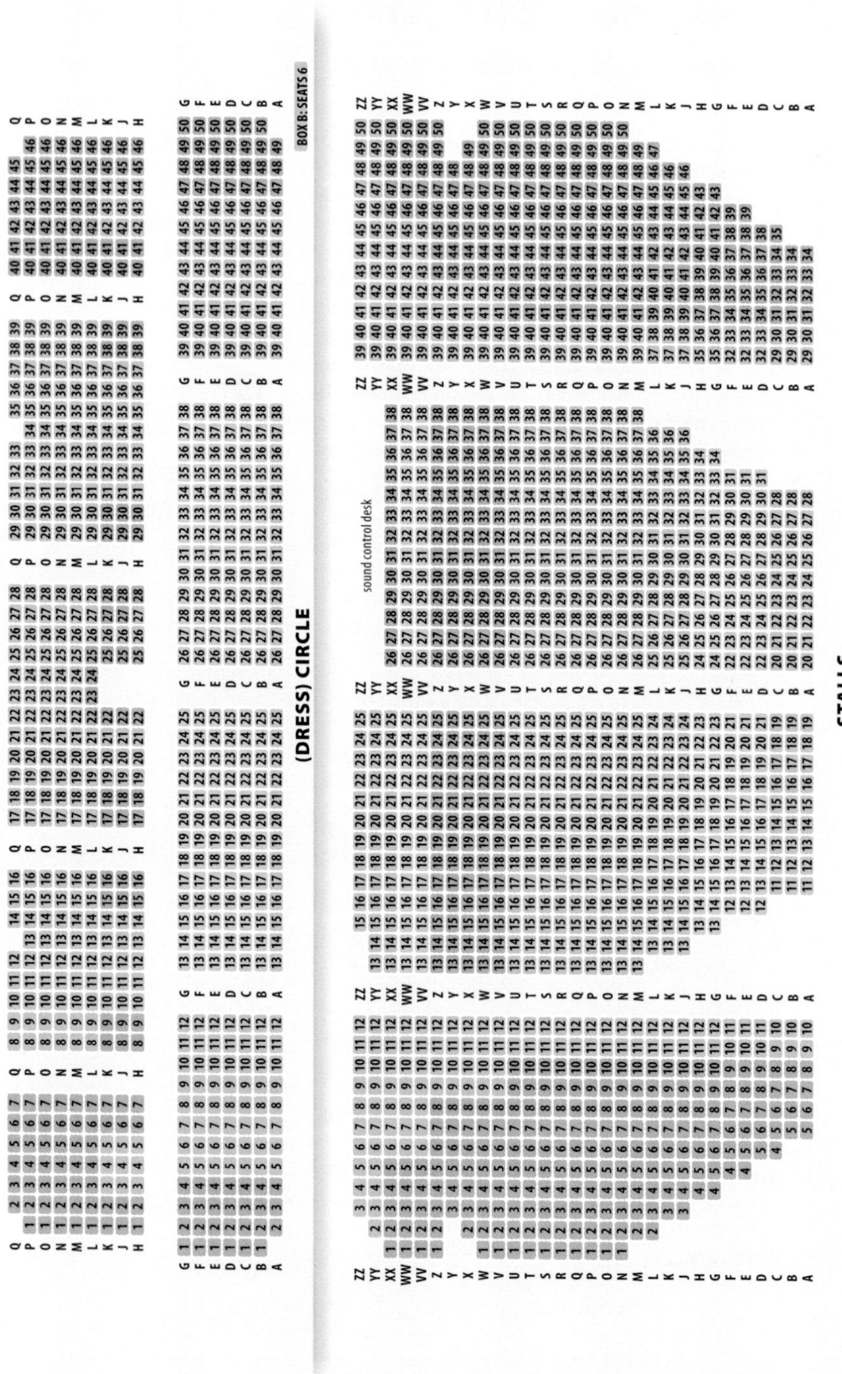

BOX B: SEATS 6

(DRESS) CIRCLE

sound control desk

STALLS

Dominion Theatre

Tottenham Court Road, London. W1P 0AG   B2

Intended as a live theatre, the Dominion ended up a cinema for over 40 years, playing long-running spectaculars like **South Pacific** and **The Sound of Music**. A vast musical theatre house since the 1980s, filling it takes some doing. Infamous, papally blessed, disaster **Bernadette** (1990) had the few brave audience members (including the Monkey) sniggering at the "leaky doughnut" and "homicidal coat hanger". Later shows **Grease** and **We Will Rock You** fared much better, and visits here are usually enhanced by attractively sunny staff.

BOX OFFICE:
0870 169 0116
0161 385 3211

ONLINE BOOKING:
www.dominiontheatrelondon.org.uk

 Tottenham Court Road (exit 3)

Euston

Great Russell Street

2000

Air Cooled only

 stalls from row Q back, and in circle

STALLS: With 28 rows in four blocks, "near front and central" is best. The circle overhangs row K, but has little impact on views until cutting off the very top of the stage from row T back. The stage is high, the orchestra pit cavernous when used. A Theatremonkey.com reader in row A "missed a small amount of rear-stage action". Rows behind draw appreciation for comfort and view. Twenty rows back, charging top price begins to seem a little greedy but, as prices fall beyond row Z, value rises. Those in seats VV15 and 16 found the view "fabulous" and those in row WW got clear views "at least comparable to second-price rear stalls elsewhere".

Both side blocks have an acute viewing angle if seated too far forward, and rear corner stage action can go missing. Beyond row T, it improves for many seats, and pricing is keener from row V, making seats on the central aisle attractive. Further forward, too, centre aisle seats are popular, with some "close enough to see actors' faces" (Q11 and 12). Don't despair of the cheapest seats either: those in seats YY49 and 50 were "pleasantly surprised", advising that, if cheaper tickets with good views and comfort are required, "these are the ones". Wheelchair spaces in XX, YY and ZZ are fair value for the distant view, better than the box alternative.

(DRESS) CIRCLE: This is vast, yet the front section feels quite close to the stage. Row A suffers restricted legroom for those over 5ft 6in. It has aisle rails that pedants might avoid; everyone else gets a handy discount for the inconvenience. Boxes or lighting may intrude into sightlines from end seats. All other seats are preferable to side block stalls. Central seats from B to G are a treat.

Behind, it's easy to imagine looking at a 20ft-tall Julie Andrews on screen, but an actor on a stage is different. With a stage extended over the orchestra pit, those in seats H to K6–9, 15–18, 27–30, 38 and 39 may find safety rails in view when actors stand too far forward. However, the legroom is excellent. The Monkey's feeling is that, unless with particularly fussy friends, these seats are fine – noting this information only "for the record". Also worth noting are L22 to 25 behind a stairwell wall. The view isn't great for shorter theatregoers, with slightly tighter legroom for the tallest.

Furthest back, the rake is steep and the stage distant. Centrally, one Theatremonkey.com reader recommends P17 to 20, giving these seats a "Great!!!" rating as they could "see everything super-clearly". Comparable to rear stalls, with a little more vertigo, there's a little less legroom but no circle overhang. Off in the side blocks, L to Q1 to 7 and 40 to 46 do feel tucked into corners – a final choice.

Entry to the last circle rows is via gantry-like stairs from the circle foyer, sharply contrasting with the vast marble flights thus far. Front-block inhabitants get level access, but, come the revolution, comrades… Seats here may seem slightly smaller than the stalls, but still acceptable.

Dress circle boxes: The nearest fifth of the stage isn't easily visible, so leaning or shuffling your chair a little may be required. Motorised wheelchair users can park here, and there's space for carers.

B 14 15 16 17 18 19 20 21 22 23 24 25 26 27 28 29 30 31 32 33 B
A 14 15 16 17 18 19 20 21 22 23 24 25 26 27 28 29 30 31 32 33 A

(DRESS) CIRCLE

13
12 12 12
11 11 11
10 10 10
9 9 9
8 8 8
7 7 7
6 6 6
5 5 5
4 4 4
3 3 3
2 2 2
C B A

D 10 11 12 13 14 15 16 17 18 19 20 21 22 23 24 25 26 27 28 29 30 D
C 11 12 13 14 15 16 17 18 19 20 21 22 23 24 25 26 27 28 29 30 C
B 13 14 15 16 17 18 19 20 21 22 23 24 25 26 27 28 29 B
A 16 17 18 19 20 21 22 23 24 25 26 27 A

34
35 35 35
36 36 36
37 37 37
38 38 38
39 39 39
40 40 40
41 41 41
42 42 42
43 43 43
44 44 44
45 45 45
A B C

9 9
8 8 8
7 7 7 7
6 6 6 6
5 5 5 5
4 4 4 4
3 3 3 3
2 2 2 2
1 1 1
D C B A

STALLS

31 31 31
32 32 32
33 33 33
34 34 34 34
35 35 35 35
36 36 36 36
37 37 37 37
38 38 38 38
39 39 39 39
40 40 40 40
41 41 41 41
42
A B C D

DONMAR WAREHOUSE THEATRE

Donmar Warehouse Theatre

Earlham Street, London. WC2H 9LX   **B8**

This is easy to miss, so walk down the left side of the Cambridge Theatre, pass a shopping mall and look for the wavy neon sign. There's usually a long returns queue (suffering from starvation, hypothermia or heatstroke, depending on time and season) as this theatre is famed for amazing casting, outstanding producing and ticket demand outstripping supply. Part of a converted brewery warehouse, the brainchild of impresario Donald Albery and dancer Margot Fonteyn (get it? Don-Mar!), this venue is successful out of all proportion to its size. The best way to secure tickets is to join the Friends scheme (see the Donmar website).

BOX OFFICE:
0870 060 6624
020 8544 7424

ONLINE BOOKING:
www.donmarwarehouse.com

 Covent Garden

 Charing Cross

🅿 Newport Place, China Town (T), Shelton Street

🚻 252

❄ Air Cooled only

STALLS: Four rows of benches, with the circle above safely out of sightlines, surround a large square stage on three sides. So close to the stage that the atmosphere created is incredibly intimate, every seat feels connected to the action.

Prices are now differentiated only according to whether you're in a front or side block. At previews, both blocks are the same price. Those seated in a side block nearest the back of the playing area often see a rear view of the actors most of the time. Choose seats close to the "centre block" end if possible, the wheelchair position at D31 being a good example to follow. Theatremonkey.com readers in seats A37 and 38 had a "great view of actor only about 6ft away" but further back they'd have been at eye level rather than knee level to the actors. A circle view is an alternative, feels the Monkey.

One observation that B41 "has ample legroom and padded bench [is] surprisingly comfortable" raises two points. Legroom varies in row A, depending on stage height, but is usually cramped. Elsewhere it's a little better, with central B and C9 and 30 having more. Being benches, with only numbers designating your share, they can cause stress. Not all theatregoers muck in and shuffle along until comfortable. "I arrived first," reports one Theatremonkey.com reader, "later we all kinda squeezed up – and I lost ground. Everyone else was sitting comfortably and I was the only one like a sardine in a tin."

(DRESS) CIRCLE: This sits above the stalls on three sides, with a thick rail around the front, treble height at the corners. Those in A12, 14, 33 and 35 will find the rail in view. A further rail, across row B, affects sightlines little except for short theatregoers.

As benches again, similar issues arise as for the stalls. Those taking up A9 and 10 found "decent views and no real space problems" and "the most comfortable theatre bench seats". B23 and 24 are reported to have "plenty of legroom", although a backrest that's "too upright", and a good view "apart from front end blocked by a bar". The Monkey prefers B to avoid the front rail, and would take stalls A first, then central circle, side circle and side stalls from preference. At bottom price, circle row B is good value.

Row C is sadistically installed half-way up one wall, with another in front to lean on. Gymnastics are required to perch here, and the row is half a buttock too short. "Thanks to ever-reliable Monkey seating advice, after reading that the bench on which I'd booked five seats was half a seat short, I was able to get an extra place at the last minute. Otherwise we'd have had to form a human pyramid, which would have been even more distracting."

The view is great but, in summary, "I've been uncomfortable in B, and bothered by the bar in A, but C is the absolute worst. After my second visit, [I'll] never accept another balcony seat. Whoever designed them, which all pitch slightly forward, was not on speaking terms with whoever planned the human body." Happily, a tall person could comfortably stand in row C, avoiding lesser legroom elsewhere.

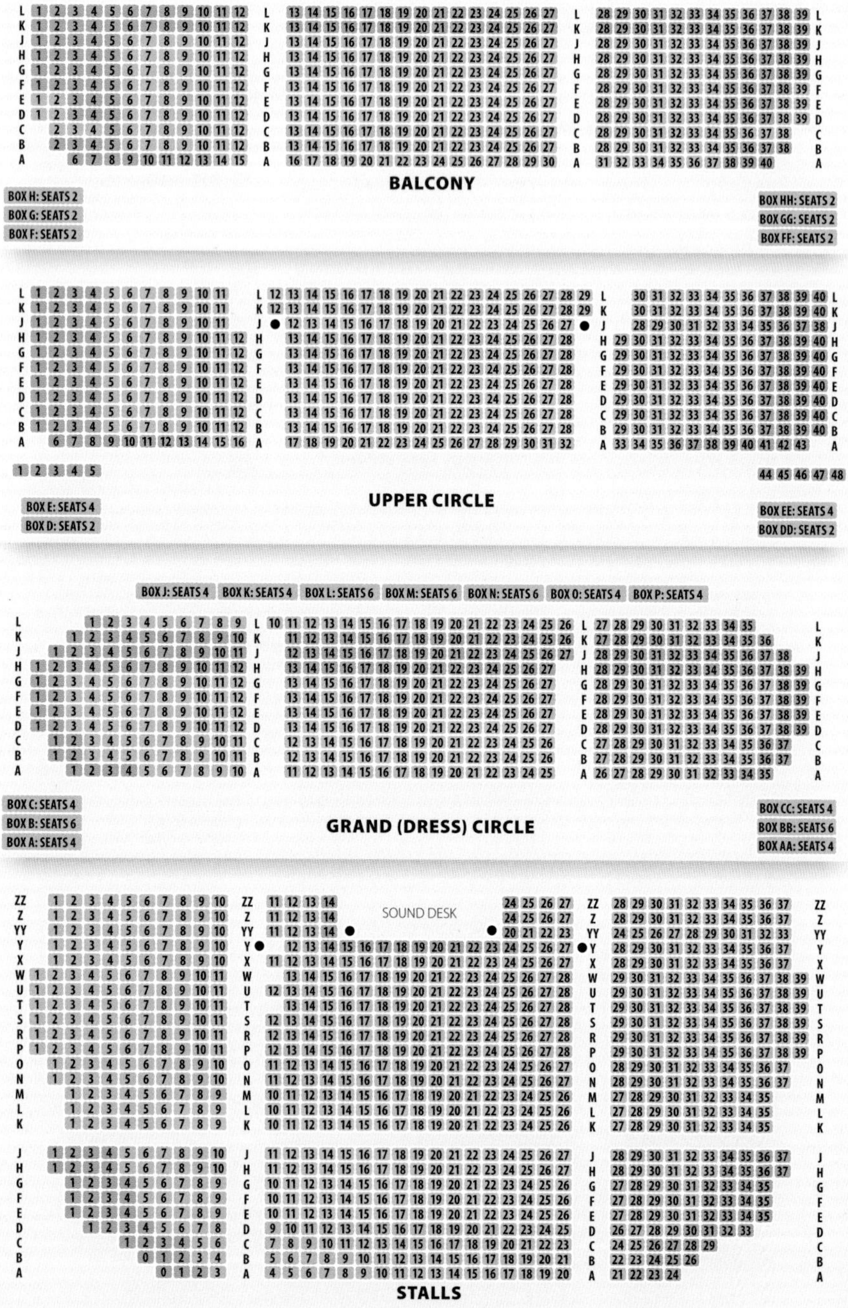

BALCONY

BOX H: SEATS 2
BOX G: SEATS 2
BOX F: SEATS 2

BOX HH: SEATS 2
BOX GG: SEATS 2
BOX FF: SEATS 2

UPPER CIRCLE

BOX E: SEATS 4
BOX D: SEATS 2

BOX EE: SEATS 4
BOX DD: SEATS 2

BOX J: SEATS 4   BOX K: SEATS 4   BOX L: SEATS 6   BOX M: SEATS 6   BOX N: SEATS 6   BOX O: SEATS 4   BOX P: SEATS 4

GRAND (DRESS) CIRCLE

BOX C: SEATS 4
BOX B: SEATS 6
BOX A: SEATS 4

BOX CC: SEATS 4
BOX BB: SEATS 6
BOX AA: SEATS 4

SOUND DESK

STALLS

DRURY LANE (THEATRE ROYAL)

Drury Lane (Theatre Royal)

Catherine Street, London WC2B 5JF   C37

As much museum as entertainment venue, it's worth reading up about George III's "Kings" and "Princes" sides, the Baddeley Cake and resident spooks before visiting. One famous spectre haunts the upper circle, the evidence clear after matinees (assuming that's ectoplasm, not melted ice cream). On stage, another, clown Joe Grimaldi, kicks lazy actors as required.

BOX OFFICE:
0844 412 2955
0870 830 0200
020 7087 7500

ONLINE BOOKING:
www.seetickets.com

Covent Garden/Temple/Holborn

Charing Cross

Parker Street

2200

Air cooled (ineffective)

stalls from row L back, and all circles

STALLS: Central fifth row and back appreciate best the vast stage. Outermost seats can suffer scenery-disrupted sightlines and noisy speakers. Further forward, those in B9 to 15 "had to look up slightly", their children needing booster cushions, and in C22, C23 and D17 "were far too close" feeling that "big shows would look better from afar". A few rows back, H9 to 17 "were perfect". Best of all is row K (K16 to 20 possibly "the most amazing place to sit"), a few millimetres higher than J and on a wide aisle. Side view wheelchair spaces here are also acceptable.

Seats L12 and 13 are "far enough back to see the whole stage, close enough to engage". The circle overhangs M (J at the sides). In M8 and 9, the dress circle "may appreciate overall staging more easily", but others are happy enough. "S29 to 33 [have] wonderful views and just enough legroom for [a 6ft tall person]." Further back, where the overhang is most noticeable, seats are lower and legroom tighter, prices fall to compensate. Purists may also wish to avoid seats around the large sound desk in rows Z and ZZ.

GRAND (DRESS) CIRCLE: Only row H back notice the circle overhang. Otherwise, "the dress circle is best for appreciating the whole spectacle". Theatremonkey.com readers agree on row A views, but not legroom – ranging from "fine" to fit for "hobbits". Stalls are safer for the taller; others will find central rows B to D unbeatable. Further out, C1 to 3 "are totally worth it at a discount" and K3 and 4 "didn't feel like we were all the way over at the side". Behind, H gets "the impact of set and lighting" while L "has a very restricted view of the stage top, missing atmosphere". Worth considering only if discounted, perhaps.

Boxes: Comfortable boxes J to P provide more legroom than row L in front, but share circle overhang issues. Of the side boxes, pick C and CC first if discounted and not shared with speakers. Above these D, E, DD and EE provide similar views from a higher angle.

UPPER CIRCLE: This offers good-value views and variable legroom: "adequate for 5' 8'' person, and steep steps" (C27 and 28); "slightly cramped" (D23 and 24); "rock hard seats" (E21 and 22). If cheaper, compensating for the overhang at row H, seats K24 to 28 "felt near the stage, with fantastic views [but] legroom cramped".

Extreme edge seats may lose nearside stage action, while aisle rails block centre stage from A16, 33 and B and C12 and 29. "Fine if discounted." Seats 12 and 29 in rows K and L are behind pillars. Acceptable if willing to lean, Row L is first pick, 12 slightly before 29.

BALCONY: "Steep enough to give a good view, wouldn't have wanted to be at the back." Others report a long climb up, vertigo, heat and uncomfortable seats. Rail-fronted rows A and B are discounted favourites. One Theatremonkey.com reader in A "leaned to look through the bars and didn't need binoculars much". Others in D27, 29 and 30 thought their seats "brilliant", in row H reported "set tops missed, leaned forward once" and in K20 to 22 "missed facial expressions, can see behind set". Outermost row C to F seats are usually cheaper, compensating for missed side action or aisle rails in view. Fit climbers with good eyesight will be happy up here.

BOX C: SEATS 2　　　　　　　BOX B: SEATS 4

BOX E: SEATS 2　　**DRESS CIRCLE**　　BOX F: SEATS 2

STALLS

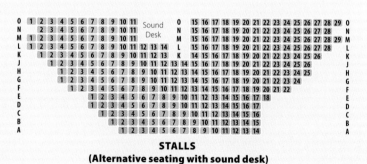

STALLS
(Alternative seating with sound desk)

Duchess Theatre

Catherine Street, London. WC2B 5LA   **C36**

Architect Ewen S. Barr cleverly overcame "Ancient Lights" laws when designing this theatre in 1929. Prohibited from blocking neighbours' daylight, he sunk the stalls as deep as possible with the entrance foyer above. This kept the roofline low enough to satisfy planners, and so one of London's neatest little venues was born.

BOX OFFICE:
0844 412 4659
0844 579 1973
0870 830 0200
020 7087 7500

ONLINE BOOKING:
www.nimaxtheatres.com

 Covent Garden/Temple/ Holborn

 Charing Cross

P Parker Street

475

No air conditioning

Seemingly at odds with its name, the Duchess seems to attract risqué entertainments, with *The Dirtiest Show In Town, Oh Calcutta!* and the final years of extraordinary 1970s hit *No Sex Please, We're British* playing here. Its greatest claim to fame, though, is the single night run of *The Intimate Review* on 11 March 1930. With scenes scrapped in order to end before midnight, it was wittily described as "half a performance". More recently, *Stones In His Pockets* was forced by cast illness to end a highly successful run after just a month in 2006.

STALLS: These are narrow; the longest row has only 29 seats. It's normally worth avoiding the first and last four seats in rows A to E as the combination of curving row and proximity to stage can make rear-stage corners vanish. For some productions, the stage is raised, potentially inducing neck ache and restricting sightlines for those seated centrally in A and B. Discounted prices are the clue and those who, like the Monkey, are unworried by such things will grab the opportunity.

The rake begins at row G and, at full price, this row is prime. Next, try rows H and J. Theatremonkey. com readers in seats G4 and 5 found "although the seats were a little cramped, the view was very good". Unless shorter or most unlucky, the heads of those in front are very rarely sightline-blockers here. Further back, the views continue to please most, and pricing in the final rows can provide for a cheaper and comfortable evening.

Wheelchairs can be accommodated beside N2 and 28, with just acceptable views. Also be aware of a sound desk, which can replace rows N and O12 to 14. Purists may wish to avoid seats nearby.

Legroom is best in central row A, average in rows B to F (F1 and 22 have most) and better in rows G to O. Centre aisle seats are available from row G back for plays, row K for musicals, adding extra comfort to good views.

DRESS CIRCLE: This is split into two blocks across the front of row D, and the view from all seats in rows A to C is fine. Seated in row B, one Theatremonkey.com reader reports a good view and "legroom not too bad". When the stage is high, the Monkey is tempted to sit here rather than very front stalls at top price. Otherwise, there's little to choose between stalls and front dress circle. The stalls offer the advantage of legroom, while circle seats, being tiered, minimise the risk of "heads in front blocking views" for shorter theatregoers.

Further back, with rows D to F at top price, the Monkey looks to the stalls first for being closer to the stage. Prices usually drop in the last three rows, however, and these can prove fine budget choices. In particular, row H is invariably reasonably priced and feels closer to the stage than Theatremonkey. com readers usually expect from a bottom-priced ticket.

Dress circle boxes: Boxes E and F – really almost just isolated seats at the front of the dress circle – offer a side view but more legroom than average. They're perhaps worth considering if no stalls are available at the same price. Two further boxes at the rear of the dress circle provide unobstructed views, with more legroom than row H in front, and a low price reflecting their distance from the stage.

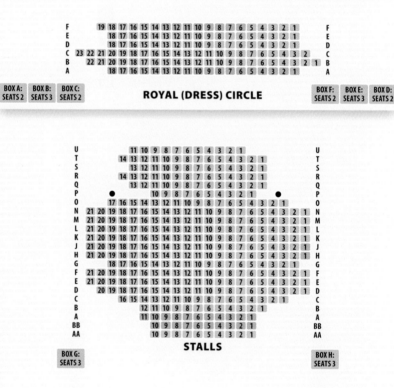

UPPER CIRCLE

BOX J: SEATS 2   BOX K: SEATS 2   BOX L: SEATS 2

BOX O: SEATS 2   BOX N: SEATS 2   BOX M: SEATS 2

ROYAL (DRESS) CIRCLE

BOX A: SEATS 2   BOX B: SEATS 3   BOX C: SEATS 2

BOX F: SEATS 2   BOX E: SEATS 3   BOX D: SEATS 2

STALLS

BOX G: SEATS 3

BOX H: SEATS 3

Duke of York's Theatre

St. Martin's Lane, London. WC2N 4BG   **B25**

Famously the original home of **Peter Pan**, and also to a ghost who slams a non-existent iron door shut at 10pm each night, this friendly theatre near Trafalgar Square seems to make even the dullest play shine. Productions queue up to play here. The owners would love to put into operation the many restoration and improvement plans, if only the flow of successful productions would allow. Violet Melnotte, most famous guardian of the theatre in Victorian times (and allegedly the door-slamming spectre), would be delighted.

BOX OFFICE:
0870 060 6623
020 8544 7424

ONLINE BOOKING:
www.ambassadortickets.com

 Leicester Square/ Charing Cross

 Charing Cross

Spring Gardens (T)

659

Air conditioned

STALLS: Rows AA to B are between the stalls boxes, creating an intimate atmosphere. Theatremonkey.com readers report "the whole cast was within touching distance" (AA5 and 6) and "BB has limited legroom". In A1 to 3 "at full price I'd go a few rows further back". Row AA is generally cheaper, to compensate for neck ache, but may be replaced by an extended stage, in which case A suffers.

Further back, C11 "feels really in on the action", D11 is perfect with "plenty of knee room", from E13 and 14 the view "wasn't blocked by heads in front", while G9 and 10 "felt a little far forward". At "restricted view" prices, the last seats in D and E can be bargains, but face box walls as much as the stage. Further back still (J21), "no elevation/rake meant centre stage blocked by the head in front". Several Theatremonkey.com readers consider rows M and N insufficiently offset to see around those in front.

Two thick goalposts in the rear stalls are the only survivors of the "Great Pillar Cull" of 1980 to improve sightlines. Now only circle overhang disrupts views, cutting the top off the set from around row P back. Despite this and a shallow rake, rows R to U generally offer acceptable sightlines plus more legroom than similarly priced circle seats.

Stalls boxes: Either side of the stage, these are comfortable but miss nearside action.

ROYAL (DRESS) CIRCLE: A fairly shallow rake renders the view average in outermost seats from D, with central row F expensive at top price. Lengthy rows place B1, 2, 21 and 22 and C1, 2 and 23 in the shadow of side boxes – restricted-view bargains for the shorter, perhaps. Seat A5 "has outstanding views but little legroom". In D12 and 13, views "are perfect (no heads in way), sound fab, legroom good, chair size adequate" but, further to the sides, D5 and 6 have "poorer legroom and sound". Wheelchair positions here are adequate, the left one perhaps better than the right.

Dress circle boxes: Boxes A and D have similar views to boxes below. B, C, E and F are further towards the circle front than the stage's edge, with a more comfortable perspective. Cheaply, B and E might be attractive for those wanting more legroom and a dress circle view.

UPPER CIRCLE: The most central row A seats are often priced identically to row U in the stalls. Better view, less legroom… your choice. Behind, "if row A leans forward, you can't see the front of the stage". Sightlines diminish, too, as the rows curve outwards, and prices fall accordingly. Expect to lose front and side segments of stage, although D16 and 17 "have a fairly good view, no reason to lean forward". Conditions can be cramped and seats may be "over priced considering comfort". A case for the stalls, again, if within budget. Rows G and H are benches, so stake your claim early and hope you're sharing with exercise enthusiasts.

Upper circle boxes: Boxes J–O offer cheap restricted-view seating with decent legroom – worth considering as an alternative to similarly priced budget upper circle seats.

UPPER CIRCLE

BOX C: SEATS 3

BOX D: SEATS 3

DRESS CIRCLE

BOX A: SEATS 3

BOX B: SEATS 4

STALLS

FORTUNE THEATRE

Fortune Theatre

Russell Street, London. WC2B 5HH   **C38**

Before entering, glance upward to see Fortuna welcome you from her lofty perch over the doorway. Beyond the main doors, a tiny foyer (don't bang your nose on the opposite wall) is kept very crowded by long-running incumbent **The Woman In Black**. The box office, apparently of beaten copper, is the most striking feature of the 1924 architecture. What beats the Monkey is how better-nourished 21st-century clerks manage to work comfortably when squeezed inside it. They do, and are always keen to help younger theatregoers, with whom the current play is particularly popular.

BOX OFFICE:
0870 060 6626
020 8544 7424

ONLINE BOOKING:
www.ambassadortickets.com

 Covent Garden/Temple/Holborn

Charing Cross

Parker Street

440

Air conditioned

STALLS: An unusual arrangement splits seats into uneven blocks either side of a central aisle. Seats on this aisle may enhance enjoyment of The Woman In Black. Otherwise, in the narrower block, many are awkwardly angled to see centre stage. Those towards the back suffer least, and fortunately the dress circle overhang at row H is generally unobtrusive.

The stage is high and extended forward by removing a few seats in row A. Here, theatregoers may feel its curve enveloping or intrusive, depending on how engrossed they are in the action. In the main block, the only considerations are potential neck ache in the front rows, and the effect of thick pillars on the first pairs of seats from row D. Central D to L are Theatremonkey.com reader favourites: in G10 to 14 "legroom is good, and the view great" (although they missed the actors' feet!). The cheaper back row is good value, while B1 and 8 to 12 and C1, D1, E1 and J1 gain extra legroom through not having other seats in front.

DRESS CIRCLE: Close to the stage, the upper circle overhang at row E doesn't impede views. Thick metal rails across the front and restricted legroom worry most here. An aisle again divides seating into uneven blocks, placing some seats further out to the sides than might be expected.

The larger block offers an adequate view from all but the outermost two seats in rows C to F, provided rails can be tolerated. One person notes that from B14 and 15 "the metal bars affect views at a couple of points where action nears the audience". Elsewhere, the venue's design, dating from less well-nourished times, is evident. From F11 and 12 "I have never felt so much like a sardine! At 6', things can be difficult but legroom was outrageous. Someone's head blocked the middle of the stage too. It really is substandard at top price." Over the aisle, a very few outermost seats may sometimes be cheaper, but row L in the stalls wins in the Monkey's mind for comfort and view.

Dress circle boxes: "Though views to the sides were limited, we had a much better view, much closer to the stage plus plenty of room to stretch out than in front-row upper circle seats." Some find the speakers here noisy.

UPPER CIRCLE: High above the dress circle, it shares a similar layout and ornate ironwork across the front. "The seats are rather small with no legroom" is a common observation. Fine foundry work also goes unappreciated. For example, from A13 and 14, "We had to watch the first half through a gap in the safety rail. Legroom was cramped... We moved to a box at the interval." Things improve slightly two rows back: Theatremonkey.com readers in C7 and 8 had a good view but "couldn't see a couple of sequences at the very, very front of the stage". The last rows feel remote. Central row G is a budget option for shorter theatregoers; taller folk really should aspire to stalls or cheap boxes if possible.

Upper circle boxes: These share similar sightlines to dress circle boxes beneath, just from a higher angle. They're potentially good value for those seeking a little legroom, and willing to compromise on view.

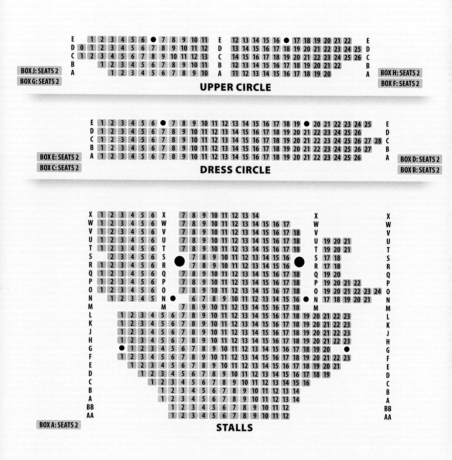

BOX J: SEATS 2
BOX G: SEATS 2

UPPER CIRCLE

BOX H: SEATS 2
BOX F: SEATS 2

BOX E: SEATS 2
BOX C: SEATS 2

DRESS CIRCLE

BOX D: SEATS 2
BOX B: SEATS 2

BOX A: SEATS 2

STALLS

Garrick Theatre

Charing Cross Road, London WC2H 0HH   B27

Named for the great 18th-century actor David Garrick, whose portrait still hangs in the stalls bar, this theatre opened in 1889 on an awkward site created by the redevelopment of Charing Cross Road. The dressing rooms are in a block separate from the rest of the theatre, linked to it by an underground passage. Traditionally, actor-manager Arthur Bourchier pats passing actors' backs on the stairway to the stage. Only problem is that he died in 1927. A Mrs Ebbsmith shares haunting duties – the original was found floating in the Thames in 1895, a ticket for Pinero's **The Notorious Mrs Ebbsmith** at the Garrick in her purse. Spooky.

BOX OFFICE:
0844 412 4662
0844 579 1974
0870 830 0200
020 7087 7500

ONLINE BOOKING:
www.nimaxtheatres.com

 Leicester Square

 Charing Cross

 Spring Gardens (T)/ Newport Place, China Town (T)

🎫 650

❄ Air conditioned

♿ stalls from row L back, and both circles

STALLS: The U-shaped auditorium creates "an amazingly intimate theatre". With the dress circle above supported by many pillars and overhanging the stalls at row G, sitting forward pays dividends. The stage can be uncomfortably high for some, but many relish the intimacy. Theatremonkey.com readers in BB1 and 2 had unobstructed views: "Had to look up, but were close to the action. Plenty of legroom – recommended." Row D "is still below the action", but otherwise front stalls gain praise: E8 and H11 and 12 "are excellent thanks to staggered seats and a good rake".

End seats in rows C to L afford lesser viewing angles to centre stage. F22 and 23, E21, H1 and 23 are officially "restricted view", either behind pillars or near protruding box walls. Seats nearby suffer, too, and are worth avoiding without discounts. Pillars at rows N and R remove views ahead from centre aisle seats (the Monkey prefers the other restricted-view seats further forward). Also, "from row J to N seating is bizarrely not staggered – putting heads directly in front". A show staged on several levels isn't comfortably viewed from N back either.

Stalls boxes: These miss some action close to and at the back of the stage.

DRESS CIRCLE: Shorter people may find the bar across row A an issue; others won't notice. Otherwise, apart from the first and last three seats in each row at the ends of the deeply curved circle, the view is usually unobstructed and fair value. Outermost end seats in B and C are usually cheaper, with B and C2, B26 and C27 perhaps worth a try if willing to lean. Centrally, E17 "is good, with plenty of legroom… upper circle overhang can decapitate actors on a high-level stage, but seeing the normal stage floor isn't a problem". Wheelchair users may find the same from their space in this row. Taller folk may find stalls more comfortable.

Dress circle boxes: Boxes D and E offer a less acute viewing angle than B and C, but all require some leaning and shifting of chairs. An option worth considering for legroom comfort at a discount.

UPPER CIRCLE: The disused balcony above doesn't affect sightlines; a double-height rail in the centre aisle does from A10 and 11, B11 and 12, C13 and 14, D12 and 13 and E11 and 12. The circle's curve to the side box walls causes end seats in all rows to be officially designated "restricted view". If on a budget, the Monkey advises maybe taking those adjacent to the full-priced ones – and bribe the plutocratic occupant into letting you lean into their airspace (brush hair and teeth before asking, perhaps). Centrally, similarly priced rear stalls win on legroom; upper circle seats win for view. Row A is usually cheaper to allow for the bar in front and reduced legroom; the Monkey prefers C or D with less leaning required.

Upper circle boxes: Boxes J and H are slightly better than G and F, if all are priced similarly to upper circle seats. Again, an option for legroom rather than view.

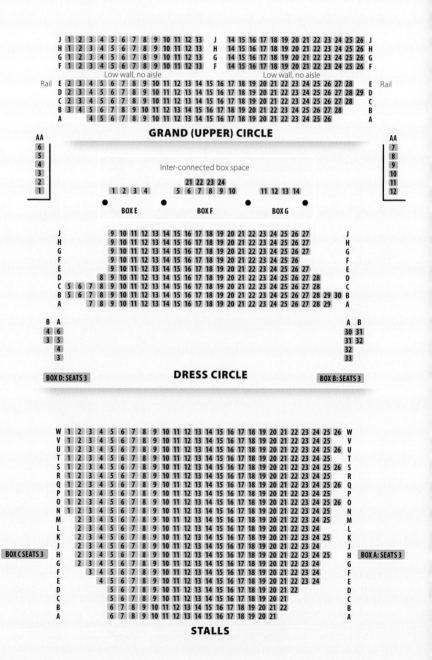

GRAND (UPPER) CIRCLE

Inter-connected box space

BOX E   BOX F   BOX G

DRESS CIRCLE

BOX D: SEATS 3   BOX B: SEATS 3

BOX C SEATS 3   BOX A: SEATS 3

STALLS

GIELGUD THEATRE

Gielgud Theatre

Shaftesbury Avenue, W1V 8AR **B12**

Opened in 1906 as the Hicks Theatre, it became the Globe three years later. In 1994, to avoid confusion with Sam Wanamaker's South Bank reconstruction, it became the Gielgud. His portrait keeps an eye on box office managers to this day. Delfont Mackintosh completed a stunning refurbishment in October 2007, one satisfied customer noting that "the Gielgud has the nicest women's toilets of any theatre I've ever been to" – a triumph indeed.

BOX OFFICE:
0844 482 5138
020 7812 7498

ONLINE BOOKING:
delfontmackintosh.co.uk

 Piccadilly Circus

 Charing Cross

P Newport Place, China Town (T)

970

Air Cooled only

STALLS: All rows are staggered to reduce head-blocking. Sightlines are improved by making rows A to D lower and placing the stage at about eye level (for a 5ft 7in Monkey). Curved row A gives more legroom to A9 to 19 but less at either end. Behind these, E15 "is central with excellent legroom and sound". Row J is slightly lower than H and "cramped for a 6ft person". The rake makes K or L prime, thereafter the shorter may prefer being further forward; everyone else should find further back pleasing.

The dress circle overhangs at row K, is potentially intrusive from R but only cuts top stage views noticeably from row T. Side boxes and slips overhang outermost seats from row D back, possibly obscuring high corner action. Rear stalls have a reasonable rake, making T to W comparable value with similarly priced upper circle seats. Row W "has pretty good views". Seats E24, G24 and N1 usually have nothing in front; E4 and G2 allow stretching for at least one leg.

Stalls boxes: Losing side stage action, these are worth taking at third price or below for comfort rather than view.

DRESS CIRCLE: With the upper circle high above, only rows H and J may feel a trifle claustrophobic. Rows B to D13 to 23 afford prime viewing – and are comfortable for those up to around 5ft 10in. Row A provides similar views but may be more cramped. If cheaper, outermost ends of these rows can be a bargain. B5 and 30 offer extra legroom or can be removed to afford wheelchair users decent sightlines. With the whole rear central dress circle at top price, row J has a fine view but is only just comfortable for a 5ft 7in Monkey. Dropped to second price, value increases greatly.

At the circle's sides, those in A3 and 33 can almost touch the stage. There's a decent view, too, if willing to lean. Other seats afford tight legroom for anyone over 4ft 5in or so. Behind, B4 and 31 have a little more room, but miss over a third of the action.

Dress circle boxes: Boxes B and D at the sides offer similar views and value to stalls boxes at third price or less.

Boxes E, F and G form a single plush Royal Albert Hall-style box space behind (and looking slightly down on) row J. Two rows of fixed seats (avoid 21 to 24 if over 5ft 6in) provide a "private room looking out" atmosphere. The very top (and, often, any extended front) of the stage isn't visible, but otherwise it's all rather inviting.

GRAND (UPPER) CIRCLE: The tight curve causes most off-centre seats to lose a crescent of stage corner; double-height aisle rails also intrude into end seat vision. Good design and new seats provide adequate legroom for those under around 5ft 9in in the front section, though row A (along with rear-section seating) is cramped. At the front, C16 and 17 are "reasonable value", C8 and 9 "less so due to the curve". Central D and E can also prove cheaper bargains. Row F suffers poor legroom and F7 "is high, but [we] could hear and see everything". Of the outermost seats, rows furthest back notice restricted views least.

This circle's edge row AA requires leaning to see more than two-thirds of the stage, and there's little legroom. Theatregoers should take anything else first unless they're card-carrying circus stars.

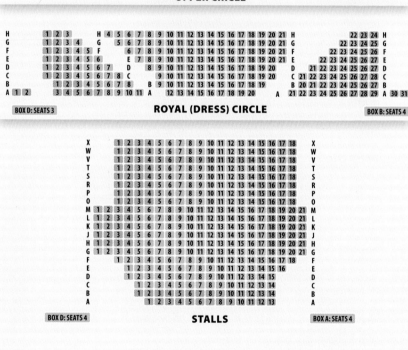

GALLERY (BALCONY)

UPPER CIRCLE

BOX D: SEATS 3

ROYAL (DRESS) CIRCLE

BOX B: SEATS 4

BOX D: SEATS 4

STALLS

BOX A: SEATS 4

Haymarket (Theatre Royal)

Haymarket, London. SW1Y 4HT   **B18**

The original 1720 building operated mostly without a performance licence until 1766. That year, lessee Samuel Foote lost his leg to a horse-riding joke played on him by the Duke of York. A charter was his compensation. A well-cared-for theatre, the foyer at Christmas is always one of the most tastefully decorated in town.

BOX OFFICE:
0845 481 1870
020 7930 8800

ONLINE BOOKING:
www.trh.co.uk

 Piccadilly Circus

 Charing Cross

 Whitcomb Street (T))

880

❄ Air Cooled only

STALLS: Aim for central stalls with their superior viewing angles. Auditorium walls narrow before row G for boxes, and the circle overhangs end seats here. G21, with nothing in front, offers abundant legroom value; F1 and G1 are nearly as generous.

Stage height varies, with rows A and B sometimes removed or sold cheaply to compensate for neck ache or lost action. The Monkey likes row A for legroom, and doesn't mind the discomfort at low prices. Other opinions are split: "B1 to 4 have brilliant views, feeling part of the drama even though nothing below the mid-calf is visible. Legroom seems less than row behind – centre appeared better"; "C may be too close for some"; "D felt too close – had to look up. Narrow seats too"; while also from D "superb – caught every nuance".

The dress circle overhang is annoyingly intrusive from row T back. Theatremonkey.com readers in V3 and 4 would be "reluctant to pay top price for these" but "felt very involved and could see and hear almost everything [apart from] top of the scenery". Row W is usually cheaper than V, though offering similar views. The wheelchair replaceable seat X18 shares the same rear stalls sightline issues.

Stalls boxes: Boxes A and C are expensive but offer fine legroom. Chairs need careful positioning to make the most of available views.

ROYAL (DRESS) CIRCLE: Without noticeable intrusion from the upper circle overhang, and decent legroom for those under 5ft 10in except in row A, there are many fine seats here. Central rows B and C are arguably the best in the house (taller theatregoers may prefer the stalls). Theatremonkey.com readers report that row E is "comfortable", seats F4 and 5 are "fair value" and F17 to 21 have good views and legroom. Outermost corners can suffer odd viewing angles and reduced sightlines: those in A3 to 7 "missed front stage action" and in A1, 2, 30 and 31 had to peer around boxes.

Dress circle boxes: Like stalls boxes below, these are average value when discounted (position your chair correctly). Box D is often used for technical equipment. Some exciting-looking monitors were housed there when the Monkey visited… one can be tuned to football, allegedly.

UPPER CIRCLE: A plastic safety screen, used instead of conventional aisle safety rails, bothers some nearest the central aisles in rows A to C. In C9 "you can live with it but it's highly annoying". More centrally, row B "has views seriously compromised by row A heads leaning forward over the bar". Further back, D7 and 8 are "are only passable if cheap". Rows F and G feel distant, and in G3 "the screen impacted slightly on stage-front view but didn't cover any action" though G11 and 12 "felt quite far away".

With the circle curve removing stage edges, all side block seats are designated "restricted view". Take centre aisle seats if possible and don't pay too much. Row A has tight legroom; elsewhere only those over around 5ft 9in should feel cramped.

GALLERY (BALCONY): This is behind and above the upper circle, and thick metal bars affect views from all seats. Theatremonkey.com readers consistently loathe sitting here. "AVOID gallery seating!"; "C offers hard bench seats; couldn't stand lack of legroom. Hot. Fidgeted all night to see much of the stage"; "[in] E1 anyone larger will find squeezing between the seat dividers tight, with very limited fidgeting room. View distant, wish I had opera glasses."

BALCONY

GRAND (UPPER) CIRCLE

ROYAL (DRESS) CIRCLE

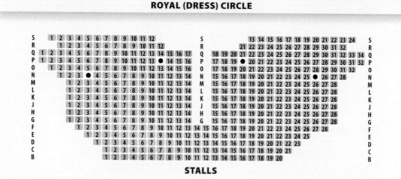

STALLS

Her Majesty's Theatre

Haymarket, London SW1Y 4QR   **B19**

Appreciate this theatre's beauty from the opposite pavement, taking in the central dome. In 1904, what would become the Royal Academy of Dramatic Art was founded here. Foyer box office staff demonstrate daily master classes in international relations and foreign trade diplomacy, dispensing tickets to worldwide fans with patient professionalism.

Due to the way in which *The Phantom of the Opera* is staged, some seats cannot be guaranteed to offer continuous full views. Prices reflect the level of any restriction

STALLS: The front row sparks regular fan debate, with opinions ranging from "cramped even at 4ft 11in" to "had no comfort problems, saw all the fine details". All agree that cheaper B10 to 12 "are great, discounted for 'conductor in view', which isn't a problem". Dry ice effects make the row cold (no camp fires, please). A row behind, a wooden block in view meant that a C11 occupant "could see how effects worked". Magic fans avoid, perhaps.

BOX OFFICE:
0844 412 2707
0870 830 0200
020 7087 7500

ONLINE BOOKING:
www.seetickets.com

 Piccadilly Circus

Charing Cross

Whitcomb Street (T)/ Spring Gardens (T)

1200

Air Cooled only

stalls from row H back, and all circles

Those central seats free of circle overhang and pillars offer the best experience and "terrific views and legroom adequate for 5ft 10in" (G15 and 16). Just behind, rows J to L between seats 4 and 24 usually satisfy, providing "the full effect, good sound, but with cramped legroom for [a 6ft tall person]" and seat backs that are "too straight for comfort". Outermost seats may have sightline problems and pillars appear from row N. Skip seats positioned directly behind these – R12 "is the worst in the house" – and be prepared to lean if taking seats either side of them. Wheelchair space at S12 also loses a little view; transfer to a seat if possible.

ROYAL (DRESS) CIRCLE: In the central section, rows C to E are usually a good choice for shorter theatregoers worried about heads blocking their sightlines in the stalls. Selfish people can cause problems (people in front lean and block views) and row A has limited legroom, but generally it's easy to get involved in the show here. Personal Monkey pick is H23, cheap due to pillar intrusion. By leaning left, it lines up with the side of the stage, thus obscuring very little

Side section seats generate comment as much due to audience behaviour as theatre design. A Theatremonkey.com reader in D7/ 8 "had a peculiar viewing angle, with people leaning into my view". Choosing carefully, top-price seats near the centre aisle generally please: A27 "is close to all action, having clear sightlines". Further along, they disappoint: C5 "was too off centre".

Outermost tickets are far cheaper, with good reason: a Theatremonkey.com reader in B32 "could hardly see front-left stage" and those further back may miss the stage top.

GRAND (UPPER) CIRCLE: In A18 to 21 "circle ledge and bar are low, only slightly blocking views" and "leaning back beheads the cast". Generally, aside from the tight legroom throughout, central seats are praised: D12 to 15 "have a better view than more expensive seats". E15 to 18 required a Theatremonkey.com reader to "peer around tall head in front" but those in H15 to 18 only lost the Phantom occasionally. Outermost seats are "restricted view". From B29 and 30 "it's impossible to see a thing without leaning". Being further back improves sightlines slightly: F24 "was great with no seat in front... only bottom left stage corner was lost" and in H26 and 27 "only corner-stage key moments were missed".

BALCONY: This is above and behind the upper circle, and is remote from the stage but not vertigo-inducing. Beware front and row end rails. Opinions range from "Saw everything" (A14) to "steer clear, compared with similarly priced seats elsewhere the view is distant and the rake appalling". A budget option only

Main Auditorium

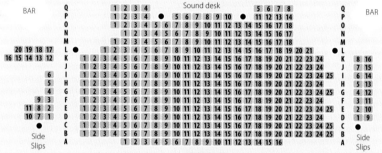

STALLS

The 'Basement' Auditorium

Leicester Square Theatre

5, Leicester Place, Leicester Square, London WC2H 7BP   B14

Once the Notre Dame Hall for the church above, Punk's heyday saw it used for the first ever concert by The Sex Pistols. Blondie and The Clash also played here before its transformation into a dance hall. Anarchy returned with a conversion to theatre use in 2002 for edgy musical **Taboo**. New lessees in 2008 have invested £600,000 to create a quality two-space venue accommodating a mixture of plays and comedy events.

BOX OFFICE:
0844 847 2475

ONLINE BOOKING:
leicestersquaretheatre.com

 Leicester Square

 Charing Cross

P Newport Place,
China Town

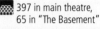 397 in main theatre,
65 in "The Basement"

❄ Air conditioned

Main auditorium

Now one of the most comfortable theatres in London. Brand-new seats that are well positioned (also heavily bolted down, so forget sneaking a pair for your lounge) impress greatly. The ceiling's night-sky colour scheme helps make a fairly low room seem open and airy, while contrasting carpeting with acoustic underlay helps the sound reach all corners clearly.

Two handy bars with circulation space in front serve a central block of seats in long rows facing a wide, shallow-ish stage. Either side of the central block are two areas of slip seats between bars and stage. The auditorium is not raked, but seats are positioned so they're offset to those in front, and the stage is high enough to prevent sightline issues. To date (and with many full houses) no problems have been recorded. "Given the size of the venue, it would be difficult not to feel part of the action."

The front row shouldn't cause neck ache for anyone. From row B, the Monkey noticed that scenery placed at the edges of the wide stage may obstruct views from outermost seats, but doesn't anticipate this being a difficulty at most productions.

Moving back through the theatre, every seat has clear sightlines. The real purists might decide that the first and last four seats feel a little less central, but views are fine – best beyond row D – with middle seats showing off the stage to best perspective.

At the rear of the central block, a sound desk position is well away from any seating, and won't distract. Two usher seats (sorry, not for public use) by the entrance stairs may attract envious glances.

Slip seats are usually cheap bargains. On the high numbers side, two rows of eight seats run parallel to the wall, facing the main seating block front-on across a wide aisle space. Viewing is sideways on and, though theatregoers in the seat nearest the stage may be conscious of the pillar beside it, there's no sightline intrusion. Seats furthest from the stage have a great viewing angle – and are almost within arm's reach of the bar.

On the low numbers side, an interesting arrangement sees six seats in a line parallel to the wall (as on the other side of the theatre), with a row of three and a row of two behind them. Then there's a gap, then two rows of front-facing seats (first a row of five, then four behind) all angled to face the stage. The Monkey liked the two nearest the aisle in particular.

Legroom is comfortable in all seats for all but the very tallest (over 6ft 5in or so). In front row slips and the first and last seats in row B, it's unlimited, with nothing in front of them. The new seats are also wide, "accommodating most broader figures admirably" as politer advertisements might say.

"The Basement" auditorium

Once forgotten storage space, this is now a small theatre with three short rows of traditional (and removable) tip-up seats. These face a square metre or two of floor-level playing area, with a projection screen behind. Behind the seats are small tables and standing room, which, together with a corner bar, all help create a warm, club atmosphere.

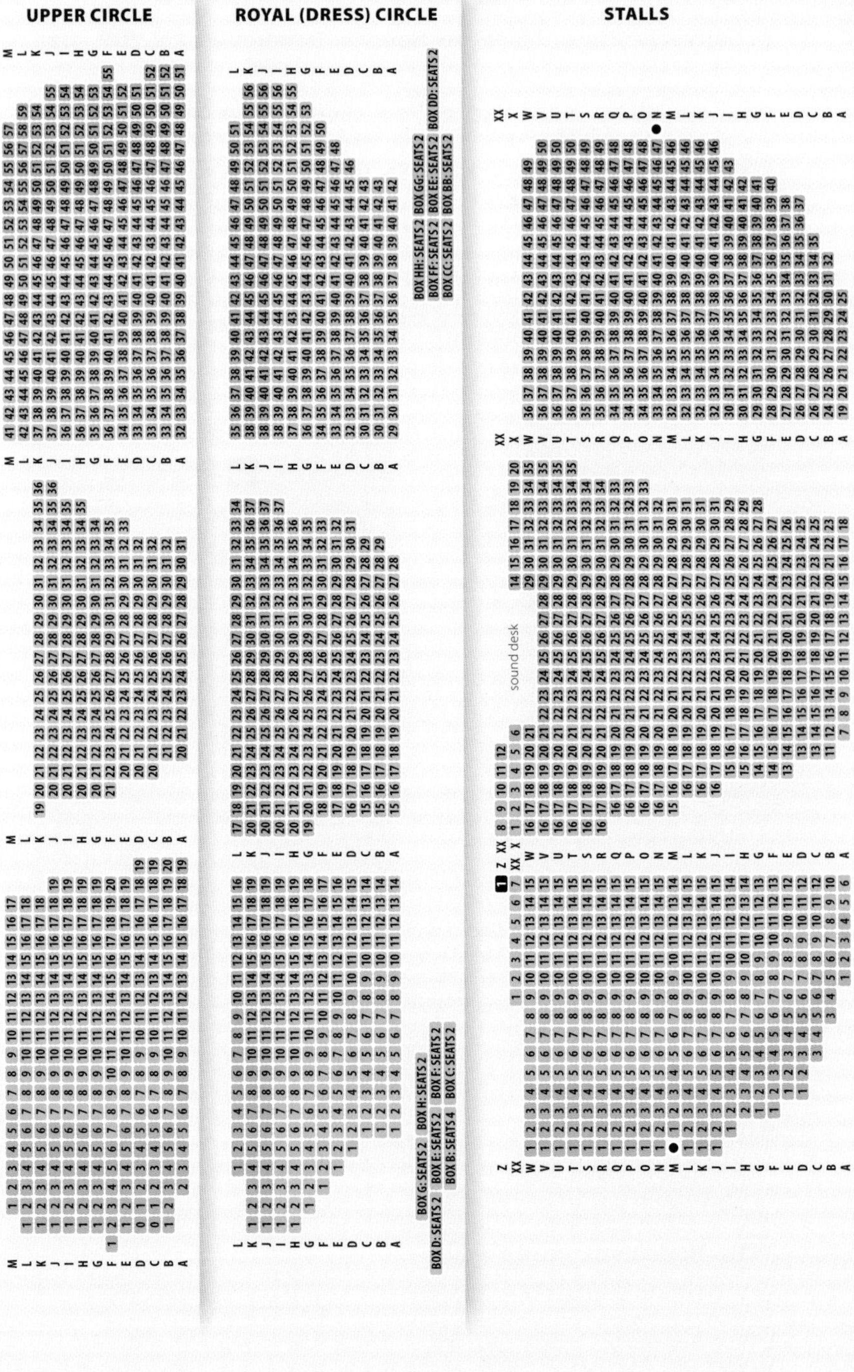

UPPER CIRCLE

ROYAL (DRESS) CIRCLE

STALLS

sound desk

BOX HH: SEATS 2 BOX GG: SEATS 2
BOX FF: SEATS 2 BOX EE: SEATS 2 BOX DD: SEATS 2
BOX CC: SEATS 2 BOX BB: SEATS 2

BOX G: SEATS 2 BOX H: SEATS 2
BOX D: SEATS 2 BOX F: SEATS 2 BOX C: SEATS 4
BOX B: SEATS 2

LONDON PALLADIUM THEATRE

London Palladium Theatre

Argyll Street, London. W1V 1AD   **A1**

Arguably London's favourite and most famous entertainment venue. Stage greats are recalled in displays running the length of the box office corridor beside the theatre entrance. Some wonder at the size of this room: in the days of twice-nightly variety, it could deal quickly with 2,000 people, admitting them directly to the auditorium via long-removed connecting doors.

BOX OFFICE:
0844 412 4655
0870 830 0200
020 7087 7500

ONLINE BOOKING:
www.seetickets.com

Oxford Circus

Euston

Poland Street (T)

2298

Air conditioned

stalls from row M back, and upper circle

STALLS: The finest seats are in central rows G to O, with noticeable rake and maximum legroom. Seats G21 to 28 "are close enough to see actors' expressions, not so close for neck strain or losing the wider view", I27 and 28 "are superb, couldn't see any seats I'd rather be in" and L16 to 18 offer "perfect viewing". The Monkey's personal choice is J20 to 27. Further forward, those in the first three rows may miss footwork and also notice the conductor bobbing into view. Legroom isn't great in outermost row A seats, but B1, 2, 3, 32 and 33 and D37 often have nothing in front of them.

Further back, P32 and 33 "were perfectly good but front rows are better value". The circle overhang at N becomes noticeable at row R but pricing sometimes compensates, and rows V to XX suffer particularly. This area is similarly priced to upper circle seats, so decide between relative comfort here (even if slightly less generous than front stalls) or view upstairs. Z1 is the "secret" seat, not sold for safety reasons, but often grabbed by standees.

Side block seats are almost all situated outside the proscenium. Box overhangs and pillars are a presence, not an active intrusion, but viewing angles can feel uncomfortable. Avoid the outermost four seats – those in H41 and 42 "could not see the rear of the stage at all" – and be aware that front rows may be "restricted view", missing side action or having loudspeakers in front. Of wheelchair positions, O48 is best, but try transferring to a seat if possible.

ROYAL (DRESS) CIRCLE: Only occupants of row J back notice circle overhang. Elsewhere, new seating has partially alleviated previous severe legroom problems. Views are excellent, but those over 5ft 9in or so may prefer stalls. B20, 21, 27 and 28 may, for views, be the "best seats in the house". C31 and 32 offer a "perfect" view with "cramped but not dire" legroom. Legroom in D16 to 19 "is a little tight" but with an "excellent" view. F24 to 27 offer "fantastic view and sound". Further back, row J may feel "a little distant" compared to front upper circle seats, which may be "cheaper for similar views".

Dress circle boxes: Those with the most obstructed views are often kept for technical use. The most frequently used (B, C, BB and CC at dress circle level and E, F, FF and EE above) offer fair, sideways views and decent legroom. Box E occupants were "quite impressed, even though you can't see the right hand side". CC was "just OK [with a] slightly restricted view" for one Theatremonkey.com reader and those in box BB "couldn't see a thing due to large speakers". Stalls are superior at top price.

UPPER CIRCLE: This is high, but the front is not particularly distant from the stage or vertigo-inducing. Row end bars don't affect sightlines, but thick front safety rails bisect actors for those in row C. Rows A and B are designated "restricted view" and priced accordingly. Other views are clearer, for example from row E where one Theatremonkey.com reader was "able to avoid leaners in A". Circle curve and box intrusions give outermost seats an awkward viewing angle but M43 to 46 may "provide fab cheap views, and you can lean without disrupting others". Good to know, should the mood (or large head brigade) strike.

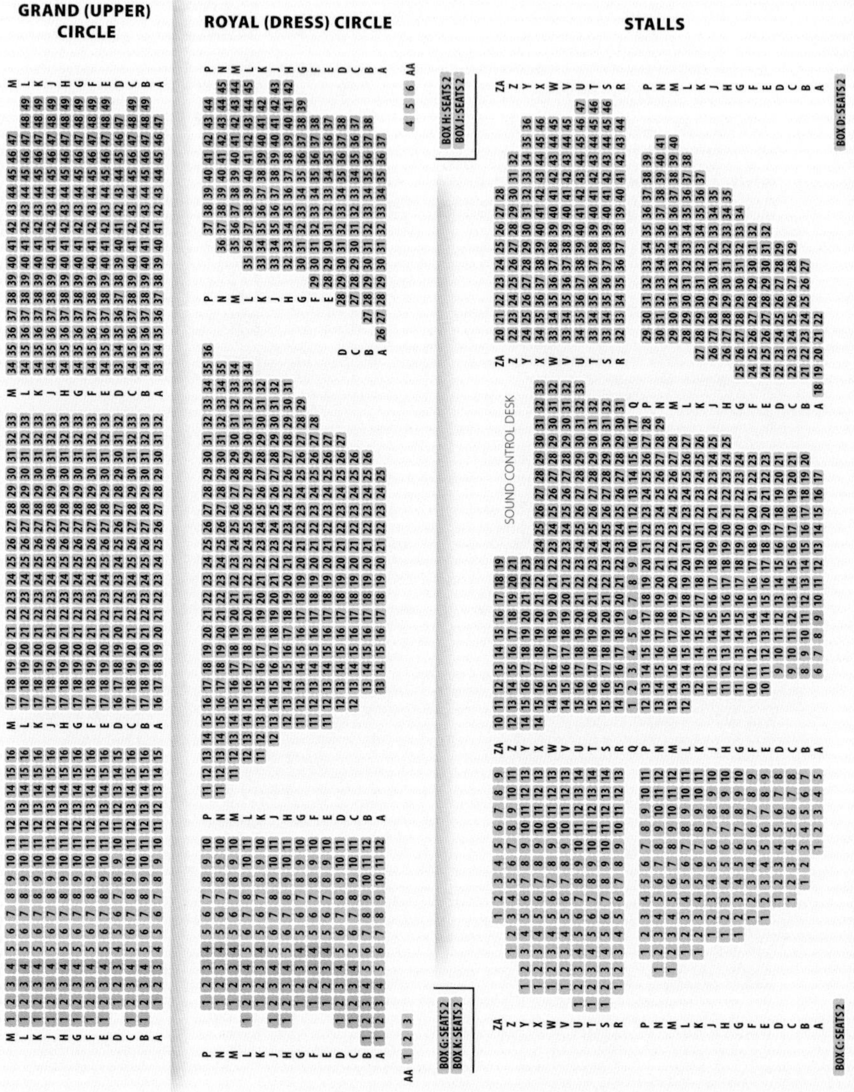

GRAND (UPPER) CIRCLE

ROYAL (DRESS) CIRCLE

STALLS

BOX H: SEATS 2
BOX J: SEATS 2

BOX D: SEATS 2

SOUND CONTROL DESK

BOX G: SEATS 2
BOX K: SEATS 2

BOX C: SEATS 2

Lyceum Theatre

Wellington Street, London. WC2E 7RQ   **C34**

Forever associated with actor Henry Irving, the current 1904 building closed on Gielgud's rousing "Long Live The Lyceum!" in 1939. It returned to theatrical use only in 1996. Lavishly restored in a rather purple manner, it's interesting how the original designer ended the ornate ceiling patterns just before the cheaper seats in the stalls and upper circle.

BOX OFFICE:
0844 844 0005
0161 385 3211

ONLINE BOOKING:
lyceumtheatrelondon.org.uk

 Covent Garden/Temple/ Holborn

 Charing Cross

P Parker Street

2082

❄ Air conditioned

O═O stalls from row S back, and both circles

STALLS: Theatregoers in front-row stalls may notice a peripatetic conductor, who occasionally blocks views. Those in A may also miss action "when characters are lying down or crouching". Still, the whole row, plus outermost seats back to M, is discounted to allow for such inconveniences. Many rate them worthwhile: typically "not particularly restricted, just cheap for being row ends" and they may miss some of the extreme left action "but you get involved" (F31 and 32).

Elsewhere, seating is a matter of personal preference. In B "there's possibly a better overall view from the dress circle, but here you feel part of the show". Some caution that the "first two or three rows are too close" and advise that J11 and 12 "have excellent views and great legroom, the only place to see this show". Centrally, aisle-facing N1 to 5 and 52 to 60 provide extra legroom.

Further back, the dull purple-painted dress circle overhang makes for a gloomy atmosphere beneath from row R, with stage views lost from T. Far corners feel slightly isolated from the action and rear central seats may notice the sound desk. Shorter folk may find the tiered dress circle preferable for looking over heads in front; otherwise it's a reasonable choice (unless purple-phobic, perhaps).

Stalls boxes: Theatremonkey.com readers report: "I liked this side view"; "better than circle boxes"; "ideal for a small child. Left stage is cut, but they can stand without others objecting, and it's very near the stage." Chairs here can be moved to assist comfort and sightlines.

ROYAL (DRESS) CIRCLE: Safety rails "slightly restrict views if sitting back in row A seats," and "a protruding light gantry on the circle front also masks front stage for those under 5ft in row A." Aisle rails are noticeable at A12, 13, 25 and 26. Elsewhere, outermost seats may feel slightly detached from the action. More centrally, most are delighted. From B27 and 28 "we could see everything clearly" and in C "the cast felt close". Even F17 to 19 "are worth paying top price for".

Further back, the steep rake begins to create a distant feel. Still, the circle overhang creates restricted-view bargains at the very back. Anybody observing flying animals from here, particularly after interval bar visits, may wish to reassess their lifestyles.

Dress circle boxes: These are priced proportionally to the views they offer, and the fact that you may share with unusual characters… Chairs are movable to maximise enjoyment.

GRAND (UPPER) CIRCLE: This is steeply raked, but once seated only the most vertigo-prone won't adjust to its height. Prices are deliberately kept family-friendly here. Those under 5ft may find row A sightlines slightly imperfect. Otherwise, only outermost seats, and a few discounted ones behind aisle safety rails, offer less than totally favourable viewing. Even then, from A33 and 34, theatregoers "can lean on the rail for a perfect view – the same as everyone else's, but discounted". Elsewhere in A "I could see easily, but… could see how effects were created".

Further back, L28 and 29 "are a very, very good price… central and can see everything… legroom [if 5ft 7in or above] can be a little uncomfortable" – a summary applicable to many seats here. Finally, standing places behind row M are a not-so-secret bargain: "stood back to watch the big set pieces, then used binoculars to see faces in detail". Perfect for the fit-but-bankrupt.

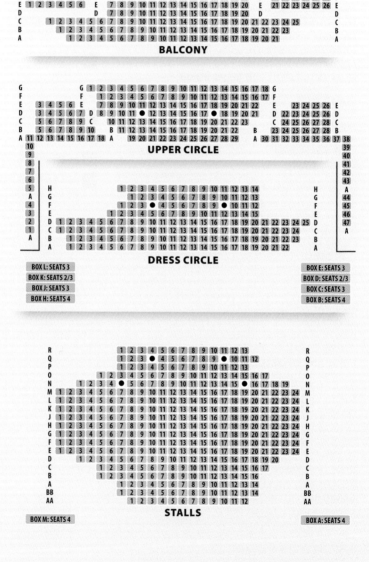

BALCONY

UPPER CIRCLE

DRESS CIRCLE

BOX L: SEATS 3		BOX E: SEATS 3
BOX K: SEATS 2/3		BOX D: SEATS 2/3
BOX J: SEATS 3		BOX C: SEATS 3
BOX H: SEATS 4		BOX B: SEATS 4

STALLS

BOX M: SEATS 4   BOX A: SEATS 4

LYRIC THEATRE

Lyric Theatre

Shaftesbury Avenue, London. W1V 7ES

B10

The oldest theatre on Shaftesbury Avenue, this 1888 workhorse handles a regular flow of larger plays and smaller musicals. One famous manager, Tom Pitt, created a rooftop garden here, and was once kept out of his own office by fear of a mouse within. Modern theatregoers rarely notice that the façade incorporates part of an 18th-century doctor's house, but mostly did notice how far costumes were skimped during a raunchy 2006 revival of **Cabaret**.

BOX OFFICE:
0844 412 4661
0844 579 1972
0870 830 0200
020 7087 7500

ONLINE BOOKING:
www.nimaxtheatres.com

 Piccadilly Circus

Charing Cross

Denman Street/Newport Place, China Town (T)

959

Air conditioned

stalls from row K back, dress and upper circles

STALLS: Front rows usually please theatregoers: for example, BB5 "has adequate legroom and good eye contact with performers". Little craning is required: occupants of B6 to 10 "did not miss a thing" and the experience from C "felt like TV come to life". Outermost seats in rows E to M have box walls almost directly ahead. Extra legroom compensates those in E1 and 24, otherwise typically "F1 has a slightly sideways view [and] having to look upwards doesn't help". Central seats satisfy most: in "K10–11, could see whole stage without turning my head".

Further back, one Theatremonkey.com reader (central row N) highlights the poor rake: "had difficulty seeing over heads in front". Dress circle supporting pillars in rows N and Q acutely affect views and value for many: "O backwards is most certainly not worth £42.50. Good legroom though."

Stalls boxes: Lose nearside action, moving chairs helps. Acceptable below top price.

DRESS CIRCLE: Shallow, and overhung by the circle above at row C, with pillars from F. Row A, with acceptable legroom and only the potential hazard of lighting clamped before outermost seats, is popular. Behind, the problem of leaning audiences adds to architectural shortcomings: "B6, C5, 6 and 22: heads blocked centre stage, while curving circle cut off the edge". Seats D7 and 8 "are overpriced", and poor tiering "meant no clear view".

More centrally, C13 and 14 "had perfect views, but were uncomfortable" and D16 to 20 "were OK when discounted" but offered a "restricted view past about 19 onwards". The benefit of a central row location evaporates at row E, a familiar cry being "obstructed view from heads in front and no rake". A few seats in rows G and H are discounted as they're behind pillars; the rest can be expensive.

Dress circle boxes: Boxes C, D and E can take a wheelchair. The loss of near edges and back corners are acceptable at third price or less; take E and L first, moving chairs to maximise views.

UPPER CIRCLE: Seat size and legroom are the major complaints here, with many theatregoers sitting sideways and being uncomfortable. For example, "I'm 5ft 10in. If you are, too, do not sit here [A32]... I survived only because seats near me were empty, so I sat the whole show sideways."

Central seats offer a clear view back to row D, thereafter only seats E13 to 16 are unaffected by pillars. A Theatremonkey.com reader in row E observes that, generally, "the back of this circle is perhaps not the best place to comfortably enjoy a show, with knees jammed hard against the seat in front". Side block seats have lesser viewing angles, and claustrophobics may find the lack of outermost side aisles a problem. Folk in extensions A1 to 12 and 36 to 47 must lean forward to see anything from their side ledge positions above the boxes.

BALCONY: This sits high above the stage but isn't particularly vertigo-inducing. F back feels noticeably distant from the stage. Rails and the circle's curve, plus lack of side aisles, make outermost seats missable. Central seats here are preferable to rear upper circle ones for the budget conscious, but be aware of limited legroom – particularly in row A – and a safety rail at D7 and 20 that bothers some.

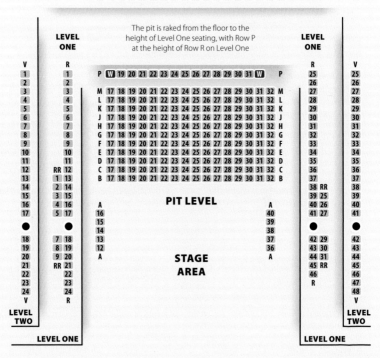

| T | 16 | 17 | 18 | 19 | 20 | 21 | Sound desk | 28 | 29 | 30 | 31 | 32 | 33 | T |
| S | 16 | 17 | 18 | 19 | 20 | 21 | 22 | 23 | 24 | 25 | 26 | 27 | 28 | 29 | 30 | 31 | 32 | 33 | S |

LEVEL ONE

The pit is raked from the floor to the height of Level One seating, with Row P at the height of Row R on Level One

LEVEL ONE

PIT LEVEL

STAGE AREA

LEVEL TWO

LEVEL ONE

LEVEL TWO

LEVEL ONE

National Theatre Cottesloe

South Bank, SE1 9PX C46

Conceived as a scenery storage facility, the primary object of the adaptable Cottesloe Theatre is to stage exciting new work or innovative versions of classics. It sometimes has unusual seating configurations, or is used for all-standing promenade performances. Its second function is to quickly sell out of tickets for important new première works, allegedly. Consider taking the National's reasonably priced "priority mailing list" membership

BOX OFFICE:
020 7452 3000

ONLINE BOOKING:
www.nationaltheatre.org.uk

 Waterloo

 Waterloo

P Under building

 400

❄ Air conditioned

O➡O stalls from row K back, dress and upper circles

This venue's layout means the terms stalls, dress circle and upper circle don't apply. The "pit" is on ground level nearest the stage, with levels one and two around and above.

Pit level: Seating is normally in a single block at one end of the room, with a playing area in front, either at floor level or on a raised stage. Main central block seats rise steeply from stage up to level-one height, meeting the auditorium entrance doors. Most offer good views and sufficient legroom for all but the longest legged. Rows F to J are generally at optimum height to take in the performance. Row P has space for wheelchairs; row R for transferees, with adequate views. A metal balustrade in front of row P makes it necessary to lean forward to get a clear view. Short row A sometimes runs down the side of the stage, affording a decent side view, sometimes limited legroom and potential obstructed sightlines for shorter theatregoers.

If the stage is raised, the front of it can be high, although seats here may be cheaper. Rows can be removed, and end seats can be discounted if factors like scenery or extra lighting disrupt sightlines. These changes are confirmed to the box office during previews, and affected advance ticket holders quickly informed. If seats have been held off sale awaiting assessment, they can be grabbed once released, providing prime front-row views or discounted bargains.

When seating is adjusted to create a central stage, or even one laid out in "islands" among the audience, the front row may have less legroom if seating is too close to the stage.

Level one: This has a single long row of seats on either side of the theatre, with an extra few behind. A thick metal rail, supporting pillars and dark front panels give sitting here the feel of relaxing on a tower-block balcony. "Views decline the closer you get to the stage" so, with the usual stage-at-one-end configuration, aim for lower numbers ends of row. Those nearest the stage lose up to a fifth of the side (or more, depending on the production) and most need to lean at some point. Prices are low enough to make sitting here a reasonable budget choice or second pick if seats below are unavailable. Row RR often consists of "bar-stool" seats with footrests awkwardly positioned. Shorter theatregoers may wish to avoid these, and should also be aware that their row R views can be affected by the circle wall in front.

If the theatre is set up with a central stage, views improve considerably. For promenade performances, without pit seating, chairs made available here will allow an overall view of the action as actors and audience mill around below.

Level two: This is directly above level one, with similar layout and views and the extra issue of being higher up. The theatre strives to keep prices low here, a decent budget option that pleases most. Rows S and T, usually central and facing the stage, are more than adequate; expect to lean forward to see over bars, and be aware of the "control room" nearby.

Seats here are "restricted view" for some productions, and many may be sold on the performance day only, to personal callers at the box office – theatregoers often rejoice at securing difficult-to-obtain tickets for a hit production.

SLIPS

	J	1 2 3 4 5 6 7 8 9 10 11 12 13 14 15 16 17 18 19 20 21 22 23 24 25 26 27 28 29 30 31 32 33 34 35 36	J	28
1	H	1 2 3 4 5 6 7 8 9 10 11 12 13 14 15 16 17 18 19 20 21 22 23 24 25 26 27 28 29 30 31 32 33 34 35 36	H	29
2	G	1 2 3 4 5 6 7 8 9 10 11 12 13 14 15 16 17 18 19 20 21 22 23 24 25 26 27 28 29 30 31 32 33 34 35 36	G	30
3	F	1 2 3 4 5 6 7 8 9 10 11 12 13 14 15 16 17 18 19 20 21 22 23 24 25 26 27 28 29 30 31 32 33 34 35 36	F	31
4	E	1 2 3 4 5 6 7 8 9 10 11 12 13 14 15 16 17 18 19 20 21 22 23 24 25 26 27 28 29 30 31 32 33 34 35 36	E	32
5	D	1 2 3 4 5 6 7 8 9 10 11 12 13 14 15 16 17 18 19 20 21 22 23 24 25 26 27 28 29 30 31 32 33 34 35 36	D	33
6	C	1 2 3 4 5 6 7 8 9 10 11 12 13 14 15 16 17 18 19 20 21 22 23 24 25 26 27 28 29 30 31 32 33 34 35 36	C	34
7	B	1 2 3 4 5 6 7 8 9 10 11 12 13 14 15 16 17 18 19 20 21 22 23 24 25 26 27 28 29 30 31 32 33 34 35 36	B	35
8	A	1 2 3 4 5 6 7 8 9 10 11 12 13 14 15 16 17 18 19 20 21 22 23 24 25 26 27 28 29 30 31 32 33 34 35 36	A	36
9				

SLIPS

(DRESS) CIRCLE

		Two wheelchairs		Two wheelchairs	
V		8 9 10 11 12 13 14 15 16 17 18 19 20 21 22 23 24 25 26 27 28 29			V
U	4 5 6 7 8 9 10 11 12 13 14 15 16 17 18 19 20 21 22 23 24 25 26 27 28 29 30 31 32 33				U
T	4 5 6 7 8 9 10 11 12 13 14 15 16 17 18 19 20 21 22 23 24 25 26 27 28 29 30 31 32 33				T
S	4 5 6 7 8 9 10 11 12 13 14 15 16 17 18 19 20 21 22 23 24 25 26 27 28 29 30 31 32 33				S
R	4 5 6 7 8 9 10 11 12 13 14 15 16 17 18 19 20 21 22 23 24 25 26 27 28 29 30 31 32 33				R
P	4 5 6 7 8 9 10 11 12 13 14 15 16 17 18 19 20 21 22 23 24 25 26 27 28 29 30 31 32 33				P
O	4 5 6 7 8 9 10 11 12 13 14 15 16 17 18 19 20 21 22 23 24 25 26 27 28 29 30 31 32 33				O
M	4 5 6 7 8 9 10 11 12 13 14 15 16 17 18 19 20 21 22 23 24 25 26 27 28 29 30 31 32 33				M
L	4 5 6 7 8 9 10 11 12 13 14 15 16 17 18 19 20 21 22 23 24 25 26 27 28 29 30 31 32 33				L
K	4 5 6 7 8 9 10 11 12 13 14 15 16 17 18 19 20 21 22 23 24 25 26 27 28 29 30 31 32 33				K
J	4 5 6 7 8 9 10 11 12 13 14 15 16 17 18 19 20 21 22 23 24 25 26 27 28 29 30 31 32 33				J
H	4 5 6 7 8 9 10 11 12 13 14 15 16 17 18 19 20 21 22 23 24 25 26 27 28 29 30 31 32 33				H
G	4 5 6 7 8 9 10 11 12 13 14 15 16 17 18 19 20 21 22 23 24 25 26 27 28 29 30 31 32 33				G
F	4 5 6 7 8 9 10 11 12 13 14 15 16 17 18 19 20 21 22 23 24 25 26 27 28 29 30 31 32 33				F
E	5 6 7 8 9 10 11 12 13 14 15 16 17 18 19 20 21 22 23 24 25 26 27 28 29 30 31 32				E
D	4 5 6 7 8 9 10 11 12 13 14 15 16 17 18 19 20 21 22 23 24 25 26 27 28 29 30 31 32 33 34				D
C	4 5 6 7 8 9 10 11 12 13 14 15 16 17 18 19 20 21 22 23 24 25 26 27 28 29 30 31 32				C
B	5 6 7 8 9 10 11 12 13 14 15 16 17 18 19 20 21 22 23 24 25 26 27 28 29 30 31				B
A	6 7 8 9 10 11 12 13 14 15 16 17 18 19 20 21 22 23 24 25 26 27 28 29 30				A

STALLS

National Theatre Lyttelton

South Bank, SE1 9PX   **C46**

This is a mid-sized, conventionally shaped house with an adjustable proscenium arch. At the interval, half its safety curtain rises from the floor, to meet the descending part in the middle. So far, decorous audiences have resisted the temptation to feed mobile telephone users spotted during Act One into the closing gap.

BOX OFFICE:
020 7452 3000

ONLINE BOOKING:
www.nationaltheatre.org.uk

🚃 Waterloo

🚇 Waterloo

🅿 Under building

▦ 900

❄ Air conditioned

⊙═⊙ stalls from row K back, dress and upper circles

STALLS: As in the larger Olivier, rows A to D are waves, narrower seats without armrests or rake. Central row A is a good choice, offering legroom and proximity to the stage. The ends of both it and the three rows behind can be a gamble, however, with sideways viewing angles and (depending on how wide the proscenium opening has been set for the production) scenery and staging potentially affecting sightlines. Ill-considered staging sometimes creates a problem elsewhere in the front stalls, too, particularly when sets feature multiple rooms. Kindly, the theatre does discount the most affected seats once they're made aware of an issue.

With a reasonable rake from row E, central H to L are prime viewing positions, elevated just enough to look down comfortably on the playing area. They're also raised sufficiently to see round most heads in front and provide adequate legroom for all but the tallest. Behind, R16 "has a very good view and legroom". Dress circle overhang becomes an issue from around row T, and is surprisingly noticeable for a modern theatre. The Monkey feels there are better viewing perspectives available at similar prices in the circle above, conceding that during the annual "£10 season" these rear rows (while not actually £10, more like £20 or so) become fair value.

(DRESS) CIRCLE: A steep rake gives all seats a clear view of the stage. Prime seats, and usually below top price, rows A and B6 to 31 offer great value in the Monkey's view. Audiences are able to take in the whole stage without encountering similarly priced rear stalls problems of overhang and distance. In B17, 18 and 31 "you could see everything well. Rake and pitch were adequate, providing excellent legroom", though one much taller Theatremonkey.com reader found the latter less so. Behind, central seats are of similar quality. Outer ones are also acceptable but more vulnerable to staging eccentricities and disturbance from those leaving via the circle's front exits.

The very back row was a Monkey haunt for many years until prices were raised. Now, row J and the ends of row H seem expensive considering distance from the stage. The Monkey now prefers row A stalls, despite potential problems, as they're cheaper and closer to the action. During the annual "£10 season", rows J and H return to Monkey favour, bargain prices stirring happy memories.

Dress circle slips: These are perched on two narrow ledges above and at either side of the circle, outside the proscenium. With nine seats on each side, the first three are on one level, with a further six behind them on another, set single file with no noticeable rake. The view is sideways to the stage and particularly distant from seats 1 to 5 and 28 to 32. "Slip seat 7 had loads of legroom; good view for only £10." They're usually sold at bottom price on the day of the performance to personal callers at the box office.

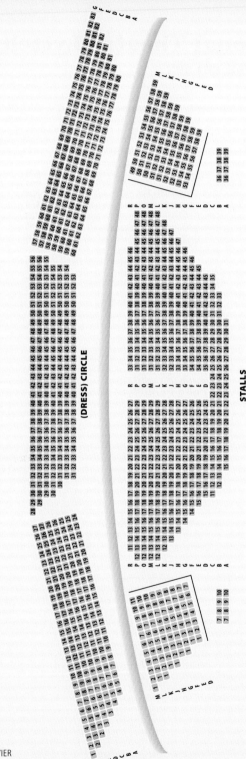

(DRESS) CIRCLE

STALLS

NATIONAL THEATRE OLIVIER

National Theatre Olivier

South Bank, SE1 9PX   **C46**

Outside, Denys Lasdun's grey building (intended to weather to white) may have been inspired by Ole Kirk Christiansen. Inside, the National Theatre operates an unbeatable and probably unique cultural supermarket. The Monkey first encountered Shakespeare, Chekhov and Ibsen here – ushers were hired for their names in the 1980s. Laurence Olivier formed the company in 1963, the players moving from the nearby Old Vic into the current building 13 years later.

BOX OFFICE:
020 7452 3000
ONLINE BOOKING:
www.nationaltheatre.org.uk

 Waterloo

 Waterloo

 Under building

 1160

 Air conditioned

Largest of the trio, this is an ancient Greek-influenced, fan-shaped auditorium. The vast stage has an impressive drum revolve capable of moving whole sets into view, plus enough "flying space" to hoist a double-decker bus. Some consider it hard to work in; the Monkey always finds it breathtaking.

STALLS: A central area contains some of the best seats in the house, flanked by two steeply tiered wings of seating, banked high to link stage to circle. The front three rows are removable – outermost seats are often replaced by stage extensions, central ones by an aisle and steps. They're also narrower, lacking armrests, and there's no rake. Intended to be waves (generating waves of enthusiasm from wave-resembling rows), they're the cheapest in the house and usually a bargain.

From A30 "value is good, the actors close, legroom fine, neck/backache possible". The rake begins at row D in the central block. It's steep, giving decent views everywhere. Theatremonkey.com readers report F40 as "part of the action" and H41 and 42 as good value with excellent views. Though not actually "a tenner" (nearer to £30), rows G and H become even better value during the annual summer "£10 season". Further back, a considerate Theatremonkey.com reader notes, in M12, "my head moving to take in the scenery didn't obscure the view for anyone else". Further along, an occupant of seat M27 "felt close to stage" and found good legroom. Wheelchair users gain similar views from their spaces in row R.

The wing sections are cheaper as views vary; occasionally the box office discounts outermost tickets if staging obstructs sightlines significantly. Sit close to the centre to minimise the risk, but beware the centremost seat next to a wall topped with potentially irritating rails and a drop beyond. Rear rows, almost against the front wall of the circle, offer the best overall views; theatregoers in front rows can nearly touch actors on any extended stage. Legroom in all seats is adequate for all but the tallest.

(DRESS) CIRCLE: This has more seats than the stalls, adequate legroom for most and no overhangs. Distance from the stage at the back and the irritating, not view-blocking, handrails at row ends are issues. Some theatregoers comment on poor sound in the more expensive centre section, particularly when actors work without microphones. The Monkey prefers front side areas, though central rows offer fine views. Behind, for example, from D10 "views are very clear, just a little bit far back from the action… legroom very good" and those in E15 and 16 were "hovering above the stage".

Central back rows seem expensive, comparing view and sound against similarly priced stalls. Towards the auditorium's edges, the curve creates an amphitheatrical looking-down-a-cone effect, but the cheapest seats are attractive. In G68, for example, "the rake is really steep, so you can see perfectly". During the annual "£10 season", outermost rows A to C and central D often become even better value. The Monkey saw its first National Theatre production from B4, becoming hooked for life on the Olivier. Say no more…

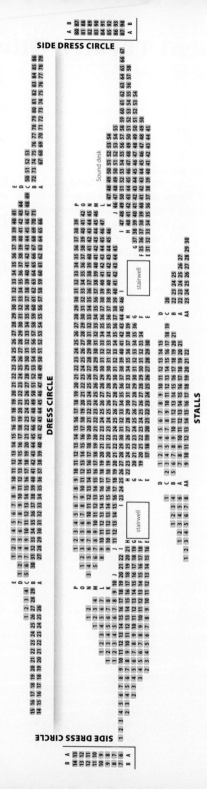

SIDE DRESS CIRCLE

DRESS CIRCLE

STALLS

Sound desk

stairwell

stairwell

SIDE DRESS CIRCLE

NEW LONDON THEATRE

New London Theatre

Drury Lane, London. WC2B 5PW　　　　　　　　　　**C40**

The original London production of **Grease**, featuring one Richard Gere, was staged here in 1973, but this theatre is more famous as the original home of **Cats** in 1981. Sadly, the cast cat-flap has been replaced by a conventional stage door. The star dressing room still retains, allegedly, its ensuite litter tray, and the main public bar is named for T. S. Eliot.

BOX OFFICE:
0844 412 4654
0870 830 0200
020 7087 7500

ONLINE BOOKING:
www.seetickets.com

 Holborn

 King's Cross/St Pancras

P Parker Street, under this theatre

940

Air conditioned

STALLS: Front stalls can be configured to provide either a conventional "end proscenium" or a "thrust" stage. The thrust version currently prevails, so advice is mostly based on this. Rows from AA to I can be added, extended or removed; they can also be renumbered according to production requirements.

In conventional proscenium layout, a stepped front section can be formed. Sightlines are good, though the stage is high for row AA; outermost seats are cheaper, compensating for missing nearside corner action. In thrust configuration, there are fewer rows and seldom tiering between seats, but they're offset to allow peering around heads. The stage is generally low, too, making the front row comfortable for most.

Behind, central rear stalls may be renumbered, but concrete tiering makes them otherwise unalterable. In central row E, "be prepared for blocked views" as row D is almost on the same level. The rest of E offers better viewing and, thanks to the wide aisle, excellent legroom. Behind, the steep rake ensures prime sightlines: "H, I and J were the best seats we could possibly have. Just like watching 'Cinerama', with full peripheral vision." Seats I23, 24, 45 and 46 on gangways combine unobstructed views with extra legroom. Behind, J11 to 15 and 41 to 45 are behind stairwell walls topped with a bar. Set back from it, sightlines are unaffected for those over 5ft tall, with good legroom a bonus.

Further back, rows O and P feel a fair way from the stage but offer cheap panoramic views, even if occasionally the stage top is missed.

Side block sections curve inwards for intimate stage views. In proscenium style, a safety rail badly affects views from rows E to I. In thrust layout, it vanishes and only the outermost seats miss rear-stage corners. Seats K47 to 54 may be in front of a sound desk. N1 and 2 can be removed to provide good wheelchair viewing positions, or substituted for normal chairs if preferred by disabled users.

DRESS CIRCLE: "A lot of stairs to negotiate to get to your seats." It's a narrow shelf, sometimes extended down the sides of the theatre with rows A to C renumbered accordingly. A high metal bar runs across the front, double height at aisle ends. Beyond it is a short lip of concrete before the plunge to the stalls.

Row A may lose some view, but gains legroom. Avoid cramped seats D1 and 44, also positioned behind sightline-blocking rails. Other end seats suffer aisle rail intrusions far less seriously. Those in central D and E feel reasonably close to the stage, but Theatremonkey.com readers in D25 and 26 "froze under an air-conditioning vent". There's less legroom here compared to the three front rows. At top price, the stalls are "first choice" over circle seats for many theatregoers.

Aisle seats in side blocks again suffer rail problems, with sightlines "possibly not so good as central ones, although the way shows are performed means there are no really bad views". Those closest to the stage end may peer through lighting equipment and miss action in the rear corners, but prices usually reflect this. Be aware that, frequently, these seats are bench style – arrive early to stake out your portion. Consider, too, whether you'll be comfortable with a lower backrest and shorter seat.

Bar/Refreshment Sales Area

Sound Desk

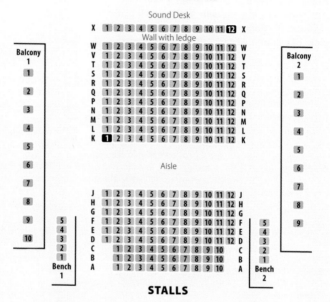

Wall with ledge

Aisle

STALLS

New Players Theatre

The Arches, Villiers Street, London. WC2N 6NG   **B30**

Beneath the arches of Charing Cross Station, this theatre's claim to fame was as launching point for **The Boyfriend** in 1953. Rebuilt in 1989, it was home for many years to the wonderful Players Theatre, who nightly served slices of authentic "music hall" as it would have been a century ago. Economics forced them into a peripatetic existence, but catch them if you can (see www.playerstheatre.co.uk). The theatre has since alternated periods of darkness with professional and amateur work. A lovely space, which the owners hope to exploit in future.

BOX OFFICE:
020 7478 0135

ONLINE BOOKING:
www.newplayerstheatre.com

 Charing Cross/ Embankment

 Charing Cross

 Spring Gardens

276

Air conditioned

STALLS: Sections are divided by a wide aisle in front of row K. Rows A to C are removable from the flat floor, depending on productions. The stage can be high for those in A. Shorter theatregoers may wish to miss B and C, as peering around heads in front could prove awkward. Inventive pricing sometimes compensates for these shortcomings, and row A usually has more legroom than the pair behind.

Things improve from row D back, with seating nicely raked on steps rather than a sloping floor. There's usually acceptable legroom for all but the tallest, and staying two seats in from the aisle minimises distraction by late-arriving audience members. Row G is about right for taking in the whole stage and seeing clearly over those in front. About a third of the way back, K offers outstanding legroom and looks down from a comfortable height. Sometimes (alas, producers seem to have realised this now) they're slightly cheaper than seats in front, too; the Monkey likes them, anyway.

By row L, the rake seems slightly shallower, only improving again at P. Behind these, rows R and S begin to feel further away, perhaps partly due to the varying rake. Row W has a wall behind, a place for those in X to put a drink if seated or to lean if the row is removed – the Monkey feels that these possibilities are reason to avoid it. Those in row X do need to be tall enough to see over the wall, and also tolerant of a sound desk behind and potential noise from the rear stalls bar. Come to think of it, in music hall days, a servery here did a nice line in hot steak sandwiches for consumption during the performance. One tradition worth reviving, perhaps…

Stalls benches: Either side of the front stalls are two raised alcoves containing benches. About a quarter of the rear stage isn't visible, but these seats are often sold cheaply when not commandeered for technical equipment. At second price or higher, central seats are usually preferable. Arrive early to stake your claim to a reasonably sized portion of bench. Note also that, while there's only one row either side, computer booking systems usually dub it "row A" regardless.

SIDE BALCONIES: Over and above the stalls aisle staircases, along the longest side walls run narrow balconies. Seats here are arranged in single file (one behind the other), not raked but with generous legroom. To see anything, you lean outwards over the bar at the balcony's edge, which the Monkey feels makes a change from leaning forwards. Be aware of your fellow audience members behind while leaning, and expect things to become competitive for the best viewing angle. Around a fifth of the nearest side of the stage is not visible, even with a little contortion, as the balconies don't project very far into the centre of the house. Factor in the problem of those in front of you leaning outwards to see more, and anyone seated here may have a hard time enjoying the show.

Wheelchair users are accommodated in spaces replacing seats 3, 4 and 5 in balcony 1, easily reached from the foyer. When booking, it may be worth checking that your wheelchair's seat is high enough to see over the wall here.

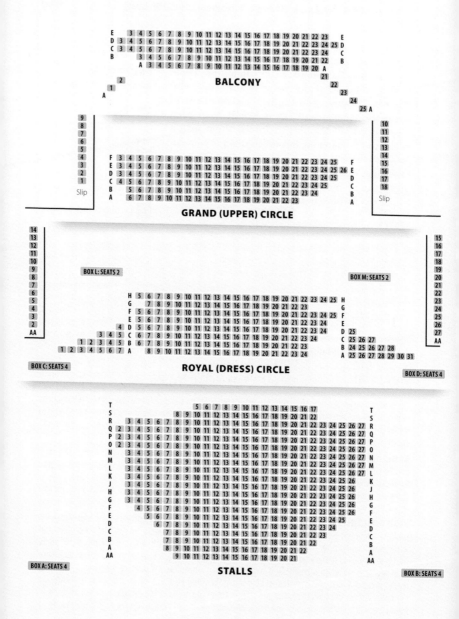

BALCONY

GRAND (UPPER) CIRCLE

ROYAL (DRESS) CIRCLE

STALLS

BOX C: SEATS 4

BOX L: SEATS 2

BOX M: SEATS 2

BOX D: SEATS 4

BOX A: SEATS 4

BOX B: SEATS 4

Slip

Slip

NOEL COWARD THEATRE

Noel Coward Theatre

St Martin's Lane, London. WC2N 4AH

B24

Starting life as the New in 1903, it honoured Sir Bronson Albery from 1973 until 2006, when Noel Coward replaced him. Designed as the larger counterpart of Wyndham's Theatre, with which it shares a stage door, medium-sized musicals as well as plays sit equally well here. During the 2006/9 run of **Avenue Q**, many Theatremonkey.com readers rated venue box office staff highly for their sensitivity towards inexperienced younger ticket buyers.

BOX OFFICE:
0844 482 5141
020 7812 7498

ONLINE BOOKING:
delfontmackintosh.co.uk

 Leicester Square

 Charing Cross

P Newport Place, China Town (T), Spring Gardens (T)

886

❄ Air conditioned

STALLS: "A15 to 18 are amazingly close. The stage is a bit high, but you get used to it." Front stalls are popular for view, comfort, sound and air-conditioning. Central row AA usually offers outstanding legroom. Even outermost seats win praise. Further back, the rake is noticeable from row F, pronounced from K, and those as far back as L echo the comment (from G7 to 10) that "I wouldn't hesitate getting these again". Seats H25 and 26 are good "even for a short person", while if emotion is your thing K19 to 22 may be "ideal for seeing actors' expressions".

By row O, some feel that circle overhang begins to intrude; price reductions in P and Q, and further ones in R and S can raise value significantly. For the shorter, the upper circle is often a decent similarly-priced alternative. A sound desk may replace seats in the back two rows..

Stalls boxes: These are beside and just above the stage, and one Theatremonkey.com reader advises "Don't touch them as they are extremely side on..." If discounted, they may be worthwhile for the legroom.

ROYAL (DRESS) CIRCLE: Without circle overhang issues, most centre block seats are highly praised. A19 and 20, for example, with no steel bar or high front obscuring views, are praised: "Sound is excellent, and I could see actors' expressions. Legroom was no problem either for the average person." Further back, "G14 didn't feel far away, and was comfy with enough legroom for me at 6ft 1in". Either side of the main block, four short rows offer mostly fair value, only corners of A missing much. Outermost seats in B and C offer a little more legroom, too.

Dress circle boxes: Beside the stage, boxes C and D have similar issues to A and B below. Facing the stage, box M "is a good last-minute option if cheap" as it's roomy with a clear view. Box L is similar but, unlike M, can't accommodate a wheelchair user.

GRAND (UPPER) CIRCLE: "Views from the front few rows are dizzy, but excellent value if cheap." "Much higher than the dress circle… I would only take the first three rows." Safety rails (double height at seats A6 and 23 and AA14 and 15) and the possibility of rows F and G being replaced by distracting lighting operator positions are the only other issues aside from vertigo. Otherwise, central seats are summed up as "good view if cheap, but felt distant" (F18 and 19).

Row AA seats 26 people on a narrow ledge bench curved along the side wall. "Views are practically nonexistent, backache severe; they are probably not worth even a tenner." "Avoid AA slips if you can." Legroom is tight here and in row A. Other rows should be acceptable to those under about 5ft 10in.

BALCONY: This shelf directly under the theatre roof has a view of the decorative ceiling. Double-height front rails (triple at aisle ends) affect row A sightlines and spoil skydivers' launches. Expect the stage to appear "very distant, with actors' expressions missed" although "sound is good". Rows D and E suffer least rail intrusion and "the first and last seats in the central block are a bit wider than normal." Like upper circle AA slips, balcony ones are also worth avoiding. Legroom here and in row A is poor; elsewhere, it's most comfortable for those under about 5ft 11in.

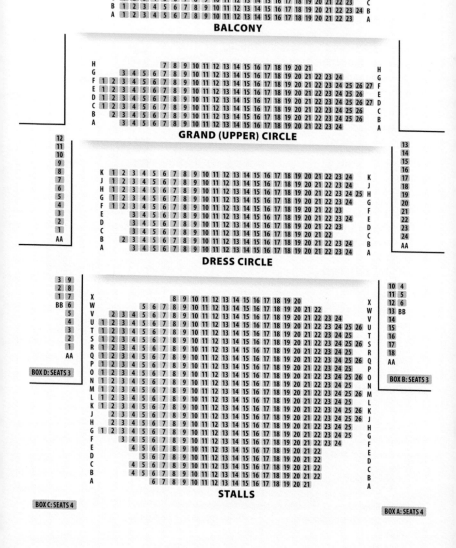

BALCONY

GRAND (UPPER) CIRCLE

DRESS CIRCLE

STALLS

BOX D: SEATS 3

BOX B: SEATS 3

BOX C: SEATS 4

BOX A: SEATS 4

NOVELLO THEATRE

Novello Theatre

Aldwych, WC2B 4LD **C35**

Following a 2005 restoration, the theatre was renamed for its most famous rooftop apartment tenant. Careful decorative research turns the clock back to 1905, making arrival by horse-drawn carriage feel obligatory. Former rented office space is now put to good use providing extra restroom facilities.

BOX OFFICE:
0844 482 5170
020 7812 7498

ONLINE BOOKING:
delfontmackintosh.co.uk

 Covent Garden/Temple/ Holborn

 Charing Cross

 Parker Street

🏛 1015

❄ Air conditioned

STALLS: "Beautiful and intimate." Those in rows B and C risk neck ache, particularly if A is replaced by an extended stage. Central seats provide optimum viewing. The rake is noticeable from row G back, and is effective throughout. A few theatregoers report that row F seats tilt awkwardly and conditions are cramped for the taller. Consider F3 and 24 and G1 and 25, usually with nothing in front although they may lose stage edge action. Circle overhangs intrude from central row T and ends of row O back .Behind, V is often cheaper than U for similar views. A sound desk replacing central rows W and X usually disturbs few, if installed.

Stalls boxes: Boxes A and C require leaning to see only around half the stage. Lighting and speaker installations can add to problems.

DRESS CIRCLE: Theatregoers in outermost seats may notice box fronts intruding a centimetre into their stage views, while those in seats from row G back will notice circle overhang. These flaws apart, clear views are enjoyed by all. Legroom varies from "minimal" in F4 and 5 to "surprisingly large" in G11. Central seats, except in row K, usually have most legroom. In row K, legroom oddly tapers as numbers rise. In seat K6 "the overhang is annoying, views are clear if distant" but low prices may make them good value.

Between circle and stage, those in slips AA and BB must lean to see more than two-thirds of the action. If nothing else is available, BB3 and 4 offer the most acceptable views and comfort available here. Wheelchair users will prefer space at A23 and 24 over places at AA10 and 11 or BB4 and 5.

Dress circle boxes: Boxes B and D suffer similar problems to those below. B offers a retiring room and separate entrance from the street. The antique loo here is a hoot.

GRAND (UPPER) CIRCLE: Row E back loses top stage view to circle overhang, while aisle bars enter sightlines of outermost seats in AA, A , B and C. Shorter theatregoers in row A may find circle front mounted lighting in vision. Circle curve removes around a tenth of front corner stage for outermost seats, noticeably from row D back, and you may have to lean to see stage front action.

Central B and C are satisfactory; E and F compare favourably with rear stalls for view but not legroom, and G and H for value with balcony seats. Seats B7 to 20 plus central C and D and C to F ends (which curve back slightly) are fine for those up to about 5ft 8in; taller folk may prefer stalls. Seats C1 and 26 offer a little stretching room for one leg. A fuse box limits legroom for A12 and, particularly, for A13 – a bargain if you're under 4ft 5in.

Those in side slips AA1 to 7 and 18 to 24 see nothing without leaning. From AA11 and 12 " we leaned around the rails. OK only if you can't afford better." Otherwise, choose centre balcony every time.

BALCONY: This hovers almost directly above the stage but "once used to the height, it's no problem". Double safety rails blight row A sightlines but provide a sense of security without roping folk together. Legroom in row A is tight if over 5ft 5in; elsewhere, it's acceptable for those up to 5ft 7in. Seats B1 and D1 have a little more legroom, though circle curve reduces sightlines. The Monkey felt that E7 to 17 best combine cheap views with acceptable legroom for those up to around 5ft 9in.

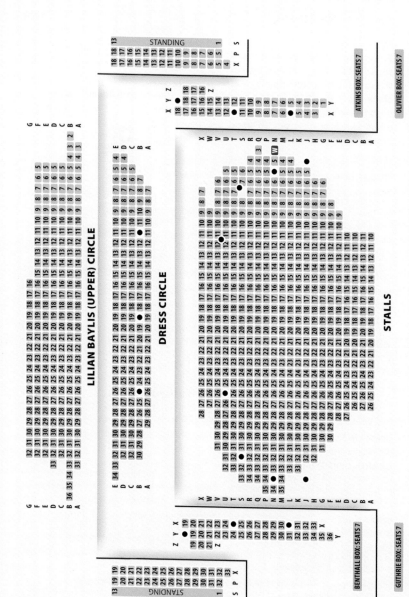

STANDING

ATKINS BOX: SEATS 7

OLIVIER BOX: SEATS 7

LILIAN BAYLIS (UPPER) CIRCLE

DRESS CIRCLE

STALLS

BENTHALL BOX: SEATS 7

GUTHRIE BOX: SEATS 7

STANDING

OLD VIC THEATRE

Old Vic Theatre

Waterloo Road, London. SE1 8NB

Lilian Baylis famously brought culture to the masses here from 1914 until her death in 1937. The Old Vic Company (later the nucleus of the National Theatre) followed her lead post-war, reopening the theatre in 1950. Under Kevin Spacey's artistic direction since 2004, some interesting new work and revivals have been presented. His inventive "signing box" at the stage door is a noteworthy addition.

BOX OFFICE:
0870 060 6628
020 8544 7424

ONLINE BOOKING:
www.ambassadortickets.com
www.oldvictheatre.com

 Covent Garden/Temple/ Holborn

 Waterloo

 Waterloo/on street after 6pm

1067

Air conditioned

STALLS: Rows A to D can be replaced by a stage extension but, when present, according to a Theatremonkey.com reader, A, B and C "were slightly raised, then dipped from D to H, then rose again" so tall heads "may spoil views here". Otherwise, central J to M are prime: "I could see expressions [from J19/20]. Good rake and stage height meant I didn't have to look up. Legroom, too, was more than adequate." The wheelchair space in row N is acceptable, but by R poor rake and large heads in front may spoil views.

Victorian horseshoe design minimises circle overhang, but requires view-intrusive pillars at the sides of N and centre of V back. Affected seats often have acceptable legroom and became popular with taller folk willing to lean, until prices were increased. Despite potential pillar intrusion or stage top losses, more central and lower-priced U to X are preferable to circle seats for tall people and vertigo sufferers. A sound desk rarely affects enjoyment when installed here.

Boxes: These are sold only once customers fully understand the eccentricities. "Olivier box: front seats had very sideways view. Seat 8 was decent, 7 very restricted; one person had to sit on an uncomfortable ledge. Steer clear if possible." The same applies to dress circle boxes.

DRESS CIRCLE: Seats B12 to 25 offer clearest views; stalls provide greater comfort for taller people. Aisle rails are a hazard for outermost seats. Other officially "restricted view" seats, mostly found behind pillars from row B back, intrigue many: D17, with an annoying pillar in view, is "not fatal, with good legroom for my 5ft 10in". Along with the overhang-restricted seats of row E, these tickets can become a little pricey considering their sightlines.

To the sides, long rows stretch from circle front to stage boxes. Designated "restricted view", the best seats are closest to the circle end. Seat Y16 "was a very pleasant surprise", its occupant sat "a little bit sideways, but… legroom OK for 5ft 11in". Further along, from Y1 to 3, "a little moving is needed [and] half the stage is 'missing' – fine for centre-stage cabaret only".

Dress circle boxes: These are as eccentric as the stalls boxes, and likewise sold only after counselling by qualified box office professionals.

LILIAN BAYLIS (UPPER) CIRCLE: High and curved, it's set far enough back from the stage to provide clear, if distant, views from all seats except those behind safety rails. Outermost seats suffer most, with some in central row A also aware of a problem. Worst affected seats are often discounted for those aged under 26 – who might wish to check for front-row stalls at the same price before committing to them. Central B to D, plus A for the shorter legged willing to look over rails, provide worthwhile alternatives to rear stalls with the whole top stage in view and no pillars. Further back, rows F and G feel, in the Monkey's opinion, a long way from the stage but they're cheap. Lighting equipment can sometimes be placed here, potentially irritating purists.

Like rows X to Z below, benches X and P between circle and stage boxes are officially "restricted view", missing between a fifth and half the stage depending on how far along the row you go. Arrive early to claim your allocated portion of bench. Standing room in S, available once all other seats have been sold, is a final budget option. Lighting can again replace some seats here.

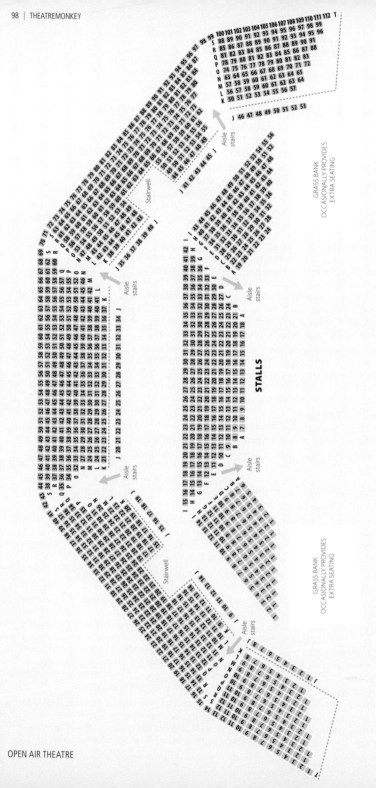

STALLS

GRASS BANK
OCCASIONALLY PROVIDES
EXTRA SEATING

GRASS BANK
OCCASIONALLY PROVIDES
EXTRA SEATING

Aisle stairs

Aisle stairs

Aisle stairs

Aisle stairs

Aisle stairs

Stairwell

Stairwell

OPEN AIR THEATRE

Open Air Theatre

Inner Circle, Regent's Park, London. NW1 4NP

A magical "must" for theatregoers every summer since 1932. Surrounded by trees, **A Midsummer Night's Dream** plays nowhere better, and their musicals are usually of a high standard. Audiences also regularly enjoy unscheduled walk-on performances by stage-struck Regent's Park wildlife.

BOX OFFICE:
0844 826 4242

ONLINE BOOKING:
www.openairtheatre.com

 Baker Street

Euston

On street

1240

 provided by prevailing weather

Arrive early to enjoy picnic facilities, great barbeque and the longest theatre bar in London. In the afternoons, the "high numbers half" of the theatre is considered the "shady side" – with less sun dazzle (sleeves and sunblock are recommended). "It can be flipping freezing in the evenings – blanket/woollens are advisable." Leave best clothes at home, carry paper towels to dry seats and bring something waterproof to sit on. Performances are never cancelled due to weather alone. If a show is rained off, you can exchange your tickets for any future normal repertory performance. Sunday and other special shows continue regardless of weather

FRONT STALLS: A fan of stepped, concrete seating rises with a good rake from the stage. Central front rows offer a wonderful experience. Aisle seat A18, with outstanding legroom, is the Monkey's favourite. The only issue is the noisy speakers occasionally sited on the stage front. Overall, central D offers the best combination of viewing angle, height and intimacy with the play. Rows C, B and A are nearly as good, and there's usually an opportunity to swell this venue's funds by buying central row F and G seats at a small premium above top price. Rows H and I likewise provide comfortable viewing and, being further from the speakers, experience more balanced sound.

Side blocks offer almost equally good, if slightly angled, views. Sitting further back and close to centre aisles provides best overall sightlines, with F to I nearly equivalent to centre block seating. Beside the side blocks, grassy banks on stage level may provide limited sprawling places if all seats are sold and production staging allows.

Behind row I, a wide aisle also hosts row J in the space against the rear wooden grandstand wall. There are outstanding legroom and stage views here, with some seats removable to accommodate four wheelchairs. Central places are best, outer ones are also very acceptable.

REAR STALLS: Nicely raked concrete steps are surrounded by wooden walls. Short theatregoers may wish to minimise sightline intrusion by taking row O back. Outermost seats are next to a long drop, not an aisle. Abseiling is banned; vertigo sufferers may wish to avoid rear rows. Fence posts at the ends of each row K segment may irritate those seated directly behind. The fences give a "box like" feel to the row, shaving an inch off legroom. Elsewhere, comfort is at least adequate for everyone up to around 5ft 10in.

Some theatregoers may become conscious of stubby metal supports for the winter tarpaulin, which enter (but don't block) views from aisle seats in rows P to R. Stairwell fencing makes two otherwise enticing off-centre block segments in rows O to R less attractive.

Central blocks are often priced equally with front stalls. They're good for taking in the wide stage but, without armrests and with a little less legroom, about fair value.

Further back, the steep rake behind row O makes these blocks' distance from the stage oddly noticeable, particularly when walking down the stairs afterwards. Optical trickery aside, good sound and reasonable pricing add to their appeal. A sound desk may replace seating around seats T53 to 62 for musicals; purists may wish to sit elsewhere. Perhaps try the pairs of row T seats facing down the stairs, with nothing else in front, which are Monkey favourites. Those in the cheapest seats at the ends of row T may find overhanging foliage dropping leaves on them.

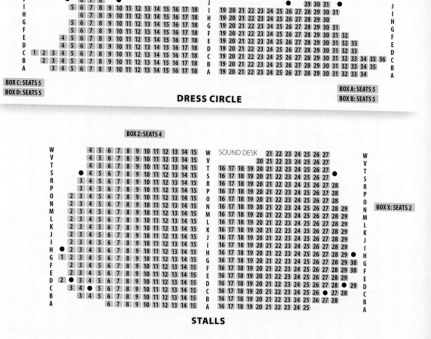

BALCONY

GRAND (UPPER) CIRCLE

BOX G: SEATS 4
BOX H: SEATS 4

BOX F: SEATS 4
BOX E: SEATS 4

DRESS CIRCLE

BOX C: SEATS 5
BOX D: SEATS 5

BOX A: SEATS 5
BOX B: SEATS 5

BOX Z: SEATS 4

SOUND DESK

BOX X: SEATS 2

STALLS

PALACE THEATRE

Palace Theatre

Shaftesbury Avenue, London. W1V 8AY

B5

This has a magnificent terracotta exterior and marbled interior. Originally an opera house, 94 years later it famously missed becoming home to **The Phantom of the Opera** when **Les Misérables** transferred instead.

STALLS: Stage height changes, but centre stalls please most. Oddly, legroom seems to vary widely. Theatremonkey.com readers report that rows G, I, O and R attract most knee-popping warnings from those over 5ft 10in; row D gets most praise. The feeling is that "proximity to the stage [makes] a little discomfort worth it" (H8 and 9), especially in the most central seats. Unusually, further from the aisle, sightlines are fine and it's only in the front corners that pillars become an issue. Seats A6 and 25 are removable to allow musicians access to the orchestra pit, seats behind for auditorium to stage stairs.

Further back, circle overhang becomes an issue at around row P, along with the unusual wall mirrors that "reflect action" (P8). From T25 to 27, Theatremonkey.com readers had "a decent lower-half stage view, but the top half was blocked". At the back, some wheelchair spaces (e.g. W23 and W27) are unimpressive. Prices usually fall to reflect both sightline and potential sound-desk distraction issues, but "just fair" is the highest rating applied by most.

Stalls boxes: Side box Y loses a third of the stage; sitting far right helps a little. Rear box Z is described as terrible and distant "with top and front stage obscured."

DRESS CIRCLE: Theatremonkey rates seats 11 to 26 in rows B to D the finest in the house. In sharp contrast, row A is dire, hazards including (A25, 26) "being intolerably uncomfortable even at 5ft 6in" and (A13) "circle mounted stage lighting blocks view". Outermost seats suffer rail intrusions and sometimes lose action to circle curve. Other central seats satisfy most but, by row H, overhang and poor ventilation render the seats "stunning only if discounted" (H23). Row J is a remote shelf, feeling rather isolated behind everybody else.

Dress circle boxes: Boxes B and D "are very restricted, avoid unless legroom is required". Boxes A and C lose around an eighth of the stage: "A and C seats 1 to 3 are excellent at restricted-view prices. 4 doesn't see much. Noisy, though, due to nearby speakers."

GRAND (UPPER) CIRCLE: "Cramped, but sightlines are superb from B at reduced prices." A is generally discounted for restricted legroom as well as view. Theatremonkey.com readers in seats A15 and 16 "lost about one-third of the stage without leaning forward", the inevitable repercussion behind (B34, 35) being "the view wasn't bad, until blocked by everyone in front leaning". This is less of a problem by D but, after that, E suffers overhang. Outermost seats peer through rails, "single restricted-view F and G seats have fewest problems" and C8 has a little more legroom.

Upper circle boxes: With only an eighth of the stage missed, readers regularly make row G their own: "Very fair price for view, would happily book again." "I always prefer box privacy and extra legroom, this one [G] is a bargain." F and H, with inferior sightlines, are cheaper but less fun.

BALCONY: "The stage is a long way down" cried one Theatremonkey.com reader, finding that a 60ft drop merited view-blocking rails across the front. Row ends have further bars, guarding against staircase accidents but affecting side block aisle seat sightlines. Vertigo sufferers, and anyone over 5ft 9in, should sit elsewhere. Row A is only for brave, short theatregoers. When those in rows A to C lean forward, those in D crane to see. Further back, from L14, "distance from the stage was OK, but the rake is not steep enough". Row P is a remote and heart-stopping 104ft from the front. The Monkey advises using back stairs to evacuate members of your party if vertigo strikes.

BOX OFFICE:
0844 412 4656
0870 830 0200
020 7087 7500

ONLINE BOOKING:
www.seetickets.com

 Leicester Square/ Tottenham Court Road

 Charing Cross

P Newport Place, China Town (T)

1480

❄ No – portable units sometimes used

○=○ stalls from row K back, and all circles

DRESS CIRCLE

```
J  1 2 3                    J      9 10 11 12 13        14 15 16 17 18    J  19 20 21 22 23 24 25 26    J
H  1 2 3 4 5 6 7 8          H    9 10 11 12 13 14 15 16 17 18 19 20 21 22 23 24  H  25 26 27 28 29 30 31 32  H
G  1 2 3 4 5 6 7 8          G    9 10 11 12 13 14 15 16 17 18 19 20 21 22 23 24  G  25 26 27 28 29 30 31 32  G
F  1 2 3 4 5 6 7 8          F    9 10 11 12 13 14 15 16 17 18 19 20 21 22 23 24  F  25 26 27 28 29 30 31 32  F
E  1 2 3 4 5 6 7 8          E    9 10 11 12 13 14 15 16 17 18 19 20 21 22 23 24  E  25 26 27 28 29 30 31 32  E

D  1 2 3 4 5 6 7 8 9 10 11  D  12 13 14 15 16 17 18 19 20 21 22 23  D  24 25 26 27 28 29 30 31 32 33 34  D
C  1 2 3 4 5 6 7 8 9 10 11  C  12 13 14 15 16 17 18 19 20 21 22 23  C  24 25 26 27 28 29 30 31 32 33 34  C
B  1 2 3 4 5 6 7 8 9 10 11  B  12 13 14 15 16 17 18 19 20 21 22 23  B  24 25 26 27 28 29 30 31 32 33 34  B
A  1 2 3 4 5 6 7 8 9 10     A  11 12 13 14 15 16 17 18 19 20 21 22  A  23 24 25 26 27 28 29 30 31 32     A
```

BOX BL: SEATS 4
BOX AL: SEATS 3

BOX BR: SEATS 4
BOX AR: SEATS 3

```
                           ZB  1 2 3 4 5        6 7 8 9 10   ZB
                           ZA  1 2 3 4 5        6 7 8 9 10   ZA
                           Z     1 2 3 4        5 6 7 8       Z
Y  1 2 3 4 5 6 7 8 9        Y  10 11 12 13 14 15 16 17 18 19 20 21 22 23 24  Y  25 26 27 28 29 30 31 32 33  Y
X  1 2 3 4 5 6 7 8 9        X  10 11 12 13 14 15 16 17 18 19 20 21 22 23 24  X  25 26 27 28 29 30 31 32 33  X
W  1 2 3 4 5 6 7 8 9        W  10 11 12 13 14 15 16 17 18 19 20 21 22 23 24  W  25 26 27 28 29 30 31 32 33  W
V  1 2 3 4 5 6 7 8 9        V  10 11 12 13 14 15 16 17 18 19 20 21 22 23 24  V  25 26 27 28 29 30 31 32 33  V
U  1 2 3 4 5 6 7 8 9        U  10 11 12 13 14 15 16 17 18 19 20 21 22 23 24  U  25 26 27 28 29 30 31 32 33  U
T  1 2 3 4 5 6 7 8 9        T  10 11 12 13 14 15 16 17 18 19 20 21 22 23 24  T  25 26 27 28 29 30 31 32 33  T
S  1 2 3 4 5 6 7 8 9        S  10 11 12 13 14 15 16 17 18 19 20 21 22 23 24  S  25 26 27 28 29 30 31 32 33  S
R  1 2 3 4 5 6 7 8 9        R  10 11 12 13 14 15 16 17 18 19 20 21 22 23 24  R  25 26 27 28 29 30 31 32 33  R
P  1 2 3 4 5 6 7 8 9        P  10 11 12 13 14 15 16 17 18 19 20 21 22 23 24  P  25 26 27 28 29 30 31 32 33  P
O  1 2 3 4 5 6 7 8 9        O  10 11 12 13 14 15 16 17 18 19 20 21 22 23 24  O  25 26 27 28 29 30 31 32 33  O
N    2 3 4 5 6 7 8          N    9 10 11 12 13 14 15 16 17 18 19 20 21 22 23  N  24 25 26 27 28 29 30 31  N
M    2 3 4 5 6 7 8          M    9 10 11 12 13 14 15 16 17 18 19 20 21 22 23  M  24 25 26 27 28 29 30 31  M
L    2 3 4 5 6 7 8          L    9 10 11 12 13 14 15 16 17 18 19 20 21 22 23  L  24 25 26 27 28 29 30 31  L
K      3 4 5 6 7            K  8 9 10 11 12 13 14 15 16 17 18 19 20 21 22      K  23 24 25 26 27 28 29      K
J      3 4 5 6 7            J  8 9 10 11 12 13 14 15 16 17 18 19 20 21 22      J  23 24 25 26 27 28 29      J
                           H  9 10 11 12 13 14 15 16 17 18 19 20 21 22 23
G  1 2 3 4 5 6 7 8          G  9 10 11 12 13 14 15 16 17 18 19 20 21 22 23  G  24 25 26 27 28 29 30 31  G
F  1 2 3 4 5 6 7 8          F  9 10 11 12 13 14 15 16 17 18 19 20 21 22 23  F  24 25 26 27 28 29 30     F
E    2 3 4 5 6 7 8          E  9 10 11 12 13 14 15 16 17 18 19 20 21 22 23  E  24 25 26 27 28 29 30     E
D                          D  8 9 10 11 12 13 14 15 16 17 18 19 20 21 22  D  23 24 25 26 27 28 29     D
C        3 4 5 6 7         C  7 8 9 10 11 12 13 14 15 16 17 18 19 20 21      C  22 23 24 25 26           C
B      1 2 3 4             B  5 6 7 8 9 10 11 12 13 14 15 16 17 18 19        B  20 21 22 23             B
A                          A  4 5 6 7 8 9 10 11 12 13 14 15 16 17 18        A
```

STALLS

Peacock Theatre

Portugal Street, London. WC2A 2HT   **C42**

University lecture hall by day, Sadler's Wells-programmed dance and specialist performance house by night. **Barnardo** was a flop here in 1980, the daft lyrics giving Theatremonkey.com its lifelong interest in failed musicals. Christmas favourite **The Snowman** is now an annual resident. An apocryphal tale has it that once, during a London Underground strike, the leading character's absence was explained by staff setting the venue's heating to "tropical". As the audience sweltered, the curtain rose to reveal a large puddle.

BOX OFFICE:
0844 412 4322
020 7863 8222

ONLINE BOOKING:
www.peacocktheatre.com

 Holborn

 King's Cross

P Parker Street

1037

Air conditioned

STALLS: Front rows are often cheaper as the high stage can cause dance audiences to miss crucial footwork. Outermost seats may have sightlines blocked by scenery and lighting, costing them stage-edge action. The circle overhang at row N "doesn't seem to impinge on the view of the top of the stage, except possibly in the last couple of rows".

Prices usually fall steadily from row S to acknowledge distance from stage and compensate for any sightline intrusions. Front and centre are prime: "G18 is excellent in every department." One Theatremonkey.com reader would elevate seat 24 (and maybe 25) in rows E to G to a good value rating "if obtainable at cheaper prices than centre tickets" as they offer good views, adding that "the viewing angle suffers a little" further forward.

In the rear stalls, the rake is really noticeable at around row P, giving a good view over the seats in front and keeping value at least fair – you can often sit further forward for the same money. Row S, if the first available below top price, saves money on the rows in front for similar views as, according to one Theatremonkey.com reader, "people on tight budgets should go for those seats without fear of losing out".

A sound desk can replace row Z5 to 8 and rows ZA and ZB6 to 10, making Y18 to 24 a no-no for those wishing to avoid extraneous noise. Seats J1 to 17, J23 to 29, B1 to 4, B20 to 23, C22, D7, D23, E8 and E24 all have extra legroom without seats directly in front. Other seating should be comfortable for all but the tallest.

DRESS CIRCLE: Further back than most dress circles, an aisle behind row D splits it into front and rear sections. Safety rails affect views slightly from A1, 10, 11, 22, 23 and 32, while a further rail across row E may disturb shorter theatregoers and those irritated by having anything at all in their eyeline. "The wide front of the circle, covering lights in front of row A, may make it less suitable for the shortest."

The front section otherwise offers clear views from most seats. Being at the back of the auditorium means these seats are far from the stage but do obtain an overall perspective – often helpful for the type of production staged here. The Monkey prefers closer front stalls at the same price. Like the stalls, side circle seats are least desirable due to potential equipment in view, obscured slivers of stage and general viewing angle. Central block row B then C, D and A (based on legroom comfort) are preferred choices, with outer seats worthwhile only once these have gone.

Rear circle seating feels very far from the stage, but offers a clear view. Rear stalls are closer to the stage and usually preferable for the same money. Again, outermost seats are second choice to more central ones if prices are similar. Wheelchair users are placed in the left section of the back row. Compared with viewing positions in theatres elsewhere, it could be worse.

Dress circle boxes: Stepped above each other at the sides of the theatre, they have side views. Box B, above A, perhaps has the slightly better angle.

```
J   1  2  3  4  5  6  7  8  9  10 11 12 13 14   J   15 16 17 18 19 20 21 22 23 24 25 26 27 28        J
H   1  2  3  4  5  6  7  8  9  10 11 12 13 14   H   15 16 17 18 19 20 21 22 23 24 25 26 27 28        H
G   1  2  3  4  5  6  7  8  9  10 11 12 13 14   G   15 16 17 18 19 20 21 22 23 24 25 26 27 28        G
F   1  2  3  4  5  6  7  8  9  10 11 12 13 14   F   15 16 17 18 19 20 21 22 23 24 25 26 27 28        F
E   1  2  3  4  5  6  7  8  9  10 11 12 13 14   E   15 16 17 18 19 20 21 22 23 24 25 26 27 28        E
D   1  2  3  4  5  6  7  8  9  10 11 12 13 14   D   15 16 17 18 19 20 21 22 23 24 25 26 27 28        D
C   1  2  3  4  5  6  7  8  9  10 11 12 13 14   C   15 16 17 18 19 20 21 22 23 24 25 26 27 28        C
B   1  2  3  4  5  6  7  8  9  10 11 12 13 14   B   15 16 17 18 19 20 21 22 23 24 25 26 27 28        B
A  1  2  3  4  5  6  7  8  9  10 11 12 13 14 15 A  16 17 18 19 20 21 22 23 24 25 26 27 28 29 30  A
```

UPPER CIRCLE

```
K   1  2  3  4  5  6  7  8  9  10 11 12 13 14   K   15 16 17 18 19 20 21 22 23 24 25 26 27 28   K
J   1  2  3  4  5  6  7  8  9  10 11 12 13 14   J   15 16 17 18 19 20 21 22 23 24 25 26 27 28   J
H   1  2  3  4  5  6  7  8  9  10 11 12 13 14   H   15 16 17 18 19 20 21 22 23 24 25 26 27 28   H
G   1  2  3  4  5  6  7  8  9  10 11 12 13 14   G   15 16 17 18 19 20 21 22 23 24 25 26 27 28   G
F   1  2  3  4  5  6  7  8  9  10 11 12 13 14   F   15 16 17 18 19 20 21 22 23 24 25 26 27 28   F
E   1  2  3  4  5  6  7  8  9  10 11 12 13 14   E   15 16 17 18 19 20 21 22 23 24 25 26 27 28   E
D   1  2  3  4  5  6  7  8  9  10 11 12 13 14   D   15 16 17 18 19 20 21 22 23 24 25 26 27 28   D
C   1  2  3  4  5  6  7  8  9  10 11 12 13 14   C   15 16 17 18 19 20 21 22 23 24 25 26 27 28   C
B   1  2  3  4  5  6  7  8  9  10 11 12 13 14   B   15 16 17 18 19 20 21 22 23 24 25 26 27 28   B
A   1  2  3  4  5  6  7  8  9  10 11 12 13 14   A   15 16 17 18 19 20 21 22 23 24 25 26 27 28   A
```

BOX B: SEATS 2

DRESS CIRCLE

BOX C: SEATS 2

```
S            1  2  3  4                         S   13 14 15 16 17 18 19 20 21 22 23 24         S
R    1  2  3  4  5  6                            R   15 16 17 18 19 20 21 22 23 24 25 26 27 28   R
Q    1  2  3  4  5  6  7  8  9 10 11 12 13 14    Q   15 16 17 18 19 20 21 22 23 24 25 26 27 28   Q
P    1  2  3  4  5  6  7  8  9 10 11 12 13 14    P   15 16 17 18 19 20 21 22 23 24 25 26 27 28   P
O    1  2  3  4  5  6  7  8  9 10 11 12 13 14    O   15 16 17 18 19 20 21 22 23 24 25 26 27 28   O
N    1  2  3  4  5  6  7  8  9 10 11 12 13 14    N   15 16 17 18 19 20 21 22 23 24 25 26 27 28   N
M    1  2  3  4  5  6  7  8  9 10 11 12 13 14    M   15 16 17 18 19 20 21 22 23 24 25 26 27 28   M
L    1  2  3  4  5  6  7  8  9 10 11 12 13 14    L   15 16 17 18 19 20 21 22 23 24 25 26 27 28   L
K    1  2  3  4  5  6  7  8  9 10 11 12 13 14    K   15 16 17 18 19 20 21 22 23 24 25 26 27 28   K
J       1  2  3  4  5  6  7  8  9 10 11 12 13    J  14 15 16 17 18 19 20 21 22 23 24 25 26       J
H    1  2  3  4  5  6  7  8  9 10 11 12 13 14    H   15 16 17 18 19 20 21 22 23 24 25 26 27 28   H
G    1  2  3  4  5  6  7  8  9 10 11 12 13 14    G   15 16 17 18 19 20 21 22 23 24 25 26 27 28   G
F    1  2  3  4  5  6  7  8  9 10 11 12 13 14    F   15 16 17 18 19 20 21 22 23 24 25 26 27 28   F
E       1  2  3  4  5  6  7  8  9 10 11 12 13 14 E   15 16 17 18 19 20 21 22 23 24 25 26 27 28   E
D       1  2  3  4  5  6  7  8  9 10 11 12       D  14 15 16 17 18 19 20 21 22 23 24 25 26       D
C          1  2  3  4  5  6  7  8  9 10 11 12    C  13 14 15 16 17 18 19 20 21 22 23 24          C
B             3  4  5  6  7  8  9 10 11          B  12 13 14 15 16 17 18 19 20 21 22             B
A                4  5  6  7  8  9 10             A  11 12 13 14 15 16 17 18 19 20                A
```

Sound desk

STALLS

Phoenix Theatre

Charing Cross Road, London. WC2H 0JP   **B4**

Granada Cinema architect Komisarjevsky tested many of his ideas for that chain's magnificent auditoria here. Older British cinemagoers may recognise the box arches and Italian frieze style surrounding the stage from their visits to suburban picture palaces of the past. A projection booth was incorporated into this theatre's balcony, but the awkward 28 degree "throw" distorted screen images.

Reverting to live entertainment, Noel Coward's Private Lives premièred here on the venue's opening night in 1930, starring the author alongside Gertrude Lawrence and Laurence Olivier. Famous names appearing since include Dustin Hoffman as Shylock in The Merchant of Venice. Today, musical Blood Brothers seems determined to keep "telling us it's not true" forever – or until Marilyn Monroe shows up, anyway.

BOX OFFICE:
0870 060 6629
020 8544 7424

ONLINE BOOKING:
www.ambassadortickets.com

Tottenham Court Road

Euston

Newport Place, China Town (T)

1000

Air conditioned

stalls from row L back, and both circles

The advance box office is on Charing Cross Road itself during the day, with the theatre entrance off the pedestrian area to the right of the building, in Phoenix Street

STALLS: Row A may be too close, as in "knees are touching stage". In seat C2, someone found that they could stretch their legs out, but the speakers were close and "detrimental to the view of stage right". Seats with high numbers at the ends of rows A and B have lights in view; back to row K, outermost seats offer strange viewing angles. Central seats are mostly hazard free: seats E5 to 11 "couldn't have been better"; F19 was "fantastic".

Rear rows offer, according to those in seats R19 to 21, "fine, clear view of faces and expressions", they could "hear all the music and talking" and felt that "value is even better when discounted" – a neat summary.

DRESS CIRCLE: Though some feel that Blood Brothers "must be viewed from front dress circle" and those in A19 and 20 "wouldn't want to be anywhere else", there are architectural issues. Row A has the least of the cramped legroom throughout, and also places a low rail in shorter visitors' sightlines (if they're sitting back in their seats). Another rail blocks centre stage for A and B14 and 15, circle overhang intrudes from row G and row K is worth missing. Otherwise, sightlines are clear from central seats, provided people with large perms aren't sitting in front. For comfort, box C is probably preferable to wheelchair transferee places at A27 and 28.

Dress circle boxes: "Box B is open, with a low edge, and somewhat exposed. Good view, though you lose about one-tenth of the stage. Blood Brothers staging means [the] right box sees more action than [the] left." Box C offers wheelchair users decent accommodation.

UPPER CIRCLE: As in the dress circle, a front rail bisects row A's show, with extra aisle end ones doubling the effect for A15 and 16 plus B14 and 15 behind. Tall inverted U-shaped handrails at the end of each row may distract a few patrons. They don't bother the Monkey, who grabs the opportunity of a quick work-out, but sitting next to them depends on personal preference – factor in your height and the circle's tight legroom when deciding. With row A providing minimal space, even for a 5ft 7in Monkey, it improves to just about "tolerable to cramped" for most above 5ft 9in in other seats; that aisle stretching space is tempting for taller theatregoers.

Otherwise, front rows feel very pleasantly close to the stage. Seats A1 to 3 and 28 to 30 lose stage corners due to theatre architecture. Rows B to D (end of row handrails aside) offer excellent viewing and are carefully priced to offer value, in the Monkey's view. Further back, tickets for rows G, H and J are usually the cheapest, providing a very decent budget alternative. If maybe a little distant, the steep rake ensures clear sightlines that usually satisfy loyal fans.

M	1	2	3	4	5	6	7	8	9	10	11	12	13	14	M	15	16	17	18	19	20	21	22	23	24	25	26	27	28	M
L	1	2	3	4	5	6	7	8	9	10	11	12	13	14	L	15	16	17	18	19	20	21	22	23	24	25	26	27	28	L
K	1	2	3	4	5	6	7	8	9	10	11	12	13	14	K	15	16	17	18	19	20	21	22	23	24	25	26	27	28	K
J	1	2	3	4	5	6	7	8	9	10	11	12	13	14	J	15	16	17	18	19	20	21	22	23	24	25	26	27	28	J
H	1	2	3	4	5	6	7	8	9	10	11	12	13	14	H	15	16	17	18	19	20	21	22	23	24	25	26	27	28	H
G	1	2	3	4	5	6	7	8	9	10	11	12	13	14	G	15	16	17	18	19	20	21	22	23	24	25	26	27	28	G
F	1	2	3	4	5	6	7	8	9	10	11	12	13	14	F	15	16	17	18	19	20	21	22	23	24	25	26	27	28	F
E	1	2	3	4	5	6	7	8	9	10	11	12	13	14	E	15	16	17	18	19	20	21	22	23	24	25	26	27	28	E
D	1	2	3	4	5	6	7	8	9	10	11	12	13	14	D	15	16	17	18	19	20	21	22	23	24	25	26	27	28	D
C	1	2	3	4	5	6	7	8	9	10	11	12	13	14	C	15	16	17	18	19	20	21	22	23	24	25	26	27	28	C
B	1	2	3	4	5	6	7	8	9	10	11	12	13	14	B	15	16	17	18	19	20	21	22	23	24	25	26	27	28	B
A	1	2	3	4	5	6	7	8	9	10	11	12	13	14	A	15	16	17	18	19	20	21	22	23	24	25	26	27	28	A

GRAND (UPPER) CIRCLE

L	1	2	3	4	5	6	7	8	9	10	11	12	13	14	L	15	16	17	18	19	20	21	22	23	24	25	26	27	28	L
K	1	2	3	4	5	6	7	8	9	10	11	12	13	14	K	15	16	17	18	19	20	21	22	23	24	25	26	27	28	K
J	1	2	3	4	5	6	7	8	9	10	11	12	13	14	J	15	16	17	18	19	20	21	22	23	24	25	26	27	28	J
H	1	2	3	4	5	6	7	8	9	10	11	12	13	14	H	15	16	17	18	19	20	21	22	23	24	25	26	27	28	H
G	1	2	3	4	5	6	7	8	9	10	11	12	13	14	G	15	16	17	18	19	20	21	22	23	24	25	26	27	28	G
F	1	2	3	4	5	6	7	8	9	10	11	12	13	14	F	15	16	17	18	19	20	21	22	23	24	25	26	27	28	F
E	1	2	3	4	5	6	7	8	9	10	11	12	13	14	E	15	16	17	18	19	20	21	22	23	24	25	26	27	28	E
D	1	2	3	4	5	6	7	8	9	10	11	12	13	14	D	15	16	17	18	19	20	21	22	23	24	25	26	27	28	D
C	1	2	3	4	5	6	7	8	9	10	11	12	13	14	C	15	16	17	18	19	20	21	22	23	24	25	26	27	28	C
B	1	2	3	4	5	6	7	8	9	10	11	12	13	14	B	15	16	17	18	19	20	21	22	23	24	25	26	27	28	B
A	1	2	3	4	5	6	7	8	9	10	11	12	13	14	A	15	16	17	18	19	20	21	22	23	24	25	26	27	28	A

BOX A SEATS 4

ROYAL (DRESS) CIRCLE

BOX C SEATS 4

Sound control desk

U		2	3	4	5	6	7	8	9	10	11								19	20	21	22	23	24	25	26	27	28	29	30	U
T		2	3	4	5	6	7	8	9	10	11								19	20	21	22	23	24	25	26	27	28	29	30	T
S	1	2	3	4	5	6	7	8	9	10	11	12	13	14	15	16	17	18	19	20	21	22	23	24	25	26	27	28	29	30	S
R	1	2	3	4	5	6	7	8	9	10	11	12	13	14	15	16	17	18	19	20	21	22	23	24	25	26	27	28	29	30	R
Q	1	2	3	4	5	6	7	8	9	10	11	12	13	14	15	16	17	18	19	20	21	22	23	24	25	26	27	28	29	30	Q
P	1	2	3	4	5	6	7	8	9	10	11	12	13	14	15	16	17	18	19	20	21	22	23	24	25	26	27	28	29	30	P
O	1	2	3	4	5	6	7	8	9	10	11	12	13	14	15	16	17	18	19	20	21	22	23	24	25	26	27	28	29	30	O
N	1	2	3	4	5	6	7	8	9	10	11	12	13	14	15	16	17	18	19	20	21	22	23	24	25	26	27	28	29	30	N
M	1	2	3	4	5	6	7	8	9	10	11	12	13	14	15	16	17	18	19	20	21	22	23	24	25	26	27	28	29	30	M
L	1	2	3	4	5	6	7	8	9	10	11	12	13	14	15	16	17	18	19	20	21	22	23	24	25	26	27	28	29	30	L
K	1	2	3	4	5	6	7	8	9	10	11	12	13	14	15	16	17	18	19	20	21	22	23	24	25	26	27	28	29	30	K
J	1	2	3	4	5	6	7	8	9	10	11	12	13	14	15	16	17	18	19	20	21	22	23	24	25	26	27	28	29		J
H			3	4	5	6	7	8	9	10	11	12	13	14	15	16	17	18	19	20	21	22	23	24	25	26	27				H
G		2	3	4	5	6	7	8	9	10	11	12	13	14	15	16	17	18	19	20	21	22	23	24	25	26	27				G
F		3	4	5	6	7	8	9	10	11	12	13	14	15	16	17	18	19	20	21	22	23	24	25	26	27	28				F
E		2	3	4	5	6	7	8	9	10	11	12	13	14	15	16	17	18	19	20	21	22	23	24	25	26	27	28			E
D		2	3	4	5	6	7	8	9	10	11	12	13	14	15	16	17	18	19	20	21	22	23	24	25	26					D
C			3	4	5	6	7	8	9	10	11	12	13	14	15	16	17	18	19	20	21	22	23	24	25	26					C
B				5	6	7	8	9	10	11	12	13	14	15	16	17	18	19	20	21	22	23	24	25	26						B
A						7	8	9	10	11	12	13	14	15	16	17	18	19	20	21	22	23	24								A
CC							8	9	10	11	12	13	14	15	16	17	18	19	20	21	22										CC
BB							8	9	10	11	12	13	14	15	16	17	18	19	20	21	22										BB

STALLS

Piccadilly Theatre

Denman Street, London. W1V 8DY   **A9**

Al Jolson once appeared here, promoting London's first "talkies". Recent history has seen varying fortunes. Converted into a cabaret restaurant in 1982, original intended resident **I** closed during a dress rehearsal. Salvaged replacement **Y** subsequently opened to the deadly comment, "Y bother?" Better management today ensures that medium-scale crowd pleasers like **Guys and Dolls** and **Grease** keep the rather oddly shaped seats filled.

BOX OFFICE:
0844 412 6666
020 8544 7424

ONLINE BOOKING:
www.ambassadortickets.com

 Piccadilly Circus

Charing Cross

Denman Street

1200

Air conditioned

stalls from row N back, and both circles

STALLS: Gracefully curved rows ensure all but outermost seats from rows CC to Q have clear centre stage focused views. The stage itself is extendable, with rows BB and CC removable. In use, they're often a popular choice when sold at reduced prices. Rows immediately behind suffer little neck ache, though perhaps shoulder problems with "high armrests" (H8 and 9). End seats look sideways and may miss edge action: F27 and 28 "are expensive undiscounted, but don't miss anything important".

Circle overhang intrudes to reduce stage top sightlines from around row R back, but pricing compensates. The rake is fine: in M28 and 29 "the sloped floor and staggered seats mean any large person in front shouldn't restrict vision", but some theatregoers advocate seatbelts. In row N, on a steep slope, one Theatremonkey.com reader felt as if "slipping forward off my seat". If braced properly, legroom is good throughout. Seats F17 to 20 "have enough space to dance"; aisle seats in rows D, H and K have even more. Furthest back, perhaps avoid seats near the sound desk, otherwise rear stalls are preferable for comfort and view to similarly priced tickets elsewhere.

ROYAL (DRESS) CIRCLE: Front, central seats offer fine sightlines. Just avoid A to C13 to 16, plus the rest of row A if you're shorter, as safety rails may be in view. Row A also has least legroom, B and the ends of C and D, which curve slightly backwards, have a shade more. Tall theatregoers may not be able to relax as much as expected. One Theatremonkey.com reader reports, in B10, "legroom was above average and the view of the stage was fantastic". This reader had a problem with the angle of the backrest: "When I relaxed into it, I found myself looking at a point on the ceiling just above the stage. The only solution was to lean forward; fine to start with but very uncomfortable later on."

From row F, things get cramped for the average-height theatregoer, too. Circle overhang is tolerable here, but becomes irritating by row J – poor rake means back rows feel distanced from the action.

Dress circle boxes: Up to an eighth of the stage is lost, making these worth considering for comfort alone. Wheelchair users get priority in box C, but it's preferable to transfer to dress circle seat A28 if possible.

GRAND (UPPER) CIRCLE: Steep raking make rows A to E feel close to the stage, and row F back potentially vertigo-inducing. Safety rails affect centre aisle views and, in seats A19 and 20, "the wall rail blocks front stage, meaning you have to sit forward". Seats C14 and 15 may be "obstructed by row A and aisle bars".

Row K back starts to feel remote, but prices allow for it: seats D4 and 5 are "better than L, but much more expensive". Still, consider that in L17 "the rake induces vertigo, the stage seems distant, music is clear but lyrics not". On the other hand, one Theatremonkey.com reader "felt a little smug paying less than those one row down". Comfort depends on height, sightlines partly on fashion: L15 "was passable, except for having some younger person with gelled spiky hair in front". As upper circles go, not a bad one.

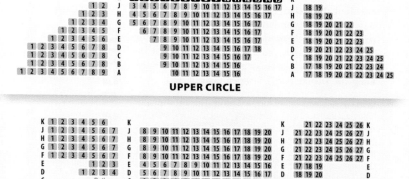

UPPER CIRCLE

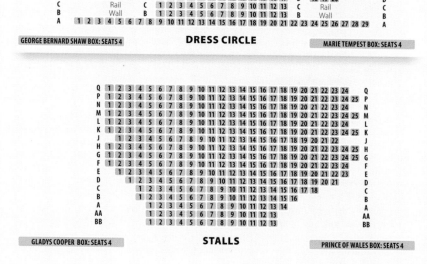

GEORGE BERNARD SHAW BOX: SEATS 4

DRESS CIRCLE

MARIE TEMPEST BOX: SEATS 4

GLADYS COOPER BOX: SEATS 4

STALLS

PRINCE OF WALES BOX: SEATS 4

Playhouse Theatre

Northumberland Avenue, London. WC2N 5DE   **C29**

"Perfect for a show as it had a friendly atmosphere", the Playhouse is the only London theatre, so far, to have a lump of station fall on it (Charing Cross in 1905). Jeffrey Archer's ownership in 1988 triggered a sympathetic restoration, pleasantly upgrading the auditorium. This charming building has seen use as a radio studio, with Tony Hancock one notable broadcaster. Now it mostly presents good drama whenever possible. Beneath the stage, the original "thunder run" (a wooden chute down which a heavy ball is bowled to produce thunder effects) survives just the other side of the under stage wall.

BOX OFFICE:
0870 060 6631
020 8544 7424

ONLINE BOOKING:
www.ambassadortickets.com

≷ Embankment

⊖ Charing Cross

🅿 Spring Gardens (T)

🚌 790

❄ Air conditioned

♿ stalls from row M back, and both circles

STALLS: Front rows BB and AA can be removed to extend the stage. If present, they're too neck-achingly close for some but provide decent value if discounted. Row A still isn't quite far enough back for others. Rows D and E win praise for comfort, but prime seating is found centrally. Outermost seats from E, including wheelchair places around G to J, may feel as if "outside the proscenium" but are less restricted than side dress circle seats. Towards the back, circle overhang at row M doesn't create any noticeable intrusion, and seats still feel nicely connected to the action. A sound desk, occasionally replacing seats in rows P and Q, may irritate purists. Everyone else usually finds rear rows superior to dress circle equivalents for both view and legroom.

Stalls boxes: Gladys Cooper and the Prince of Wales boxes flank the stage, providing sideways views missing nearside action. These are about fair at second price, but the Monkey feels rear stalls are better unless chairs are preferred over fixed theatre seats. – or one wishes to boast for some reason about sitting on a future king.

DRESS CIRCLE: The attractive balustrade circle front may be a little high for short theatregoers in row A to peer over. Central seats in this row are fine for medium-height theatregoers. Outermost seats are often discounted, and the balustrade's curve give the end pair an inch of extra leg space. Elsewhere, central block B to E is prime if substantial legroom isn't vital. Further back feels remote, even expensive, considering circle overhang from row G. Side blocks fare little better. Rails affect sightlines in rows D and E, limiting legroom for their outermost seats, too.

By row F, value near the central aisle at second price becomes average – take rear stalls first for the same money. Rear corners particularly just feel "off" the action, in the Monkey's opinion.

Dress circle boxes: George Bernard Shaw and Marie Tempest boxes offer patrons similar views to Glad and Charlie below, but with an elevated viewing angle. These are preferable to second price dress circle for legroom only.

UPPER CIRCLE: "Don't sit in the upper circle if you suffer from vertigo – lean forward too far and you could end up on the stage yourself!" The less brave may wish to sit away from the drop. Aisle end rails affect views from central block aisle seats. Sportingly, they (and the immediately adjacent ones) are usually cheaper. That "cheap seat next to them" can make a sensible budget choice for single theatregoers – or couples seat-swapping at the interval.

The circle's curve and further rails, plus occasionally lighting installations, make outermost corner seats worth missing. Tight legroom for everybody aside, view and value are pretty reasonable elsewhere for the price, with central rows B and C a decent pick. When reduced, rows from E back offer similar views more cheaply, though remoteness from stage action can be an issue.

GRAND (UPPER) CIRCLE

```
                    N   1  2  3  4  5  6  7  8  9 10 11 12 13 14        N
                    M   1  2  3  4  5  6  7  8  9 10 11 12 13 14 15 16  M
L  1  2     3 4 5 6 7 8 9   L  10 11 12 13 14 15 16 17 18 19 20 21 22 23 24 25 26  L  27 28 29 30 31 32 33        34 35  L
K  stairwell  1 2 3 4 5 6 7 K   8  9 10 11 12 13 14 15 16 17 18 19 20 21 22 23 24  K  25 26 27 28 29 30 31               K
J  stairwell  1 2 3 4 5 6 7 J   8  9 10 11 12 13 14 15 16 17 18 19 20 21 22 23 24  J  25 26 27 28 29 30 31   stairwell   J
H            1 2 3 4 5 6 7  H   8  9 10 11 12 13 14 15 16 17 18 19 20 21 22 23 24  H  25 26 27 28 29 30 31               H

                    G   1  2  3  4  5  6  7  8  9 10 11 12 13 14 15 16 17  G
F  1 2 3 4 5 6 7 8 9 10  F  11 12 13 14 15 16 17 18 19 20 21 22 23 24 25 26 27  F  28 29 30 31 32 33 34 35 36 37  F
E  1 2 3 4 5 6 7 8 9 10  E  11 12 13 14 15 16 17 18 19 20 21 22 23 24 25 26 27  E  28 29 30 31 32 33 34 35 36 37  E
D  1 2 3 4 5 6 7 8 9 10  D  11 12 13 14 15 16 17 18 19 20 21 22 23 24 25 26 27  D  28 29 30 31 32 33 34 35 36 37  D
C  1 2 3 4 5 6 7 8 9 10  C  11 12 13 14 15 16 17 18 19 20 21 22 23 24 25 26 27  C  28 29 30 31 32 33 34 35 36 37  C
B  1 2 3 4 5 6 7 8 9 10  B  11 12 13 14 15 16 17 18 19 20 21 22 23 24 25 26 27  B  28 29 30 31 32 33 34 35 36 37  B
A  1 2 3 4 5 6 7 8 9 10  A  11 12 13 14 15 16 17 18 19 20 21 22 23 24 25 26 27  A  28 29 30 31 32 33 34 35 36 37  A
```

Slip 5 4 3 2 1 (left)
Slip 6 7 8 9 10 (right)

GRAND BOX 1: SEATS 4 (left)
GRAND BOX 1: SEATS 4 (right)

DRESS CIRCLE

```
SLIP BOX 1: SEATS 4 / CIRCLE BOX 1: SEATS 4 (left)
SLIP BOX 2: SEATS 4 / CIRCLE BOX 2: SEATS 4 (right)

        M  0 1 2 3 4 5 6   M   7 8 9 10 11 12 13 14 15 16 17 18 19 20 21 22 23        O  25 26 27 28 29        O
        L    1 2 3 4 5 6   L     8 9 10 11 12 13 14 15 16 17 18 19 20 21 22           N  25 26 27 28 29 30     N
        K    1 2 3 4 5 6 7 K     8 9 10 11 12 13 14 15 16 17 18 19 20 21 22 23 24 25  M  25 26 27 28 29 30     M
        J    1 2 3 4 5 6 7 J     8 9 10 11 12 13 14 15 16 17 18 19 20 21 22 23 24 25  L  25 26 27 28 29        L
        H    1 2 3 4 5 6 7 H     9 10 11 12 13 14 15 16 17 18 19 20 21 22 23 24 25    K  26 27 28 29 30 31 32  K
        G  1 2 3 4 5 6 7 8 G     9 10 11 12 13 14 15 16 17 18 19 20 21 22 23 24 25    J  26 27 28 29 30 31 32  J
        F  1 2 3 4 5 6 7 8 F     9 10 11 12 13 14 15 16 17 18 19 20 21 22 23          H  26 27 28 29 30 31 32  H
                                                                                     G  27 28 29 30 31 32 33 34  G
        E  3 4 5 6 7 8 9 10 E  11 12 13 14 15 16 17 18  E  19 20 21 22 23 24 25 26 27 28 29 30 31 32 33 34 35  E
        D  2 3 4 5 6 7 8 9 10 D 11 12 13 14 15 16 17    D  19 20 21 22 23 24 25 26 27 28 29 30 31 32 33        D
        C  1 2 3 4 5 6 7 8 9 C  10 11 12 13 14 15 16    C  17 18 19 20 21 22 23 24 25 26 27 28 29 30 31 32     C
        B  2 3 4 5 6 7 8 9 B    10 11 12 13 14 15       B  17 18 19 20 21 22 23 24 25 26 27 28 29 30           B
        A  2 3 4 5 6 7 8 9 A    10 11 12 13 14 15 16 17 A  18 19 20 21 22 23 24 25 26 27 28 29 30 31 32 33     A
```

5 1 2 3 4   (left)   1 2 3 4 10 (right)
4 1 2 3 4   1 2 3 4 9
3 1 2 3   1 2 3   8
2 1 2   1 2   7
1 1 2   1 2   6

DRESS CIRCLE LOGE (left)
DRESS CIRCLE LOGE (right)

STALLS

STALLS BOX 1: SEATS 4
STALLS BOX 2: SEATS 4

```
ZB  1 2 3 4 5 6 7 8 9 10  ZB                                        ZB  22 23 24 25 26 27 28 29 30 31  ZB
ZA  1 2 3 4 5 6 7 8 9 10  ZA              17 18 19 20 21            ZA  23 24 25 26 27 28 29 30 31 32  ZA
Z   1 2 3 4 5 6 7 8 9 10  Z   Sound Desk     18 19 20 21 22        Z   24 25 26 27 28 29 30 31 32 33  Z
Y   1 2 3 4 5 6 7 8 9 10  Y                      19 20 21 22 23    Y   24 25 26 27 28 29 30 31 32 33  Y
X   1 2 3 4 5 6 7 8 9 10  X   11 12 13 14 15 16 17 18 19 20 21 22 23 24  X  25 26 27 28 29 30 31 32 33 34  X
W   1 2 3 4 5 6 7 8 9 10  W   11 12 13 14 15 16 17 18 19 20 21 22 23 24  W  25 26 27 28 29 30 31 32 33 34  W
V   1 2 3 4 5 6 7 8 9 10  V   11 12 13 14 15 16 17 18 19 20 21 22 23 24  V  25 26 27 28 29 30 31 32 33 34  V
U   1 2 3 4 5 6 7 8 9 10  U   11 12 13 14 15 16 17 18 19 20 21 22 23     U  25 26 27 28 29 30 31 32 33     U
T   1 2 3 4 5 6 7 8 9 10  T   11 12 13 14 15 16 17 18 19 20 21 22 23     T  24 25 26 27 28 29 30 31 32 33  T
S   1 2 3 4 5 6 7 8 9 10  S   11 12 13 14 15 16 17 18 19 20 21 22 23     S  25 26 27 28 29 30 31 32 33     S
R   1 2 3 4 5 6 7 8 9 10  R   11 12 13 14 15 16 17 18 19 20 21 22 23     R  24 25 26 27 28 29 30 31 32 33  R
P   1 2 3 4 5 6 7 8 9 10  P   11 12 13 14 15 16 17 18 19 20 21 22 23 24  P  25 26 27 28 29 30 31 32 33 34  P
O     1 2 3 4 5 6 7 8 9   O   10 11 12 13 14 15 16 17 18 19 20 21 22     O  23 24 25 26 27 28 29 30 31     O
N     1 2 3 4 5 6 7 8 9   N   10 11 12 13 14 15 16 17 18 19 20 21 22 23  N  24 25 26 27 28 29 30 31 32     N
M   0 1 2 3 4 5 6 7 8     M    9 10 11 12 13 14 15 16 17 18 19 20 21     M  22 23 24 25 26 27 28 29 30     M
L   0 1 2 3 4 5 6 7       L    8 9 10 11 12 13 14 15 16 17 18 19 20 21   L  22 23 24 25 26 27 28 29        L

K   1 2 3 4 5 6 7 8 9 10 11 12 13 14 15 16 17 18 19 20 21 22 23 24 25 26 27 28 29 30 31 32     K
J   1 2 3 4 5 6 7 8 9 10 11 12 13 14 15 16 17 18 19 20 21 22 23 24 25 26 27 28 29 30 31 32 33  J
H   1 2 3 4 5 6 7 8 9 10 11 12 13 14 15 16 17 18 19 20 21 22 23 24 25 26 27 28 29 30 31 32     H
G   1 2 3 4 5 6 7 8 9 10 11 12 13 14 15 16 17 18 19 20 21 22 23 24 25 26 27 28 29 30 31 32 33  G
F   1 2 3 4 5 6 7 8 9 10 11 12 13 14 15 16 17 18 19 20 21 22 23 24 25 26 27 28 29 30 31 32     F
E     2 3 4 5 6 7 8 9 10 11 12 13 14 15 16 17 18 19 20 21 22 23 24 25 26 27 28 29 30 31        E
D       3 4 5 6 7 8 9 10 11 12 13 14 15 16 17 18 19 20 21 22 23 24 25 26 27 28 29 30           D
C         4 5 6 7 8 9 10 11 12 13 14 15 16 17 18 19 20 21 22 23 24 25 26 27 28 29              C
B           5 6 7 8 9 10 11 12 13 14 15 16 17 18 19 20 21 22 23 24 25 26 27 28                 B
```

STALLS

Prince Edward Theatre

Old Compton Street, London. W1D 4HS

B6

Variously a cabaret restaurant, servicemen's club and home of Cinerama, it returned permanently to theatre in 1978. Leading Lady Elaine Paige set a record for opening in three successive musicals here – **Evita**, **Chess** and **Anything Goes**.

BOX OFFICE:
0844 482 5151
020 7812 7498

ONLINE BOOKING:
delfontmackintosh.co.uk

 Leicester Square/
Tottenham Court Road

 Charing Cross

 Newport Place,
China Town (T)

1619

Air conditioned

stalls from row P back,
and both circles

STALLS: "A rather funny aisle runs down the side of the auditorium", a legacy of 1992 stalls remodelling. According to some in row B, the stage is high (hence the cheaper front row) and "rear stage and feet are lost looking steeply up". Most prefer a few rows back. Row L's wide aisle allows theatregoers to "really stretch out and enjoy the show, without heads obstructing views." Remember to stay awake, though. Outermost seats here and behind have sometimes required craning to see side action. This is also true of any problems created by circle and box overhangs at the ends of row P and from central S back.

Prices usually drop to compensate for significant problems, including sound-desk disturbance, and the only likely complaint is, as expressed by a Theatremonkey.com reader in V3/4, "having a 20-stone man-mountain with a head the size of a medicine ball in front" which "would have been OK if he hadn't inclined his head all the time to the right". If he isn't in town, you should be fine.

Rear stalls boxes: Fair value when priced to account for circle overhang.

DRESS CIRCLE: An unusually high rail-topped wall, plus little legroom, makes row A unsuitable for those under 5ft 3in or tall people. Behind, centrally, B8 to 11 "are excellent" and "leaners in row A were only a slight irritant". Though row C is felt equally good, one person felt D or E even better-elevated for shorter theatregoers. Outermost seats look over loges, making them a final choice here. In the rear circle, seats F16 to 18 have aisle rails in view. Occupants of G15 to 19 "could see straight to centre stage" and had good legroom. Row L back is usually discounted to allow for circle overhang, with corner seats in rows N and O cheaper still. Row N is "a bargain, half the price of some other rows". Seats M1 to 6 have a little more legroom.

Dress circle loges: Five short rows project in tiers from the dress circle front corners. Each is self-contained, enclosed by walls and metal rails. Those in loge 4 said that it "feels private, only the seat nearest the wall slightly lost corner action". Some felt that, in loge 5, seats 1 and 2 are "a little side on and fine unless the occupant of loge 4 leans forward" but there's good legroom and "it's worth top price".

Dress circle boxes: Only sometimes missing near side action, one Theatremonkey.com reader reported their box as "better than back row dress circle". Acceptable for wheelchair users, transferees to row A could obtain more central views.

Slip seats: "Fantastic value, great legroom. Have to lean forward slightly, but the view is clear."

GRAND (UPPER) CIRCLE: Steep, with legroom that's "inadequate for 6ft 3in". Theatremonkey.com readers in seats A20 and 21 found them "comfortable for 5ft 6in and 5ft 9in". Front-section aisle seats with rails in view are usually generously discounted to "fair value". Other seats are "wonderful for [the] price" (C19) while "binoculars make seeing faces possible". Only outermost seats have less pleasing sightline angles.

Everyone seems to have to squeeze past row G. In seats H4 to 7 "a safety rail in front made my child feel OK about the height, and borrowing a booster seat helped her see over it". Seats M15 and 16 "have views comparable to cheap non-restricted seats in any theatre". Seats L1, 2, 34 and 25, behind stairwell walls, are preferable to last-resort front corner rows slips for view and legroom.

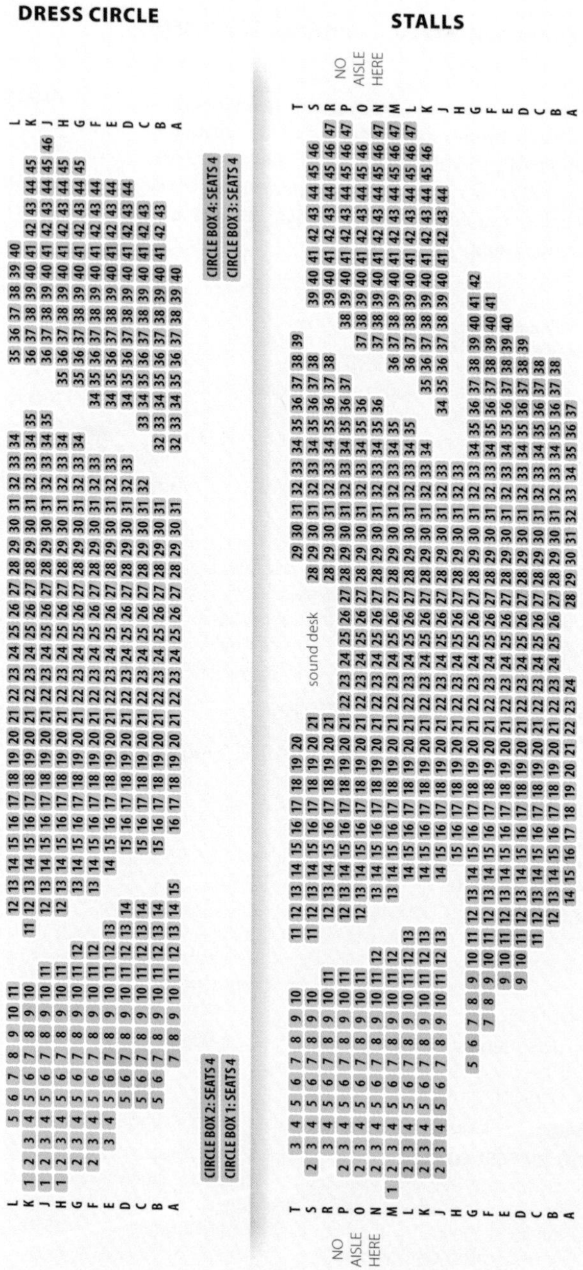
DRESS CIRCLE
STALLS
CIRCLE BOX 4: SEATS 4
CIRCLE BOX 3: SEATS 4
CIRCLE BOX 2: SEATS 4
CIRCLE BOX 1: SEATS 4
sound desk
NO AISLE HERE
NO AISLE HERE

PRINCE OF WALES THEATRE

Prince of Wales Theatre

31 Coventry Street, London. W1D 6AS B16

Following its 2004 makeover, this feels literally like the flagship of the Delfont Mackintosh empire. Streamlined surfaces, white walls and glass combine to evoke the Queen Mary and other liners of a more gracious age; there's even the Delfont Room for cabaret. Should **Mamma Mia** ever close, **Anything Goes** can be the only replacement. Within the auditorium, seats are so luxurious that you'll want to take one home. Sadly, the foyer gift shop doesn't sell them. For the ladies, the stalls level restroom, with 13 cubicles, adds further comfortable convenience(s) to their visits.

BOX OFFICE:
0844 482 5115
020 7812 7498

ONLINE BOOKING:
delfontmackintosh.co.uk

 Piccadilly Circus

Charing Cross

P Whitcomb Street (T)

1125

Air conditioned

STALLS: A keyboard player inhabits a hollow in central row A. Either side, seating wraps around a sloping stage, set almost at nose level for someone 5ft 5in tall. With the advantage of nobody in front, and a discount allowing for any craning when scenery rises, these are popular with regular customers. Seats at row ends may seem "removed from action", offering lesser quality sightlines and "ear-popping" speaker proximity. Front and centre, in B33 and 34 occupants may "feel the energy of the performance", and those in rows D to H report near perfect conditions.

Circle overhang at row E begins removing views from row N back, with row T losing around three-fifths off the top of the stage – luckily, in Mamma Mia it isn't an issue, as action happens at a lower level. With sensible pricing, a decent rake and well-staggered seats, only top-price central row P may seem a little expensive. Beside the sound desk, T20 "has plenty of room to get up and have a jig about". Only purists may wish to avoid both it and any dancing occupant.

Sensible pricing keeps most side section seating fair value. An oddly placed false proscenium wall snips views from the ends of rows J and K, negating the advantage of extra legroom in K2. Still, aisle-facing J2 to 13 and 34 to 44 have plenty. Claustrophobics should note that outer row ends have boxes overhanging and no side aisle from row K back. Seats S39 to 46 have a potentially noisy access corridor behind. Wheelchair users may prefer spaces created at T38 and 39 to those here.

DRESS CIRCLE: In the Monkey's opinion, this feels closer to the stage than any similar circle in London, but those in high heels should beware the very steep rake. Dangers are minimised with double-height aisle end rails (which worry almost nobody in A15, 16, 31, 32 or seats behind). Row A's overhanging bar, which incidentally makes the 5ft 7in Monkey feel safely "tucked in" for the show, also helps. A few shorter folk might prefer being a row back: B28 and 29 "have brilliant views and are comfortable", an opinion echoed from many other central block seats.

The Monkey feels central H preferable to rear stalls row P, despite a slight reduction in legroom compared with rows in front. Central rows J to L are also attractively priced, and worth considering over side stalls for overall stage views without intrusive circle overhang.

Side block seats focus well on centre stage, only a few corner ones losing a sliver of extreme edges to circle curve and rails. Outermost seats from row F back don't have aisles beside them. E3, like row A, has more legroom than usual. Shelf-like K and L have less as the rows taper to the wall, though centre aisle seats on L are well priced. Good seat design maximises comfort throughout.

DRESS CIRCLE BOXES: Architecturally stunning, boxes 1 and 3 see three-fifths of the stage without leaning. Lean and the whole stage is visible, but legroom is reduced. Still, they're fair value if cheaper. Boxes 2 and 4 were once spotlight operator positions. Narrow, vertigo-inducing shelves, box office staff generally show customers these before purchase. Suitable for adventurous types with a head for heights, willing to stare into an abyss

UPPER CIRCLE

Row L: 1 2 3 5 6 7 8 9   10 11 12 13 14 15 16 17 18 19
Row K: 1 2 3 5 6 7 8 9   10 11 12 13 14 15 16 17 18
Row J: 1 2 3 4 5 6 7 8 9 10   11 12 13 14 15 16 17 18 19 20 21 22 23
Row H: 1 2 3 4 5 6 7 8 9 10 11 12   13 14 15 16 17 18 19 20 21 22 23 24 25
Row G: 1 2 3 4 5 6 7 8 9 10 11 12 13   14 15 16 17 18 19 20 21 22 23 24 25 26
Row F: 1 2 3 4 5 6 7 8 9 10 11 12   13 14 15 16 17 18 19 20 21 22 23 24 25
Row E: 1 2 3 4 5 6 7 8 9 10 11 12   13 14 15 16 17 18 19 20 21 22 23 24
Row D: 1 2 3 4 5 6 7 8 9 10 11 12   13 14 15 16 17 18 19 20 21 22 23 24
Row C: 1 2 3 4 5 6 7 8 9 10 11 12 13   14 15 16 17 18 19 20 21 22 23 24 25 26
Row B: 1 2 3 4 5 6 7 8 9 10 11 12 13   14 15 16 17 18 19 20 21 22 23 24 25 26
Row A: 1 2 3 4 5 6 7 8 9 10 11 12 13   14 15 16 17 18 19 20 21 22 23 24 25 26

DRESS CIRCLE

10 STANDING PLACES

Row L: 1 2 3 4 5 6 7 8 9 10 11 12 13 14 15 16 17 18 19 20
Row K: 1 2 3 4 5 6 7 8 9 10 11 12 13 14 15 16 17 18 19 20 21 22
Row J: 1 2 3 4 5 6 7 8 9 10 11 12 13 14 15 16 17 18 19 20 21 22 23 24 25 26 27 28 29
Row H: 1 2 3 4 5 6 7 8 9 10 11 12 13 14 15 16 17 18 19 20 21 22 23 24 25 26 27 28 29
Row G: 1 2 3 4 5 6 7 8 9 10 11 12 13 14 15 16 17 18 19 20 21 22 23 24 25 26 27 28 29
Row F: 1 2 3 4 5 6 7 8 9 10 11 12 13 14 15 16 17 18 19 20 21 22 23 24 25 26 27 28
Row E: 1 2 3 4 5 6 7 8 9 10 11 12 13 14 15 16 17 18 19 20 21 22 23 24 25 26 27 28 29
Row D: 1 2 3 4 5 6 7 8 9 10 11 12 13 14 15 16 17 18 19 20 21 22 23 24 25 26 27 28
Row C: 1 2 3 4 5 6 7 8 9 10 11 12 13 14 15 16 17 18 19 20 21 22 23 24 25
Row B: 3 4 5 6 7 8 9 10 11 12 13 14 15 16 17 18 19 20 21 22 23 24
Row A: 8 9 10 11 12 13 14 15 16 17 18 19 20 21 22 23 24 25 26 27 28

Loge 1: 3 2 1   7 6 5 4 3 2 1 A

Loge 2: 29 30 31 32 33 34 35 36 A   3 2 1

STALLS

10 STANDING PLACES

Row W: 9 10 11 12 13 14 15
Row V: 7 8 9 10 11 12 13 14 15 16   22 23
Row U: 3 4 5 6 7 8 9 10 11 12 13 14 15 16 17 18 19 20 21 22 23 24
Row T: 2 3 4 5 6 7 8 9 10 11 12 13 14 15 16 17 18 19 20 21 22 23 24 25 26
Row S: 1 2 3 4 5 6 7 8 9 10 11 12 13 14 15 16 17 18 19 20 21 22 23 24 25 26 27
Row R: 1 2 3 4 5 6 7 8 9 10 11 12 13 14 15 16 17 18 19 20 21 22 23 24 25 26 27 28
Row Q: 1 2 3 4 5 6 7 8 9 10 11 12 13 14 15 16 17 18 19 20 21 22 23 24 25 26 27
Row P: 1 2 3 4 5 6 7 8 9 10 11 12 13 14 15 16 17 18 19 20 21 22 23 24 25 26
Row N: 1 2 3 4 5 6 7 8 9 10 11 12 13 14 15 16 17 18 19 20 21 22 23 24 25 26 27
Row M: 1 2 3 4 5 6 7 8 9 10 11 12 13 14 15 16 17 18 19 20 21 22 23 24 25 26
Row L: 1 2 3 4 5 6 7 8 9 10 11 12 13 14 15 16 17 18 19 20 21 22 23 24 25
Row K: 2 3 4 5 6 7 8 9 10 11 12 13 14 15 16 17 18 19 20 21 22 23 24 25
Row J: 2 3 4 5 6 7 8 9 10 11 12 13 14 15 16 17 18 19 20 21 22 23 24
Row H: 2 3 4 5 6 7 8 9 10 11 12 13 14 15 16 17 18 19 20 21 22 23 24 25
Row G: 3 4 5 6 7 8 9 10 11 12 13 14 15 16 17 18 19 20 21 22 23 24 25
Row F: 3 4 5 6 7 8 9 10 11 12 13 14 15 16 17 18 19 20 21 22 23 24
Row E: 3 4 5 6 7 8 9 10 11 12 13 14 15 16 17 18 19 20 21 22 23
Row D: 4 5 6 7 8 9 10 11 12 13 14 15 16 17 18 19 20 21 22 23
Row C: 4 5 6 7 8 9 10 11 12 13 14 15 16 17 18 19 20 21 22
Row B: 5 6 7 8 9 10 11 12 13 14 15 16 17 18 19 20 21 22
Row A: 5 6 7 8 9 10 11 12 13 14 15 16 17 18 19 20 21
Row BB: 6 7 8   20 21 22

Sound Desk

Queen's Theatre

Shaftesbury Avenue, London. W1V 8BA

B13

The original 1907 frontage matched that of the Gielgud, with which it shares a block. Lost to the Blitz in 1940, it was replaced by today's concrete and glass. In September 2009, a massive upgrading programme began, but **Les Misérables** spins on regardless.

BOX OFFICE:
0844 482 5160
020 7812 7498

ONLINE BOOKING:
delfontmackintosh.co.uk

 Piccadilly Circus

 Charing Cross

Newport Place, China Town (T)

1045

Air conditioned

stalls from row L back, and both circles

STALLS: An extended orchestra pit creates trios of bargain seating either side. Microphones cunningly disguised as cobbles bother few. Limited legroom worries some in row BB 8 and 20. Behind, seats A13 and 14 are discounted for "conductor in view" and A5 to 7 and 20 to 22 for stage curving. Full price outermost seats behind these also suffer less favourable viewing angles, with circle overhang clipping top stage views from row K. The 2009 upgrades improve viewing angles, but these are still seats most acceptable only when discounted.

More central seats from row D provide the best views and usually have "good legroom and sound" (G11 and 12). Compensating for circle overhang and reportedly muffled sound on occasion, seats M25 and 26 allow views of "all the stage floor effects sometimes missed further forward".

Behind, overhang-affected seats seem expensive. Centre ones suffer least: Theatremonkey.com readers in Q12 felt "slightly out of the action" but "the overhang blocks, but doesn't ruin, the experience as it does for end seats", and in row R found ample legroom but not best views". Some outermost seats are priced to compensate, T4 and 24 most reasonably. Furthest back, in the cheapest stalls, a disappointed Theatremonkey.com reader in row V found "sound was average, but we couldn't see projections or barricade top properly".

DRESS CIRCLE: Aisle rails are noticeable from the corners of the first three rows. Outermost seats lose stage edge views as the circle curves, but any discounted ones make acceptable budget options. Seats A8 to 10 and 26 to 28 have little legroom, but those in B21 and 22 had "plenty of legroom for 5ft 8in". Centrally, "A25 has an excellent view but lacks legroom" and generally rave reviews follow right back to row J; even K is "not too far away". On a level with the exit doors, row L offers a little more legroom but may (L16) feel "slightly removed from the action" and "doors behind irritated".

At the circle's sides, slips A1 to 7 and 29 to 36 lose a third of rear stage; A1 and 36 have almost no legroom. Behind, loges can be replaced by wheelchair spaces – not great views without leaning, alas.

Boxes: The dress circle and upper circle boxes have been boarded up due to nightly student uprisings.

UPPER CIRCLE: Not too high, with a good rake, most seats feel close to the action and are fairly priced. Shorter folk may find peering over the wide circle wall a problem in row A, and centre aisle customers have a rail and technical equipment in view. Outermost seats back to row G suffer circle curve (cutting stage edges) plus aisle end rails in their sightlines. Central row B back, off the aisle, is first choice. From D17 and 18, Theatremonkey.com readers could "see everything (despite row A leaning)" but found the angle wasn't the best.

Further back, F19 "is little bit high, but with a good view and legroom" and, with a view of how effects work, not recommended unless for really poor students. (Also suitable for those planning a musical or their own rebellion?) Of the designated "restricted view" seats, J1 and 2 are prime, offering decent legroom and sightlines least affected by circle curve. Seats H1 and 2 are nearly as good. Centrally, J7 and 8, if discounted, offer "perfect views". They are reported to be comfortable but with small armrests. Upper circle legroom is cramped for most; row A has least. Seats A1, 2, 25 and 26 exist but are not sold, being the most cramped of all.

BALCONY (UPPER CIRCLE)

(DRESS) CIRCLE

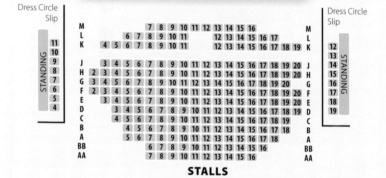

Dress Circle Slip

Dress Circle Slip

STALLS

DOWNSTAIRS

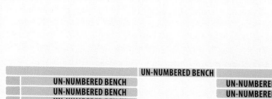

STALLS

UPSTAIRS

ROYAL COURT THEATRE

Royal Court Theatre

Sloane Square, London. SW1W 8AS

A theatre since 1888, the 2000 refurbishment impresses nearly as much as its dramatic credits. Many George Bernard Shaw productions were premiered here. Following bomb-damage repairs, in 1956 the English Stage Company began presenting landmark works considered by many to have changed theatre forever. **Look Back In Anger, The Entertainer, The Rocky Horror Show** and **Blasted** are a few of the fine, challenging pieces encouraged through programming policies continuing to this day.

BOX OFFICE:
020 7565 5000

ONLINE BOOKING:
www.royalcourttheatre.com

 Sloane Square

Victoria

Cadogan Place

Downstairs 395 seats,
Upstairs 80 seats

Air conditioned

Theatre Downstairs

STALLS: Occasionally the auditorium is drastically altered for a particular play, and you could find yourself inside a plastic tube or standing throughout. Usually, conventional seating prevails with only front rows AA, BB, A and B added or removed. Possible neck ache aside, these are generally a bargain at lower prices.

Further back, "staggered seats and a fair rake mean good views" according to Theatremonkey.com readers in seats H12 and 13, and the theatre is intimate enough for even row M to feel close to the stage. The circle overhang, affecting slightly top of stage sightlines from row K, is tolerable. Only seats at the extreme ends of rows sometimes feel "outside the proscenium" with a more acute viewing angle. Legroom is adequate throughout (best in row K) and armrests can be raised if two tickets are purchased. Wheelchair spaces behind row J11 and 12 offer fine views, those on the ends of K acceptable ones.

(DRESS) CIRCLE: The upper circle overhang doesn't affect views in this shallow circle. Double-height aisle end rails are an issue for seats A3, 4, 19 and 20. The front circle rail and its supports are potentially in the eyeline of shorter theatregoers in row A. The tight curve of the circle leaves outer seats angled towards centre stage, sometimes removing nearside corner action. Prices reflect these issues for able-bodied theatregoers but, at equal prices, wheelchair users may prefer stalls row J to the space at D2. Legroom is best in the central eight seats of B and C, and may be tight elsewhere for the tallest theatregoers.

Between circle front and stage is a row of cheap slip seats without armrests – good value view (but sometimes limited) if willing to crane. Behind are eight restricted-view standing positions, observing about one-third of the stage through shooting-gallery-style slits. They're sold on the day only, for a few pence each, to personal callers (excluding armed assassins) and can be a last-minute way in to a sold-out production.

BALCONY (UPPER CIRCLE): High above the stage, and steeply raked. Row A has very limited legroom, and often offers restricted views if the stage is extended. Front safety rails also intrude, making these a final choice for many. Behind, views are as the Monkey would expect from an upper circle. Centre seats offer clearest sightlines and greatest value, feeling reasonably involved with stage action even at a slight distance. Further out, the circle's curve and rails combine to limit views, particularly of events happening at the front corners of the stage. Taking into account legroom discomfort, many prefer to pay more for stalls instead, as price differences are generally kept small by the theatre management.

Theatre Upstairs

A simple and highly adaptable space, configured to suit each production. Audiences could be perched on bedroom furniture, shop chairs or placed on benches behind a mirror. Grandstand seating sometimes has limited legroom – try for seats with only stairs in front of them in this case. Always arrive early to select your view, as audiences are rarely assigned individual seat numbers in advance.

UPPER CIRCLE

H		1 2 3 4 5 6 7 8 9	H	10 11 12 13 14 15 16 17 18	H
G		1 2 3 4 5 6 7 8 9	G	10 11 12 13 14 15 16 17 18	G
F		1 2 3 4 5 6 7 8 9	F	10 11 12 13 14 15 16 17 18	F
E		1 2 3 4 5 6 7 8 9	E	10 11 12 13 14 15 16 17 18 19	E
D	1 2 3 4 5 6 7 8 9 10	D	11 12 13 14 15 16 17 18 19 20	D
C	1 2 3 4 5 6 7 8 9 10	C	11 12 13 14 15 16 17 18 19 20	C
B	1 2 3 4 5 6 7 8 9 10	B	11 12 13 14 15 16 17 18 19 20	B
A	1 2 3 4 5 6 7 8 9 10	A	11 12 13 14 15 16 17 18 19	A

DRESS CIRCLE

BOX D: SEATS 4

BOX C: SEATS 3

BOX B: SEATS 2

BOX A: SEATS 2

		F	1 2 3 4 5 6 7	F	
E	1 2 3 4 5 6	E	7 8 9 10 11 12 13 14 15 16 17	E	18 19 20 21 22	E
D	1 2 3 4 5 6	D	7 8 9 10 11 12 13 14 15 16 17	D	18 19 20 21 22	D
C	1 2 3 4 5 6	C	7 8 9 10 11 12 13 14 15 16 17	C	18 19 20 21 22	C
B	1 2 3 4 5 6 7	B	8 9 10 11 12 13 14 15 16 17 18	B	19 20 21 22 23 24	B
A	1 2 3 4 5 6 7 8	A	9 10 11 12 13 14 15 16 17 18 19	A	20 21 22 23 24 25 26	A

STALLS

N	1 2 3 4	N	5 6 7 8 9 10 11 12 13 14 15 16	O	1 2 3 4	O
M	1 2 3 4	M	5 6 7 8 9 10 11 12 13 14 15 16	N	17 18 19 20	N
L	1 2 3 4	L	5 6 7 8 9 10 11 12 13 14 15 16	M	17 18 19 20	M
K	1 2 3 4	K	5 6 7 8 9 10 11 12 13 14 15 16	L	17 18 19 20	L
J	1 2 3 4 5	J	6 7 8 9 10 11 12 13 14 15 16 17	K	17 18 19 20	K
H	1 2 3 4 5	H	6 7 8 9 10 11 12 13 14 15 16 17	J	18 19 20 21 22	J
G	1 2 3 4 5	G	6 7 8 9 10 11 12 13 14 15 16 17	H	18 19 20 21 22	H
				G	18 19 20 21 22	G
F	1 2 3 4 5 6 7 8 9 10 11 12 13 14 15 16 17 18 19 20 21 22	F
E	1 2 3 4 5 6 7 8 9 10 11 12 13 14 15 16 17 18 19 20 21	E
D	1 2 3 4 5 6 7 8 9 10 11 12 13 14 15 16 17 18 19 20	D
C	1 2 3 4 5 6 7 8 9 10 11 12 13 14 15 16 17	C
B	1 2 3 4 5 6 7 8 9 10 11 12 13 14 15 16 17	B
A	1 2 3 4 5 6 7 8 9 10 11 12 13 14 15 16	A

St Martin's Theatre

West Street, London. WC2H 9NZ   **B21**

Typically, the younger sister gets the hand-me-downs – the St Martin's is no exception. The Mousetrap moved across the yard from elder sibling the Ambassadors in 1974, and has been running here ever since. Its fabulous panelled auditorium is unique. Beautifully refurbished throughout in recent years without losing a single performance, "it's just like going back in time". Notice, too, the foyer stairwell plaque remembering young actor Meggie Albanesi, who died aged just 24 in 1923.

BOX OFFICE:
0844 499 1515
020 7836 1443
ONLINE BOOKING:
www.the-mousetrap.co.uk

 Leicester Square/ Tottenham Court Road

 Charing Cross

 Newport Place, Chinatown (T)

553

Air conditioned

STALLS: All seats here offer at least acceptable views. The first five rows curve gracefully in front of the stage. Central seats maximise views without craning. One Theatremonkey.com reader reports: "Up close it all looks more real, faults are magnified and you don't get the period feel with modern faces. Further away it's almost time travel, as though you're looking down on a show from 50 years ago." Do watch legroom: larger people next to an occupant of seat F14 "couldn't fit into the seats well [and] moved to aisle row seats behind". Its wide aisle allows row G the most legroom anywhere in the house. An occupant of seat H6 was unimpressed: "My girlfriend is 5ft 4in and still said that she could have done with a bit more legroom."

Behind, side blocks still feel connected to the stage, with only row O perhaps a little further back – though it's very fairly priced to compensate. The dress circle overhang, removing the top of the stage for row M back, affects enjoyment "not one bit" for anybody seated here.

DRESS CIRCLE: As in the stalls, circle overhang spoils nothing, and only the back row, F1 to 7, feels a little remote. The balustrade front wall may be high for shorter theatregoers in A. Circle curve and slightly side location also shave a little off the stage for A1 to 4 and 24 to 26 plus B1, 2, 23 and 24. Neither they, nor seats behind, are much cheaper either; a final pick for many if stalls or central dress circle are available.

According to a Theatremonkey.com reader, seat C10 has "plenty of leg room, ensuring no aching limbs" but someone over 6ft tall in front "obscured part of the stage – but did not spoil my enjoyment". Behind, row E has "no decent rake, no leg room and [is] very stuffy". Row F is cheaper with similar views. Taller people will find stalls row G more comfortable for the same money.

Dress circle boxes: Side boxes A and B at dress circle level are designated "restricted view", losing a slice of nearside stage. Boxes C and D at the rear of the dress circle offer clearer but distant views. The wheelchair plinth in C helpfully assists users to see over the box wall.

UPPER CIRCLE: Quirkily, front rows feel close to the stage, rear rows much further back. "Height gives the play a slightly grander dimension, allowing you to see character rather than actor." In row A, the balustrade front gives extra toe-room for some, and the rail "didn't prevent us from seeing anything relevant" (from seats A8 and 9). It's easy to peer under the rail from row A but short theatregoers in row B may notice it more. Rows from E back promise clear views at lower prices. Seats F3 and 4 are under a massive fan so their occupants moved before expiring of hypothermia: "If Theatremonkey were to recommend seats for menopausal women prone to hot flushes, these (and their equivalent on the other side) are probably more efficient than HRT."

End seats in rows B to D gain a tiny bit of extra legroom as rows curve back a little. Elsewhere, it can be cramped for those over 5ft 9in or so. Taller people may, as an occupant of seat B11 commented, be "glad to be able to swing one leg into the aisle".

UPPER CIRCLE

DRESS CIRCLE

BOX: SEATS 2

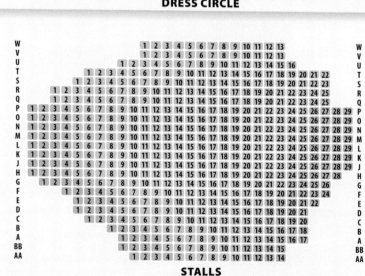

STALLS

Savoy Theatre

Strand, London WC2R 0ET C33

Forever a name associated with its neighbouring hotel and Gilbert and Sullivan, the current theatre is the third incarnation on the site. Dating from 1929, it was restored in 1990 following a devastating fire. Happily, the autumnal-toned seat upholstery was recreated, complete with unusual diamond-shaped fabric numbers. Quality musical revivals do well here, but a recent brush with opera proved less successful.

BOX OFFICE:
0870 164 8787
020 8544 7424

ONLINE BOOKING:
www.ambassadortickets.com

 Charing Cross

 Charing Cross

 Spring Gardens (T)

🚌 1157

❄ Air conditioned

STALLS: The stage can be high, and extended or given an orchestra pit by removing rows AA and BB. When these are present, they're often discounted. Row AA may be "great value of cheap" and "legroom is surprisingly good" but "you have to look up, sometimes seeing the cast only from knee upwards". Outermost seats back to row P may notice slivers of side action lost, sightlines reduced by their angle towards the proscenium. Still, good staggering allows clear views between heads in front. Central seats are popular: G16, for example, "has a good rake" and its occupant "could see faces very clearly and wouldn't want to be closer".

The only problem noted is the raised footrest counteracting any slope, so "you can't put your feet under the seat in front", an oddity in all raked rows. Try seats H1 and 28 for maximum legroom. Some also find the wooden seat backs and armrests uncomfortable. Circle overhang can intrude slightly from row O but otherwise, from T17 and 18, for example: "the view is amazing considering the distance, and sound is perfect" while "legroom is also OK for 5ft 7in me; cramped otherwise". Purists should note potential sound desk intrusion if one replaces seats in central rows U to W for musicals.

DRESS CIRCLE: Rails across the fronts of rows A and G, particularly at aisle ends, are practical but affect sightlines. Central front section seats from row B are worthwhile. From row D: "Sightlines are excellent and legroom fine." By F14 and 15 "it feels a tiny bit distant, but views are very clear and sound is great". The F1 wheelchair position is perhaps a little far over.

Circle overhang cuts into views from row K back, making rear-section top-price seats less desirable. There's also less legroom. Only seats H6, M7 and N8 are granted nothing in front by an architectural anomaly. The smaller seating section feels claustrophobically marooned (no aisle beside G to N seat 1 either), and seat O9 "is a bit too high up and far back". A hazard of the back row is that seats "are right against the wall, with a flat back".

Dress circle box: This is often used for lighting equipment. Leaning is required to see much more than half the stage.

UPPER CIRCLE: High, again with rails across the front of both sections; the polish bill could be astronomical. Seat A25 has "minimal 'rail' intrusion, but a slight lean forward is needed to see entire front stage" and legroom is tight "but you could swing them [the legs, that is] into the aisle". Against legroom advantage, outermost seats offer least favourable sightline angles. Most prefer front and centre: an occupant of D14 reports: "though the height above stage made me quite vertiginous, the actual view is fine".

In the rear section, "the difference between rows E and F is huge as theatre design seems to emphasise distance from the stage". The row G bar "is a nuisance", while rows K and L "seem a long long way away". An occupant of J11, beside the spotlights booth, "missed front stage" but for someone who's "20 stone and XXL 5ft 11in", legroom was acceptable and there was enough room alongside for a coat. This eyrie affects others differently, being reportedly vertigo-inducing but high enough "to give [a] clear view above the horizontal bars affecting some lower rows". Sound is good "as it reverberates off the back wall". At low prices, who could ask for more?

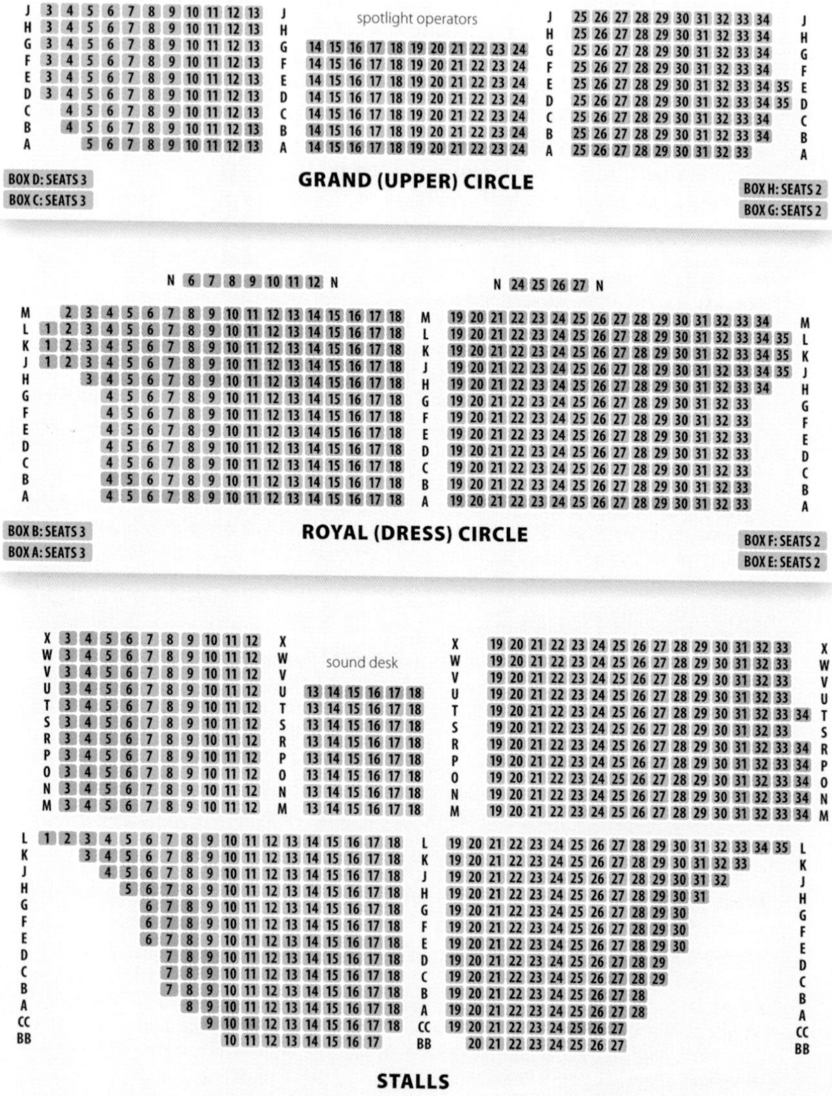

GRAND (UPPER) CIRCLE

spotlight operators

J	3 4 5 6 7 8 9 10 11 12 13																						25 26 27 28 29 30 31 32 33 34										J
H	3 4 5 6 7 8 9 10 11 12 13																						25 26 27 28 29 30 31 32 33 34										H
G	3 4 5 6 7 8 9 10 11 12 13						14 15 16 17 18 19 20 21 22 23 24						25 26 27 28 29 30 31 32 33 34										G

BOX D: SEATS 3
BOX C: SEATS 3

BOX H: SEATS 2
BOX G: SEATS 2

ROYAL (DRESS) CIRCLE

N 6 7 8 9 10 11 12 N   N 24 25 26 27 N

BOX B: SEATS 3
BOX A: SEATS 3

BOX F: SEATS 2
BOX E: SEATS 2

STALLS

sound desk

SHAFTESBURY THEATRE

Shaftesbury Theatre

210 Shaftesbury Avenue, London. WC2H 8DP   **B3**

This was the last theatre to open on Shaftesbury Avenue, in 1911. **Hair** literally brought the roof down in 1973, prematurely ending its famously successful run. More damage was done by reviews than the nightly nuclear explosion in **Out Of The Blue** – a Japanese musical running just three weeks in 1994. Theatremonkey.com readers consistently praise high levels of customer service here.

BOX OFFICE:
020 7379 5399

ONLINE BOOKING:
www.keithprowse.com

 Holborn/Tottenham Court Road

 King's Cross/St Pancras

 Museum Street

1400

❄ Air Cooled only

⊙⊙ stalls from row N back, and both circles

STALLS: Front rows can be added or removed, and are often sold cheaply. These are best, perhaps, "for fans only" because "actors' feet are cut from view and legroom is also limited". Things don't improve behind. An occupant of seat CC25 "had to look up, though less acutely than [those in] BB", concluding it's "not really worth top price". Outermost seats throughout the stalls suffer from acute viewing angles and missed action.

Mid-way back and central gets the vote of all but the tallest theatregoers. This theme is constant throughout: a Theatremonkey.com reader recommends seats L17 and 18, but "without legroom for my 6ft 6in, it's a good job that [on] one side was an aisle and on the other my wife, because we had to get very close!" Row M behind has much more legroom (and less chance of inadvertently making new friends). This fabled row is on a walkway: "You could sit legs outstretched throughout. Buy these if you can."

Further back, N26 and 27 "have perfect sightlines, though just on the proscenium edge". From row P, the low ceiling and circle overhang are noticeable and central row U may be bothered by a sound desk but, as they offer better legroom than comparably priced seats upstairs, they're worth considering. For the most budget conscious, standing spaces may miss varying amounts of stage, so "arrive early for the best spot".

ROYAL (DRESS) CIRCLE: Shorter theatregoers need to sit upright in row A to see over the rail, though some prefer a rail to a tall adult in front. "It's worth braving tight legroom for the intimate, uninterrupted view", according to a report from seats A21 to 23. Outermost seats in rows A and B suffer double-height rails, and wheelchair users may prefer boxes over transferring to A4. Elsewhere, E19 to 22 have "a great view, but not much legroom" while in H7 and 8 "the rake is not steep, so vertically challenged souls might struggle to see, but legroom is only adequate for 5ft 10in".

Dress circle boxes: Boxes A, B, E and F offer side-angled views, potentially with nearside action missed without leaning. Boxes A and E are adequate rail-view free alternatives for wheelchair users.

GRAND (UPPER) CIRCLE: This is moderately high, with safety rails that may be annoying but a Theatremonkey.com reader found they "didn't affect enjoyment". Higher rails are noticeable from aisle seats. The general wisdom is to take advantage of central tickets, particularly where prices fall around row D: theatregoers in D18, 22 and 23 "felt a lot closer to the stage than upper circles elsewhere", saw "everything from facial expressions to tiniest foot movement" and felt very comfortable with "lots of leg room".

Even better, a good rake is helpful outside the pantomime months. An occupant of D31 was amazed: "the person in front was about 6ft (I am 5ft 7in), and I could still see... that never happens!" Even the cheapest seats are praised: J6 "has lots of legroom and perfect vision". Watch only for central G, with its potentially irritating spotlight position behind.

Upper circle boxes: Boxes C, D, H and G offer similar views to dress circle boxes, from a higher angle.

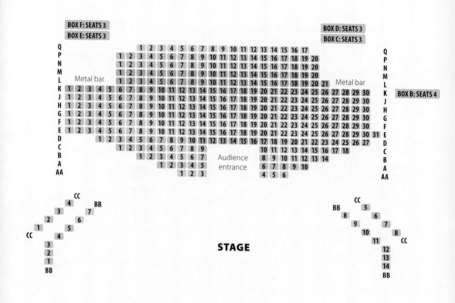

STUDIO 1

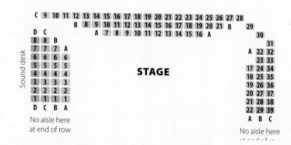

STUDIO 2

TRAFALGAR STUDIOS

Trafalgar Studios

Whitehall, London. SW1A 2DY

B28

Renowned for farce in the 50s and 60s, spicier material in the 70s then briefly as a war museum, this venue had a mixed past as the Whitehall Theatre.

BOX OFFICE:
0870 060 6632
020 8544 7424

ONLINE BOOKING:
www.ambassadortickets.com

Studio 1

"A good 'intimate' space", featuring a main bank of seats rising from the (usually) floor-level stage. Either side of the playing area, rows BB and CC can be added, sometimes extending past the proscenium towards the rear wall, creating an interesting perspective. Centrally, row AA is removable. In use, according to one theatregoer in AA4 seat 5, it's "superb [with] acting an arms length away", though those behind in row A may find heads blocking views. They may be glad of the protection available as, when absent, row A "is so close that an actor dripped sweat on my dress!".

 Charing Cross

 Charing Cross

P Spring Gardens (T)

382

Air conditioned

An audience entrance splits rows AA to D. Without aisles beside its walls, claustrophobics may wish to avoid adjacent seats. A bar above the doorway may intrude into shorter theatregoers' sightlines in D11 to 17 and possibly central row E behind. Where rows A to C curve, at B2, 3, 12 and 13, and C3, 4, 15 and 16, seats face each other slightly, knees potentially intertwining. (These are no more expensive on Valentine's Day.)

Row E was the front of the old circle, and has "a great view and loads of legroom". Row F is equally popular but by row G the seats narrow noticeably. This causes discomfort for wider theatregoers, although a narrower one was delighted "to be able to see over tall people in front". Sightlines also please elsewhere: in seats J27 and 28, for example, "even two seats off end of row, you don't feel that the viewing angle makes you miss any action". Comfort is still an issue: "K1 has superb sightlines, good acoustics, but horribly narrow seats with no armrests, and awful legroom for 5ft 6in me." Top price seems steep here.

Tall safety rails beside row L catch falling bodies and allow washing to be hung without affecting views. Second price feels fair for the penultimate rows, and cheapest Q is praised. Theatregoers in Q5 and 6 reported "no complaints about distance or view" and "no real difference" between this row and the more expensive N.

Boxes: All these offer legroom advantages. Boxes C, D, E and F, when not required for technical equipment, have clear but distant sightlines. Box B is closer to the stage, its side location sometimes obscuring nearside action.

Studio 2

Seats in the cornflake box-shaped Studio 2 surround the wide, shallow, floor-level stage on three sides. Modestly comfy padded tip-up benches lack armrests; each bench provides two seats with about 50cm of space per person. Shallow steps raise rows, with seats staggered slightly to assist seeing around those in front.

Seat 1 in rows A to D, A22, B29 and C39 are beside barriers, not aisles. A full auditorium may induce claustrophobia, short theatregoers may find corner rail ends in their eyeline, and there's a sound desk behind seats D1 to 8. Otherwise, choose by legroom: row A, B20 and 21 and C9 to 12 and 28 have most; C29 and 30, at 45-degree angles to the stage, are next; then B23 and C13 with space for one leg to the right. Seat C8 is similar, with a space to the left. Legroom is tight elsewhere, with minimal knee gap between rows for someone 5ft 7in or taller.

UPPER CIRCLE

```
J       15 14 13 12 11 10  9  8  7  6  5  4  3  2  1
H       17 16 15 14 13 12 11 10  9  8  7  6  5  4  3  2  1
G    18 17 16 15 14 13 12 11 10  9  8  7  6  5  4  3  2  1
F    18 17 16 15 14 13 12 11 10  9  8  7  6  5  4  3  2  1
E    18 17 16 15 14 13 12 11 10  9  8  7  6  5  4  3  2  1
D    18 17 16 15 14 13 12 11 10  9  8  7  6  5  4  3  2  1
C    18 17 16 15 14 13 12 11 10  9  8  7  6  5  4  3  2  1
B    18 17 16 15 14 13 12 11 10  9  8  7  6  5  4  3  2  1
A       16 15 14 13 12 11 10  9  8  7  6  5  4  3  2  1
```

DRESS CIRCLE

```
K  19 18 17 16 15 14 13 12 11 10  9  8  7  6  5  4  3  2  1  K
J  19 18 17 16 15 14 13 12 11 10  9  8  7  6  5  4  3  2  1  J
H  19 18 17 16 15 14 13 12 11 10  9  8  7  6  5  4  3  2  1  H
G  19 18 17 16 15 14 13 12 11 10  9  8  7  6  5  4  3  2  1  G
F  ●    17 16 15 14 13 12 11 10  9  8  7  6  5  4  3  2  1 ●  F
E  19 18 17 16 15 14 13 12 11 10  9  8  7  6  5  4  3  2  1  E
D  19 18 17 16 15 14 13 12 11 10  9  8  7  6  5  4  3  2  1  D
C  19 18 17 16 15 14 13 12 11 10  9  8  7  6  5  4  3  2  1  C
B  19 18 17 16 15 14 13 12 11 10  9  8  7  6  5  4  3  2  1  B
A  19 18 17 16 15 14 13 12 11 10  9  8  7  6  5  4  3  2  1  A
```

BOX C: SEATS 3   BOX A: SEATS 3
BOX D: SEATS 4   BOX B: SEATS 4

STALLS

```
S     18 17 16 15 14 13 12 11 10  9  8  7  6  5  4  3  2  1  S
R     18 17 16 15 14 13 12 11 10  9  8  7  6  5  4  3  2  1  R
Q     18 17 16 15 14 13 12 11 10  9  8  7  6  5  4  3  2  1  Q
P        17 16 15 14 13 12 11 10  9  8  7  6  5  4  3  2  1  P
O ●         15 14 13 12 11 10  9  8  7  6  5  4  3  2  1  ● O
N           16 15 14 13 12 11 10  9  8  7  6  5  4  3  2  1  N
M     18 17 16 15 14 13 12 11 10  9  8  7  6  5  4  3  2  1  M
L     18 17 16 15 14 13 12 11 10  9  8  7  6  5  4  3  2  1  L
K     18 17 16 15 14 13 12 11 10  9  8  7  6  5  4  3  2  1  K
J     18 17 16 15 14 13 12 11 10  9  8  7  6  5  4  3  2  1  J
H     18 17 16 15 14 13 12 11 10  9  8  7  6  5  4  3  2  1  H
G     18 17 16 15 14 13 12 11 10  9  8  7  6  5  4  3  2  1  G
F     18 17 16 15 14 13 12 11 10  9  8  7  6  5  4  3  2  1  F
E     18 17 16 15 14 13 12 11 10  9  8  7  6  5  4  3  2  1  E
D     18 17 16 15 14 13 12 11 10  9  8  7  6  5  4  3  2  1  D
C     18 17 16 15 14 13 12 11 10  9  8  7  6  5  4  3  2  1  C
B     18 17 16 15 14 13 12 11 10  9  8  7  6  5  4  3  2  1  B
A        16 15 14 13 12 11 10  9  8  7  6  5  4  3  2  1  A
AZ                   10  9  8  7  6  5  4  3  2  1       AZ
AY                   10  9  8  7  6  5  4  3  2  1       AY
```

Vaudeville Theatre

Strand, London. WC2R 0NH   **C32**

Voltaire once stayed in a house on this site. That was demolished to make way for this miniature gem in 1869. The beautifully neat frontage and foyer were added in 1890, with the auditorium given its present form in 1926. Visitors sometimes infer that the Vaudeville offers non-stop variety shows. In fact, the theatre is known for quality drama and comedy; the odd musical or revue also plays beautifully in intimate surroundings. Friendly, informed service is still the tradition here, and the Vaudeville remains the Monkey's favourite theatre in the West End.

BOX OFFICE:
0844 412 4663
0844 579 1975
0870 830 0200
020 7087 7500

ONLINE BOOKING:
www.nimaxtheatres.com

 Charing Cross

Charing Cross

P Spring Gardens (T)

700

Air conditioned

STALLS: Most seats offer fairly priced views, plus reasonable legroom to all but the tallest. Row AY is often at the front, with the stage rarely high enough to induce neck ache. On occasions where it is raised, price reflects the change or the row is removed. It's easy to connect with the action here, particularly from central seats, and legroom is often fine.

Watch end seats in rows B to G for less comfortable viewing angles and (sometimes) proximity to extra speakers. Otherwise, central seats back to row J offer prime sightlines, with usually adequate rake and stagger to see around heads in front. An occupant of seat D14 "found the view excellent" and "far enough back not to crane your neck whilst still being close".

The circle overhang at row M begins to encroach into stage top views a little for rows behind. This rarely causes problems, unless a set designer takes titles like Up On The Roof too literally. Pillars at the ends of row N don't appear in sightlines, but may make claustrophobics wish to avoid seats nearby. Row P, if at second price, is worth a look. The back three rows generally provide decent views, for wheelchair users, too, in row S, at acceptable prices – with greater comfort than upper circle seats for longer-legged people. Purists may wish to avoid any sound desk occasionally installed here.

DRESS CIRCLE: The front of the dress circle feels framed by side boxes and the overhanging circle above. All outermost seats peer towards the stage around these edges, with seats A1 and 19 most affected. Row A can be cramped, while C has a little less legroom, too – seat design eases things slightly here. Seat G19 is often discounted for being partly behind a pillar, and can be worthwhile for those willing to lean a little. Otherwise, front rows are popular: B12 and 13 afford "an excellent view of the whole stage". Further back, rows F to H perhaps feel more distant than similarly priced stalls seats. Row J can be fairer value if below top price.

Generally, the Monkey prefers rear stalls over rear circle at comparable prices, for comfort and relationship to the stage. Taller theatregoers may also be more comfortable downstairs.

Dress circle boxes: Boxes A, B, C and D, in pairs either side of the theatre, lose around an eighth of nearside stage. Box C can take two transferees from wheelchairs. Moderate value, these are options for legroom seekers if suitable stalls are unavailable.

UPPER CIRCLE: This feels slightly further from the stage than expected in such a small theatre. Legroom throughout is predictably tight. Like the dress circle below, outermost seats have acute viewing angles. The tops of the boxes are visible (and tricky to dust?). The front circle rail intrudes into row B sightlines and often causes those in A to lean. Central seats offer clear views from row C, though rear stalls may offer greater comfort at similar prices. Seats otherwise are invariably fairly priced, including those in more remote rows H and J. It's often worth taking the row behind a "price change" boundary in this circle for similar but cheaper views.

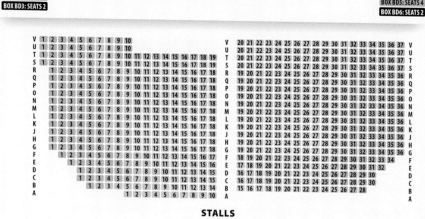

GRAND (UPPER) CIRCLE

BOX BU1: SEATS 2
BOX BU2: SEATS 3
BOX BU3: SEATS 2

BOX BU4: SEATS 2
BOX BU5: SEATS 3
BOX BU6: SEATS 2

1 2 3 4 5 ALCOVE RIGHT

ALCOVE LEFT 1 2 3 4 5

SIDE RIGHT

SIDE LEFT

BOX BD1: SEATS 3
BOX BD2: SEATS 4
BOX BD3: SEATS 2

DRESS CIRCLE

BOX BD4: SEATS 3
BOX BD5: SEATS 4
BOX BD6: SEATS 2

STALLS

Victoria Palace Theatre

Victoria Street, London. SW1E 5EA

Superstitious dancer Anna Pavlova never looked at her statue above the entrance. It vanished in 1939, being replaced by a replica only in 2006. Home to the **Crazy Gang** from 1947 for over 20 years, the theatre is now famous for musicals. Here, attending **Annie** in 1978, a tiny Monkey first caught the theatregoing bug from stalls seat V20. Next to this, and all aisle seats, the original 1910 iron row ends are a fascinating feature.

BOX OFFICE:
0844 248 5000
020 7834 1317

ONLINE BOOKING:
victoriapalacetheatre.co.uk

 Victoria

 Victoria

P Semley Place

 1517

❄ Air conditioned

STALLS: "Large, unforgiving, and feeling disconnected from two-thirds back, you can also hear Underground trains rumbling." Cheap front rows are popular for Billy Elliot. Outermost seats suffer acute viewing angles and potentially miss action. Some are discounted to compensate, others not. C1 and F32 are reported to "miss quite a bit – right is better, as more action happens left".

At top price, row F begins to draw favourable comments from taller people, while by G central seats are recognised as having "an offset helping uninterrupted views, adequate legroom, and good comfort for someone 6ft 2in" (K11 to 14). Once past half-way back, middle seats are still "far back enough to see everything" (P18 and 19) but, off to the sides, things deteriorate. Theatremonkey.com readers in seats L29 and 30 felt "detached from the action" and those in M35 and 36 "could only see right side properly". Wheelchair spaces here and at P36 have similar problems. Circle overhang clips stage top sightlines from row Q and occupants of seats T18 and 19 "noticed the sound desk a little".

DRESS CIRCLE: Rows K and L suffer slight circle overhang, and front corner seats miss some action. A tall Professor of Logic (in C17) maximises sightlines and comfort thus: "make your first choice A to D17 or 18, then stick your long legs into the aisle". Alternatively, outermost ends of rows D to H provide space as rows curve back: a Theatremonkey.com reader of 5ft 8in and boyfriend of 6ft 4in "had plenty of room, and an unspoiled view" from seats F31 and 32. Elsewhere, legroom gets tight, especially for taller people. Rear rows are described as "OK, but too far back to clearly take everything in".

Behind, alcove right seat 3 "sees the stage width but not height – though you can lean without blocking others", legroom is poor and "people wander in front". Either side, side alcove seat 2 chairs "are not fixed in place, legroom is quite good, but you miss a bit of side stage" so consider these "only after similarly priced cheap stalls".

Dress circle boxes: These are worth avoiding, unless wishing to trade views for legroom. Occupants of box 2 saw "between a third and half the show, with huge noisy speakers blocking stage right".

GRAND (UPPER) CIRCLE: This is high and steeply raked, so vertigo is possible. Theatregoers report cramped, uncomfortable conditions here, which is a shame as central sightlines are good and prices often reasonable. Rows A and B are discounted to allow for safety rails in view. In row A, "prepare to lean". Potentially, leaners in front cause problems for other rows but, by D29 for example, "views are fine", helped by staggered seats. Only outermost seats potentially suffer lesser viewing angles as the circle curves, and sound can be variable.

Theatremonkey.com readers in J33 to 35 found that "air-conditioning vents in front kept us cool". Going a row back to K saves money, offers similar views and an inch more legroom and you may "see the mechanics of how the sets worked". Circle edges are final resorts: an occupant of seat A44 found it "possibly the worst seat in the house" with a double safety bar in front, affording views that are "terrible unless leaning forward" with "no legroom unless prepared to stand".

Upper circle boxes: With similar problems to dress circle boxes, these are mostly kept off public sale.

```
D    3 4 5 6 7 8 9 10 11 12 13 14 15   D   16 17 18 19 20 21 22 23 24 25 26 27 28      D
C  2 3 4 5 6 7 8 9 10 11 12 13 14 15   C   16 17 18 19 20 21 22 23 24 25 26 27 28 29   C
B          6 7 8 9 10 11 12 13 14 15   B   16 17 18 19 20 21 22 23 24 25               B
A  5       6 7 8 9 10 11 12 13 14 15   A   16 17 18 19 20 21 22 23 24 25            26 A
```

BALCONY

```
D  2 3 4 5 6 7 8 9 10 11 12 13 14 15 16 17 18 19 20 21 22 23 24 25 26 27 28 29     D
C  2 3 4 5 6 7 8 9 10 11 12 13 14 15 16 17 18 19 20 21 22 23 24 25 26 27 28 29 30  C
B  2 3 4 5 6 7 8 9 10 11 12 13 14 15 16 17 18 19 20 21 22 23 24 25 26 27 28 29 30  B
A  2 3 4 5 6 7 8 9 10 11 12 13 14 15 16 17 18 19 20 21 22 23 24 25 26 27 28 29     A
```

BOX 7: SEATS 2
BOX 5: SEATS 2

GRAND (UPPER) CIRCLE

BOX 8: SEATS 2
BOX 6: SEATS 2

```
                           G  13 14 15 16 17 18 19 20 21  G       8 STANDING PLACES
F    3 4 5 6 7 8 9 10 11 12 13 14 15 16 17 18 19 20 21 22 23 24 25 26 27 28 29 30  F
E  2 3 4 5 6 7 8 9 10 11 12 13 14 15 16 17 18 19 20 21 22 23 24 25 26 27 28 29 30  E
D  2 3 4 5 6 7 8 9 10 11 12 13 14 15 16 17 18 19 20 21 22 23 24 25 26 27 28 29 30  D
C      3 4 5 6 7 8 9 10 11 12 13 14 15 16 17 18 19 20 21 22 23 24 25 26 27 28 29   C
B    3 4 5 6 7 8 9 10 11 12 13 14 15 16 17 18 19 20 21 22 23 24 25 26 27 28        B
A      4 5 6 7 8 9 10 11 12 13 14 15 16 17 18 19 20 21 22 23 24 25 26 27 28        A
```

BOX 3: SEATS 2
BOX 1: SEATS 2

ROYAL (DRESS) CIRCLE

BOX 4: SEATS 2
BOX 2: SEATS 2

BOX A: SEATS 4   13 STANDING PLACES

```
R              11 12 13 14 15 16 17 18 19 20 21             R
Q      8 9 10 11 12 13 14 15        16 17 18 19 20          Q

P  3 4 5 6 7 8 9 10 11 12 13 14 15 16 17 18 19 20 21 22 23 24 25 26 27 28  P
O  3 4 5 6 7 8 9 10 11 12 13 14 15 16 17 18 19 20 21 22 23 24 25 26 27     O
N  3 4 5 6 7 8 9 10 11 12 13 14 15 16 17 18 19 20 21 22 23 24 25 26 27 28  N
M  3 4 5 6 7 8 9 10 11 12 13 14 15 16 17 18 19 20 21 22 23 24 25 26 27     M
L  3 4 5 6 7 8 9 10 11 12 13 14 15 16 17 18 19 20 21 22 23 24 25 26 27 28  L
K  3 4 5 6 7 8 9 10 11 12 13 14 15 16 17 18 19 20 21 22 23 24 25 26 27     K
J    4 5 6 7 8 9 10 11 12 13 14 15 16 17 18 19 20 21 22 23 24 25 26 27     J
H    4 5 6 7 8 9 10 11 12 13 14 15 16 17 18 19 20 21 22 23 24 25 26 27     H
G      5 6 7 8 9 10 11 12 13 14 15 16 17 18 19 20 21 22 23 24 25 26        G
F        6 7 8 9 10 11 12 13 14 15 16 17 18 19 20 21 22 23 24 25 26        F
E          6 7 8 9 10 11 12 13 14 15 16 17 18 19 20 21 22 23 24 25         E
D          6 7 8 9 10 11 12 13 14 15 16 17 18 19 20 21 22 23 24 25         D
C            7 8 9 10 11 12 13 14 15 16 17 18 19 20 21 22 23 24            C
B          7 8 9 10 11 12 13 14 15 16 17 18 19 20 21 22 23 24             B
A            8 9 10 11 12 13 14 15 16 17 18 19 20 21 22 23 24             A
```

STALLS

Wyndham's Theatre

Charing Cross Road, London WC2H 0DA   **B23**

Actor Manager Charles Wyndham achieved the dream of opening his own theatre in 1899. Delfont Mackintosh beautifully restored the building, from sparkling Portland stone frontage to exquisitely pretty circular foyer and blue/cream gilded auditorium. Productions clamour to play this perfectly located venue; past ones include Madonna's 2002 West End debut in **Up For Grabs**.

BOX OFFICE:
0844 482 5120
020 7812 7498

ONLINE BOOKING:
delfontmackintosh.co.uk

 Leicester Square

 Charing Cross

P Newport Place, China Town (T)/Spring Gardens (T)

970

Air conditioned

STALLS: The stage can be high. Short theatregoers and those allergic to neck ache may wish to sit further back. Eye-level corners at the ends of row A don't enhance already sideways views of the action; rows B and C behind suffer less. Unraked rows A to D are personal Monkey favourites: C22 and 23 "like all front stalls, feel very close to the action". Most are happy further back, with good central views and adequate legroom.

Circle overhang intrudes slightly from row N, while outermost seats from row G may feel less involved in the action. Furthest back, in P "the sound varied, my seat was rather uncomfortable, and it was stuffy". Row Q faces an aisle, offering a little more legroom. It also fences row R into an alcove. Both are fair value at second price or lower. Cheap standing spaces alongside can be a bargain.

Stalls box: Box A offers decent legroom plus central sightlines, missing only stage top views.

ROYAL (DRESS) CIRCLE: This has few intrusions to spoil viewing. Circle overhang shaves a little off stage top from row C back, but aisle end rails (plus those installed beside rows A and B to help less able people) cause no problems. In row A, "it's worth braving slightly tight legroom for the view". Behind, seats D15 and 16 are "central and comfortable" but watch out for knees of long-legged people behind! Row G is on an alcove shelf, circle overhang is noticeable and rails in front of all but its central seats may disrupt sightlines. Beside it, cheap standing places may provide bargain viewing positions.

Dress circle/upper circle boxes: Paired either side of the theatre, between stage and circles, these offer sideways viewing, shaving around 15% off nearside action. Be prepared to move chairs around and lean for best sightlines.

GRAND (UPPER) CIRCLE: Far above the stage, this section offers limited legroom for anyone over around 5ft 7in. When mounted on the circle front, lighting may intrude into row A views. Central seats in rows B and C offer prime sightlines. Further out, this circle curves tightly, removing almost one-fifth of the front corner segment of nearside stage; aisle seats suffer most. Discounted, the next two or three seats in may offer better alternatives to the balcony, if available at similar prices.

BALCONY: This is behind and a little above the upper circle. The front safety rail slightly affects views in row A. Further rails across rows B and D cause no problems, and may reassure vertigo sufferers. Row C seats, flat on a ledge rather than tip-up, are a little deeper. Row D seats are slightly wider. Legroom is tight for those over around 5ft 9in; centre aisle seats permit a little stretching.

Row A has least space, except for separate corner "nests" at A5 and 26. This brace of narrow ledge seats, with straight backs and minimal legroom, faces the stage. Beside each is a deeper padded triangle. Those of average hip width, if willing to look sideways, could comfortably sit here with legs stretched parallel to the circle front wall. Theatremonkey considered permanent nesting residence, until management warned that any signs (banana skins, cable TV installation etc.) would result in its indefinite ban. With the stage not overwhelmingly distant, and prices proportionate to view, balcony seats are fair value. When sold, standing spaces are also adequate if those on lower levels are unavailable.

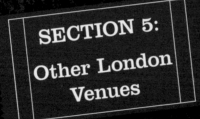

SECTION 5:
Other London Venues

Theatremonkey.com and its readers
enjoy many other venues throughout
London, and some notes gleaned on
a selection of the most famous are
shared in the following pages.

Barbican Hall

Silk Street, London. EC2Y 8DS

Within the Barbican Centre complex, this is a beautifully light and airy concert hall. A recent refurbishment ironed out most minor issues raised by concertgoers since opening, and it remains a firm Monkey favourite.

Five rows directly in front of the stage are generally good value. In row B, though, one concertgoer at an English National Opera concert performance reports being too close to the soloists: "Rare, but when the front of the platform is heavily populated I recommend D and E [for] better view and value." (Also safer if performers look unsteady on their feet!) Pricing usually reflects viewing angle and proximity to the stage, a stepped rake from row G ensures decent sightlines. Legroom is comfortable; row G has most. Wheelchair spaces in the rear stalls are fine. Outermost seats in rows G to K are "restricted view" bargains if sightlines are unimportant to classical concertgoers.

The (dress) circle, above and behind the stalls, offers best views from the central section. Side blocks are often attractively priced, providing good value in the cheaper seats slightly off the aisles. Again, rake and comfort are to high standards throughout, and only the tallest concertgoers need consider seeking extra legroom stalls.

On the highest tier, the balcony (upper circle level) is above and almost behind the circle. The Monkey likes central row D without anyone behind. Expect a clear, if distant, view and well-balanced sound. In the side blocks, seats at A to D13 to 25 and 60 to 72 are usually well priced. Comfort is equal to the rest of the auditorium.

BOX OFFICE:
0845 120 7500
020 7638 8891

ONLINE BOOKING:
www.barbican.org.uk

 Barbican/Moorgate

Moorgate

P within building complex

2020

Air conditioned

Earls Court Arena

Earls Court, Warwick Road, London SW5 9SY

Opened officially in 1937 as the Earls Court Exhibition Centre, this venue has a central open area and balconies above it that can be used as vast concert or performance spaces. Only the highest gallery has permanent seating. Below, at balcony, stalls and arena levels, portable grandstands are used and block numbers change regularly. The Monkey's advice is to check block numbering on the specific event's plan at the Earls Court & Olympia website (www.eco.co.uk) when purchasing.

When central arena seats are used, the first 12 rows of block AA are prime. Behind, the usual problem caused by a flat floor applies, so people can't see when everyone else stands. If used, block EE is sometimes elevated, and its front rows are another possibility.

Stalls are side and rear grandstands, facing either the stage or arena action. Restricted-view seats closest to the stage or arena may not be sold. Otherwise, rows back to P are usually satisfactory in all blocks until half-way down the venue. Rear stands behind EE are fair: rows from H back see most over heads in front. For arena events, choose these or central side blocks.

Second-level balcony seats are hard (but cushions are available to hire!). All seats look over bars, gangways and sometimes stairwell entrances. Theatremonkey.com readers are often delighted with "restricted view" seats near the stage. Views are through vertical bars, which are "nowhere near being in the way", so the angle of view is "awesome". For central arena events, angled corner

BOX OFFICE:
0870 903 9033
0870 830 0200

ONLINE BOOKING:
www.eco.co.uk

 Earl's Court

Moorgate

P Seagrave Road

16,000 to 19,000

No air conditioning

blocks offer good overall viewing.

Third-level fixed gallery seats are uncomfortable and a long, potentially vertigo-inducing, distance from the stage. Roof supports render some seats unusable for end-stage events. Bargains are to be found in row A, just behind balcony seats and with most legroom.

HMV Hammersmith Apollo

Queen Caroline Street, Hammersmith, London. W6 9QH

This theatre was built in 1932 during the Super Cinema era, but film was dropped completely by 1984 in favour of live events. Known to generations of Londoners for hosting great bands on their way up, the chart diet is supplemented by short runs of musicals, dance productions and comedy.

Central stalls back to row N offer best views. Outer block seats may lose rear corners of the stage, or find speakers blocking sightlines. The dress circle overhang at row U only very slightly affects views from the back two rows, making these rows a bargain when discounted. Wheelchair users allocated a raised area behind row BB – together with those using standing places beside them – also enjoy acceptable viewing.

Elsewhere, the only real problem can be seeing the stage when behind a tall person (particularly when everybody stands during a concert). There's a reasonable rake, but shorter concertgoers should try either for front rows, tiered circle seating or places on cross-aisles at J or T1 to 19 and 40 to 58. The longer-legged will also find that these last seats provide added comfort. All seats can be removed to create one large standing area for some events.

The dress circle stretches back over the foyer; rear and outermost seats are perhaps closer to Hammersmith Flyover than the stage. However, those in 079 and 80 felt that their seats weren't "really that far away", although centre blocks may be better, but "all seats are tiered so those in front don't block views". For people under 5ft tall, the circle front wall is a little high to see over, as are seats behind stairwell walls, namely K11 to 13, 24 to 26, 51 to 53 and 64 to 66. Legroom is average for all but the tallest people. Rear circle standing places provide a vantage point for those happy to hear, as much as see, the show.

BOX OFFICE:
0844 844 4748
0161 385 3211

ONLINE BOOKING:
hammersmithapollo.net

 Hammersmith

 Gunnersbury

P Hammersmith Grove

3326 plus 298 standing

No air conditioning

London Coliseum

St. Martin's Lane, London. WC2N 4ES

Once housing Broadway musicals, this is now a beautifully restored opera and ballet house. For opening night in 1904, a carriage on rails, intended to transport the King from door to auditorium box, broke down and was never used again. Faring better, the globe atop the building – always intended to revolve but rendered static in an ancient planning dispute – now does so, thanks to a 2004 overhaul.

Unusually, circles wrap around and behind the stalls, eliminating overhang problems. Central stalls "offer clear views" according to concertgoers. Stepped raking assists nicely, but be careful when finding your seat. Claustrophobics may note there are no aisles beside outermost seats from row E back. Rear stalls wheelchair spaces offer clear views.

Boxes are always popular. "Stage boxes have one-fifth restricted view, but are great for close viewing." Higher-level and rear

BOX OFFICE:
0871 911 0200

ONLINE BOOKING:
www.eno.org

 Leicester Square/
Charing Cross

 Charing Cross

P Spring Gardens (T)

2358

No air conditioning

stalls boxes facing the stage are preferable. Wheelchair spaces in stalls boxes are acceptable.

Central dress circle seats offer prime sightlines, with discounts compensating for an overhang that removes stage top and surtitle board views for row H back. Outer block seats lose a little to architectural intrusions. Three discounted rows run towards the stage, in front of boxes, with their end seats curving to face it. Seats D1 and 53 are avoidable, located almost behind box front protrusions.

Upper circle seats are "spaced as well as the stalls, but the front row lacks legroom". Outermost seats curve back for better viewing. Circle overhang removes surtitle and stage-top views from row K back.

The balcony is high above the stage, and front rows have safety rails in view. If concertgoers aren't concerned by rails, vertigo and limited legroom, balcony seats are a bargain. "Sound and air-conditioning are variable." Wheelchair users can transfer to some seats here.

O2 Arena

Peninsula Square, London SE10 0DX

Finally providing a commercially successful use for the Millennium Dome, the arena is the centrepiece of leisure facilities including the smaller horseshoe shaped IndigO2 auditorium, club space matter, restaurants, cinemas and exhibition spaces, with much more planned. Theatremonkey.com readers report that arriving, and particularly leaving, the centre by car or public transport requires patience when thousands do likewise simultaneously.

Initial impressions of the main arena, which hasn't been open long, are favourable – seats and legroom are comfortable throughout. The central floor area can either be filled with seats facing the stage or used as performance space. Around this is steeply banked lower-tier seating. Behind and above run two levels of private boxes. The front of the upper tier rests on these, running back almost 20 rows.

Arena seats suffer lack of rake if an end stage is used. Those seated beyond the first few rows may see less around any standing taller folk in front. With centrally staged arena events, having few rows removes this issue. Sensibly, seating isn't usually placed behind the view-blocking mixer desk.

BOX OFFICE:
0844 856 0202
0161 385 3211

ONLINE BOOKING:
www.theo2.co.uk

North Greenwich

Charlton

Beside venue.
Riverboat: to pier at arena

 20,000

 No air conditioning

Lower-tier seating is steeply banked, offering decent sightlines over the arena crowd to the stage. Part of 101 and 112 have side views but are very close. Audiences see clearly from 106 and 107, although they feel further back.

Boxes are "an experience [with] great view and sound" but "buy the closest ones". Above these, a Theatremonkey.com reader opines, "personally, I wouldn't go for the upper-tier seating – very steep and not particularly pleasant – you know it's bad when you see people coming down the steps backwards". Shorter concertgoers should also watch for seating behind row end, stairwell and aisle end rails, which all potentially intrude into sightlines.

The IndigO2's stalls are removable to provide standing. Seated events may have usual viewing problems. Balcony seats provide decent views, but watch out for front safety rails. Rear balcony standing space is reportedly good value.

Queen Elizabeth Hall & Purcell Room

South Bank, SE1 8XX

Detached from the Festival Hall itself, these share a separate building and foyer space but are under the same ticketing and programming administration. The Queen Elizabeth Hall offers flexible staging for a variety of events; the Purcell Room is suited to smaller music or prose performances.

BOX OFFICE:
0871 663 2500

ONLINE BOOKING:
www.southbankcentre.co.uk

 Waterloo

 Waterloo

 within complex area

880 (Queen Elizabeth Hall), 372 (Purcell Room)

Air conditioned

Queen Elizabeth Hall

All seats offer clear views of the stage and good acoustics. Choir spaces, facing the auditorium, can be a bargain when sold. Front stalls are gently raked, with wheelchair users offered prime views from central row A. Behind these, seats at B to M14 to 16 are equally good, and side blocks are also acceptable – row A having maximum legroom there.

Behind, rear stalls are more steeply raked. Row AA is on a wide aisle. It has excellent legroom, but isn't raised much above row M in front. Wheelchair spaces here are also less central – row A is preferable. Central rows BB to DD offer most value, though invariably all seats here are well priced. Rear rows LL back feel further from the stage and are best value at low prices for orchestral rather than visual events.

Purcell Room

Front rows A to C are not raked, but no sightline issues have been reported. Seats 6 to 19 are directly in front of the stage, 1 to 5 and 20 to 24 angle inward towards it.

The raked rear section offers clear views, good sound and an atmosphere-enhancing closeness to the stage. Central rows D to L are prime, with D having most legroom. Two wheelchair spaces at the ends of this row also offer decent views and value for money.

Royal Albert Hall

Kensington Gore, London. SW7 2AP

This stunning 1871 oval memorial to Queen Victoria's beloved husband, Albert, was lovingly refurbished in 2003.

Tiered choir stalls face the hall. The central arena provides either a stage area, audience standing space or seating. Row 6, seated, "has fantastic views and atmosphere until people in front stand up"; the Monkey also encountered this from row 11 back.

Stalls encircle the arena, with the stage often projecting a little in front of blocks G and O, placing them level with performers. Rear corners can yield worthwhile restricted-view seats when equipment blocks sightlines. Blocks J2, K1, K2 and L1 are reported to have "great sound and good views" and an occupant recommends "sitting in row 3 back, to avoid obstruction by heads of arena standees". Some seats swivel to improve viewing; all have acceptable legroom. Sound in block K can suffer occasionally. Watch also for rails here, particularly in aisle-adjacent front-row seats. The front wall may also create sightline difficulties for shorter folk at arena events. Block K offers wheelchair users average views.

Three tiers of boxes, many privately owned but sold to the public, are Monkey favourites. Those a quarter or more back from the stage have best viewing angles. Front rows offer variable legroom,

BOX OFFICE:
020 7589 8212

ONLINE BOOKING:
www.royalalberthall.com

 South Kensington

Victoria

at Imperial College

5222

Air cooled

depending on seat layout. A stool seat, usually number 5 in a five-person box, provides most. Chairs without arms may be substituted if larger concertgoers need them. Boxes 5 and 35 offer decent wheelchair viewing positions.

The circle safely cages audiences behind view-obscuring bars. Outermost blocks P and Y are sold cheaply because the circle curve restricts stage views. Legroom can be tight; seats with aisle stairs in front have most.

Beneath the roof, the promenade is a vertigo-inducing standing space with a wonderful atmosphere during concerts.

Royal Festival Hall

South Bank, SE1 8XX

Original decorative features were restored, and acoustics and audience comfort refined, during a two-year refurbishment completed in 2007. Stage height can be altered to maximise sightlines.

Removable padded choir benches, with oddly angled wooden backrests, lose nearside views looking down onto the stage. Aisle seats suffer minor rail intrusion. Choir seats are described by one Theatremonkey.com reader as "excellent, except for piano concertos – the [piano] lid deflects sound away". The wheelchair space is acceptable. Seats at B54 and D11, 12, 29, 30, 55, 56 have most legroom; elsewhere legroom is tight for those over 5ft 9in.

Front stalls from row C back are perfectly raked. The conductor's podium may be in front of central row A. Central rows R to T can be replaced by a sound desk. "G26 and 27 [are] excellent, level with the stage. Before G you have to look up slightly. Legroom is good."

BOX OFFICE:
0871 663 2500

ONLINE BOOKING:
www.southbankcentre.co.uk

Waterloo

Waterloo

within complex area

2788

Air conditioned

Side stalls are tiered shelves parallel to front stalls. Rails intrude slightly into row W and Z views. Seats at W1 to 4 and 30 to 33 are single, face the stage and are replaceable by wheelchairs. Seats at W5 to 17, 34 to 46 and X11 to 17, 40 to 46 are angled to the stage.

Rear stalls rise steeply behind front stalls. Row AA is on a wide aisle, providing excellent wheelchair positions. Behind a rail (perhaps an issue for shorter visitors), rows BB to XX are not staggered. Row SS back feels further from the stage and circle overhang is noticeable. Rear standing areas offer fair views. Legroom is acceptable for most people under 6ft tall.

Front grand-tier seats may have aisle rails in view. Sections behind offer steeply raked, clear sightlines. Outermost seats may have boxes in view. From row F, they have no adjacent aisle. Legroom is tight in rows B and C, and the stalls are generally more comfortable.

Boxes offer movable chairs and some wheelchair spaces, all with clear sideways views. A front rail may be in view for shorter concertgoers.

Royal Opera House
Bow Street, Covent Garden, London WC2E 9DD

The ornate 1858 horseshoe auditorium, with circles around and behind the stalls, was fully restored in 1999. Devoted followers are undeterred by sometimes high prices, knowing there are affordable tickets available. "The online interactive seating plan is helpful, with incredibly honest details and photographs."

Central row A stalls are cheaper with conductor in view. Seats at H1 to 6 and 27 to 32 behind stairwell walls are popular, given the slight rake (which improves further back).

Middle stalls circle and grand-tier seats offer fine sightlines, with the circle overhang clipping top stage/surtitle views only from seats in the outermost corners. Cheaper side benches are particularly prized by regulars, and the loss of stage top or rear corners is considered worthwhile for proximity to the stage.

Above, grand-tier boxes are highly regarded. Rear seats lose some view but are priced accordingly.

BOX OFFICE:
020 7304 4000

ONLINE BOOKING:
www.roh.org.uk

 Covent Garden

 Charing Cross

 Parker Street

 2257

 Air conditioned

Only rear central balcony seats are affected by overhang. Some side seats miss a quarter of the stage, with rails or pillars in view. Boxes similarly lose stage edge, and rear seats suffer most. Prices reliably reflect any issues.

The front amphitheatre provides decently priced, clear view central seats and well-priced, slightly restricted view, side ones. Further back is high: "Although far away, [row T] had great unobscured view (remembered binoculars). Legroom great." Just watch for row L behind stairwell walls.

Side lower and upper slips suffer progressively poorer views nearer the stage. Outermost upper slips see least through technical grids. Like some seats elsewhere, these may be classed "non-viewing" and sold cheaply, offered first to sight-impaired audience members. Decent wheelchair spaces are available in all circles.

The Linbury and Clore provide two simple studio theatres in addition to the main house.

Shakespeare's Globe
21 New Globe Walk, Bankside, London SE1 9DT

Sam Wanamaker's Shakespearian dream opened in 1997. As authentic as possible, it may boast better sanitary facilities and less audience debauchery – unless a production gets really dull, perhaps. Performances run from May to September, and are never cancelled solely due to the weather. Educational activities are offered all year round within permanent exhibition and studio spaces.

Three tiers of galleries encircle the ground-level yard. A 5ft-high stage projects almost a third into the centre, two pillars supporting its roof. Yard audiences surround the stage, standing in all weathers. Sitting on the ground or bringing chairs/shooting sticks is prohibited, a ban that is rigorously enforced. Unless able to stand for up to three hours, the Monkey's advice is to consider seating. Wheelchair users are also advised that seeing over the crowd may be difficult here; booking "gentlemen's room" places is preferable.

All three gallery levels are supported by numerous view-

BOX OFFICE:
020 7401 9919

ONLINE BOOKING:
www.shakespeares-globe.org

 Mansion House/
London Bridge

London Bridge

 Upper Thames Street
Riverboat: to
Bankside Pier

 881 plus up to 700
standing

 provided by prevailing
weather

intrusive pillars. However, even the worst of these merely put a foot-wide stripe through sightlines – comparable with restrictions in many other venues. The theatre accurately prices seats according to view, making selection simple.

Apart from the normal chairs in the "gentlemen's rooms", seating is on benches. One Theatremonkey.com reader (who was in the lower gallery section H, row B) advises: "Get seats in row A where you can lean forward, or E where you can lean back. Great view, but lack of back support is a problem." Cushions and back supports can be hired, but some find them ineffective.

Lower gallery patrons may also have to contend with views blocked by the heads of people standing in the yard. Upper gallery seats are not recommended for vertigo sufferers. Safety rails also intrude on views here. All seats nearer the stage may lose nearside or centre stage views to auditorium architecture or stage pillars.

Wembley Arena

Empire Way, Wembley, HA9 0DH

This arena was opened in 1934 to house events too small for the adjacent stadium. A £35m upgrade in 2006 provided new seating, restrooms, catering facilities and better acoustics than ever. Insulated black pipes, carrying perfectly chilled beer to counters around the concourse, are the final detail assisting its aim to be the absolute number 1 venue in London.

The central arena usually houses four blocks of seating, facing a stage. "About four rows back is best", if the stage is high. Fourteen or so rows behind, the usual "everyone stands therefore nobody sees" rule may kick in. Blocks C and D are stepped, "each step holding two rows. The front row on each step gets the better view. In C, this is the odd numbered row, in D, the even numbered ones." Seats (for example, C3) may be "tiered to see over the mixer desk", otherwise they're not sold.

Behind, E ("east terrace") rises steeply and spreads across the width of the building. It offers distant, but clear, views except

BOX OFFICE:
0844 815 0815
0161 385 3211

ONLINE BOOKING:
livenation.co.uk/wembley

Wembley Park

Wembley Stadium

Beside venue

12,200

No air conditioning

for the fact that rails slightly intrude for the front four rows. Rear corners often offer cheaper, good value sightlines. For central arena staged events, E is even better, and all blocks feel closer to the action. As there are fewer rows, the problem of too many heads in front is also reduced.

Along both sides of the arena run the grand tier (rows A to H) and upper tier (rows J to W). Wheelchair users enjoy superb sightlines from places in row A. Blocks N/S6 offer spectacularly close views. Tiered seating helps everybody see here; even far corners offer a clear, if neck-aching, sideways view. Least desirable, and rarely sold, are seats on the far side of entrance door walls and L200. Lowest numbered ends of blocks S/N1 and 2, when behind the stage, lose a third of the view. When sightlines are confirmed, though, last-minute bargains can be released here. Legroom throughout the venue is usually acceptable to all but the tallest people, and is least in grand-tier and upper-tier rows A and J.

Fringe Theatre Details

Equivalent to Off-Broadway and Off-Off Broadway, London has a thriving community of venues outside the West End. From the beauty of the Hackney Empire, Richmond and New Wimbledon – which share West End architects – to the innovative Almeida or intimate Blue Elephant, Bridewell, Union, Brockley Jack and Theatre 503 above a pub, the Monkey urges readers to visit all of them.

Contact details for venues are shown below, while current "What's on" listings and more information can be found at:

www.theatremonkey.com/fringetheatrenotes.htm

www.fringereport.co.uk

www.officiallondontheatre.co.uk

www.whatsonstage.com/offwestend

Above the Stag Theatre

Above the Stag Public House, 15 Bressenden Place, London SW1E 5DD

0844 478 0030   www.abovethestag.com

Albany Theatre

Douglas Way, Deptford, London SE8 4AG

020 8692 4446   www.thealbany.org.uk

Almeida Theatre

Almeida Street, Islington N1 1TA

020 7359 4404   www.almeida.co.uk

Arcola Theatre

28 Arcola Street, London E8 2DJ

020 7503 1646   www.arcolatheatre.com

Arts Depot

5 Nether Street, Tally Ho Corner, North Finchley N12 0GA

020 8369 5454   www.artsdepot.co.uk

Baron's Court Theatre

The Curtain's Up Public House, 28a Comeragh Road, Barons Court W14 9HP

020 8932 4747

Battersea Arts Centre (BAC)

Lavender Hill, Battersea SW11 5TN

020 7223 2223   www.bac.org.uk

Battersea Barge

Nine Elms Lane, Battersea SW8 5BP

020 7498 0004   www.batterseabarge.com

Bedford Pub's Globe Theatre

The Bedford Public House, 77 Bedford Hill, London SW12 9HD

020 8682 8940   www.thebedford.co.uk

Bernie Grant Arts Centre

Town Hall Approach Road, London N15 4RX

020 8365 5450

www.berniegrantcentre.co.uk

Bloomsbury Theatre

15 Gordon Street, WC1H OAH

020 7388 8822   www.thebloomsbury.com

Blue Elephant Theatre

59a Bethwin Road, Camberwell SE5 OXT

020 7701 0100

www.blueelephanttheatre.co.uk

Brick Lane Music Hall

443 North Woolwich Road E16 2DA

020 7511 6655

www.brick-lane-music-hall.co.uk

Bridewell Theatre

Bride Lane, London EC4Y 8EQ

020 7353 3331   www.bridewelltheatre.org

Broadway Theatre and Studio

Rushey Green, Catford SE6 4RU

020 8690 0002

www.broadwaytheatre.org.uk

Brockley Jack Theatre

410 Brockley Road, Brockley SE4 2DH

0844 847 2454   www.brockleyjack.co.uk

Bush Theatre

Sheperds Bush Green, London W12 8QD

020 8743 5050   www.bushtheatre.co.uk

Camden People's Theatre

58-60 Hampstead Road, London NW1 2PY

08700 600 100   www.cptheatre.co.uk

Canal Café Theatre
Delamere Terrace, Little Venice W2 6ND
020 7289 6054   www.canalcafetheatre.com

Chelsea Theatre
World's End Place, King's Road SW10 0DR
020 7349 7811   www.chelseatheatre.org.uk

Chicken Shed Theatre
Chase Side, Southgate, London N14 4PE
020 8292 9222   www.chickenshed.org.uk

Churchill Theatre, Bromley
High Street, Bromley, Kent BR1 1HA
0870 060 6620 www.ambassadortickets.com

Cockpit Theatre
Gateforth Street, London NW8 8EH
020 7258 2925   www.cockpittheatre.org.uk

Courtyard Theatre
Hoxton, 40 Pitfield Street N1 6EU
0870 163 0717   www.thecourtyard.org.uk

Drill Hall
16 Chenies Street, London WC1E 7EX
020 7307 5060   www.drillhall.co.uk

Edward Alderton Theatre
5 Brampton Road, Bexleyheath, Kent DA7 4EZ
020 8301 5584   www.edwardalderton.org

Etcetera Theatre
above the Oxford Arms Pub,
265 Camden High Street, London NW1 7BU
020 7482 4857   www.etceteratheatre.com

Finborough Theatre
118 Finborough Road, London SW10 9ED
0870 4000 838
www.finboroughtheatre.co.uk

Gate Theatre
11 Pembridge Road,
Notting Hill Gate W11 3HQ
020 7229 0706   www.gatetheatre.co.uk

Greenwich Theatre
Crooms Hill, Greenwich SE10 8ES
020 8858 7755
www.greenwichtheatre.org.uk

Hackney Empire
291 Mare Street, London E8 1EJ
020 8985 2424   www.hackneyempire.co.uk

Hampstead Theatre
Eton Avenue, Swiss Cottage NW3 3EU
020-7722-9301 www.hampsteadtheatre.com

Hen and Chickens
109 St Pauls Road, Highbury Corner N1 2NA
020 7704 2001   www.unrestrictedview.co.uk

Institute of Contemporary Arts (ICA) Theatre
The Mall, London SW1Y 5AH
020 7930 3647   www.ica.org.uk

Jacksons Lane Theatre
269a Archway Road, Highgate, London N6 5AA
020 8341 4421   www.jacksonslane.org.uk

Jermyn Street Theatre
16b Jermyn Street, London SW1Y 6ST
020 7287 2875
www.jermynstreettheatre.com

Kenneth More Theatre
Oakfield Road, Ilford, Essex IG1 1BT
020 8553 4466
www.kenneth-more-theatre.co.uk

King's Head Theatre
115 Upper Street, Islington N1 1QN
0844 209 0326 (agency)
www.kingsheadtheatre.org

Landor Theatre
Landor Pub, Landor Road SW9 9PH
020 7737 7276   www.landortheatre.co.uk

Little Angel Theatre
14 Dagmar Passage, Off Cross Street, Islington N1 2DN
020 7226 1787   www.littleangeltheatre.com

Lyric Hammersmith
Kings Mall, King St W6 0QL
0871 221 1729   www.lyric.co.uk

Menier Chocolate Factory

53 Southwark Street, London SE1 1RU

020 7907 7060 (agency)

www.menierchocolatefactory.com

New End Theatre

27 New End, Hampstead NW3 1JD

0870 0332733   www.newendtheatre.co.uk

New Wimbledon Theatre

Broadway, Wimbledon SW19 1QG

0870 060 6646 www.ambassadortickets.com

Old Red Lion Theatre

418 St John Street, London EC1V 4NJ

020 7837 7816 www.oldredliontheatre.co.uk

Orange Tree Theatre

1 Clarence Street, Richmond, Surrey TW9 2SA

020 8940 3633

www.orangetreetheatre.co.uk

Oval House Theatre

52-54 Kenington Oval, London SE11 5SW

020 7582 7680   www.ovalhouse.com

Pentameters Theatre

28 Heath Street, London NW3 6TE

020 7435 3648   www.pentameters.co.uk

People's Show Theatre

Pollard Row, Bethnal Green, E2 6NB

020 7729 1841   www.peopleshow.co.uk

Pleasance Theatre

Carpenters Mews, North Road, London N7 9EF

020 7609 1800   www.pleasance.co.uk

Putney Arts Theatre

Ravenna Road, Putney, London SW15 6AW

020 8788 6943

www.putneyartstheatre.org.uk

Richmond Theatre

The Green, Richmond, Surrey TW9 1QJ

0870 060 6651 www.ambassadortickets.com

Riverside Studios

Crisp Road, Hammersmith W6 9RL

020 8237 1111 www.riversidestudios.co.uk

Roundhouse Theatre

Chalk Farm Road, London NW1 8EH

0844 482 8008   www.roundhouse.org.uk

Rosemary Branch

2 Shepperton Road, London N1 3DT

020 7704 6665   www.rosemarybranch.co.uk

Rose Theatre

24-26 High Street, Kingston KT1 1HL

0871 230 1552 www.rosetheatrekingston.org

Sadler's Wells & Lilian Baylis Theatres

Rosebery Avenue, London EC1R 4TN

0844 412 4300   www.sadlerswells.com

Soho Theatre

21 Dean Street, London W1D 3NE

020 7478 0100   www.sohotheatre.com

Southwark Playhouse

Shipwright Yard, London SE1 2TF

0844 847 1656 (agency)

www.southwarkplayhouse.co.uk

Tabard Theatre

2 Bath Road, London W4 1LW

08701 696 805 (agency)

www.tabardtheatre.co.uk

Tara Studio

356 Garratt Lane, Earlsfield SW18 4ES

020 8333 4457   www.tara-arts.com

Theatre503

503 Battesrea Park Road, Battersea SW11 3BW

020 7978 7040   www.theatre503.com

Theatre Royal Stratford East

Gerry Raffles Square, Stratford E15 1BN

020 8534 0310   www.stratfordeast.com

Theatro Technis

26 Crowndale Road, London NW1 1TT

020 7387 6617   www.theatrotechnis.com

Tricycle Theatre

269 Kilburn High Road, London NW6 7JR

020 7328 1000   www.tricycle.co.uk

Unicorn Theatre

147 Tooley Street, More London,
Southwark SE1 2HZ

020 7645 0560   www.unicorntheatre.com

Union Theatre

204 Union Street, London SE1 0LX

020 7261 9876   www.uniontheatre.org

Upstairs at the Gatehouse

The Gatehouse Pub, Highgate Village N6 4BD

020 8340 3488

                www.upstairsatthegatehouse.com

Warehouse Theatre

Dingwall Road, Croydon CR0 2NF

020 8680 4060

                www.warehousetheatre.co.uk

Watford Palace Theatre

Clarendon Road, Watford WD17 1JZ

01923 225671   www.watfordtheatre.co.uk

White Bear Theatre Club

138 Kennington Park Road,
Kennington SE11 4DJ

020 7793 9193 www.whitebeartheatre.co.uk

Wilton's Music Hall

Graces Alley, Off Ensign Street,
London E1 8JB

020 7702 2789   www.wiltons.org.uk

Finally, two other important music venues in London are:

Cadogan Hall

Sloane Terrace, London SW1X 9DQ

020 7730 4500 www.cadoganhall.com

Wigmore Hall

36 Wigmore Street, London W1U 2BP

020 7935 2141 www.wigmore-hall.org.uk

Further Reading

Andrews, R. 2007. *The London Theatre Guide*. Metro Publications.

Aston, M. 1997. *The Cinemas of Camden*. London Borough of Camden, Leisure and Community Services.

Barson, S., Kendall, D., Longman, P. & Smith, J. 2003. *Scene/Unseen: London's West End Theatres*. English Heritage.

Bergan, R., Karney, R. & Burnard, J. 2004. *The Great Theatres of London*. Andre Deutsch.

Elms, S. (Ed.) 1985. *The London Theatre Scene*. Frank Cook Publications.

Eyles, A. 1998. *The Granada Theatres*. BFI Publishing.

Gee, L. 2008. *Stage Mum*. Hutchinson.

Kilburn, M. (Foreword, Zoe Wanamaker) 2008. *London's Theatres*. New Holland Publishers.

Macqueen-Pope, W. J. 1947. *An Indiscreet Guide to Theatreland*. Muse Arts.

Poynton, K. (Ed.) 2008. *Contacts*. Spotlight

Public Information Exchange, 2008. *Blue Badge Parking Guide for London*. PIE Guides

Reischel, J. (Foreword, Leslie Bricusse) 2007. *So You Want to Tread The Boards*. JR Books.

Richmond House Publishing, 2007. *The Original British Theatre Directory* (2007). www.rhpco.co.uk

Shenton, M. & Foss, R. 2004. *Harden's Theatregoers' Handbook*. Harden's.

Society of London Theatre (SOLT). 2004. *Access Guide to London's Theatres*. SOLT.

Acknowledgements

Thanks first to Henry, Theatremonkey.com reader and publisher who suggested this venture. Without him, this book would have contained even more dubious jokes. Frances for editing, particularly where it involved bananas, Martin for the fine seating plans.

To Mark for his introduction piece, of course.

Key people in Theatremonkey's history: Don, whose computer-building skills first provided a basis for the whole thing, and Victor and the team at PC Express Limited (www.pcexpress.co.uk), who now provide the vital skills needed to keep Theatremonkey hardware functioning.

Special and important are UK friends David and Tanya and transatlantic ones Brian and Sharon, whose unstinting kindness, opinions, advice and encouragement at the start of this project, and always, is invaluable.

David, Helen, Jen, Jonathon and Philippa for graphics and quotation permissions. Philip and team at London Opera Glasses Company for location details.

To those within "the business", and the countless internet-surfing guests whose contributions grew the site beyond all possible expectations and made this book what it is. Impossible to name everybody, but if the few can represent the many: Ashley, Chris, Edmund, Jake, Rachel, Simon, Thibaud – constant thanks. Abbie, Adam, Ahmet, Alexandra, Alf, Alun, Andrew, Andy, Asa, Asti, Barfly, Barry, Ben, Berni, Bryan, Carl, Carol, Charlotte, Cheryl, Christian, Christina, Colin, Cristopher, Daniel, Danielle, David, Dawn, Denise, Edythe, Elizabeth, Francesca, Frankie, Gavin, Gemma, Graham, Hannah, Harriet, Hazel, Helen, Ian, James, Jane, Jaz, Jenny, Jessica, Jim, Jo, John, Jos, Joseph, Joshua, Judy, Jules, Julius, Keith, Kevin, Kirsty, Lee, Lesley, Liam, Lisa, Lizzie, Lyn, Mark, Martin, Mary, Michael, Mila, Monika, Murray, Niall, Nev, Patrick, Paul, Peter, Phongpan P, Pip, Queenie, Rebekah, Richard, Rob, Rochelle, Rowena, Rupi, Sally, Sam, Sandrine, Sara, Sarah, Sharon, Simon, Steve, Steven, Stuart, Sue, Talabi, Tanya, Teresa, Terri, Terry, Tim, Tom, Tony, Tracey, Trevor, Truds, Verine, Wayne, William, Wim, Xanthe, Zena. Thanks for your time and email.

Finally, and absolutely not least, those unsung but vital folk who assist the public in box offices and telephone rooms, front of house and elsewhere to make each visit special. This last round of applause is for you.

Map

OTHER VENUES

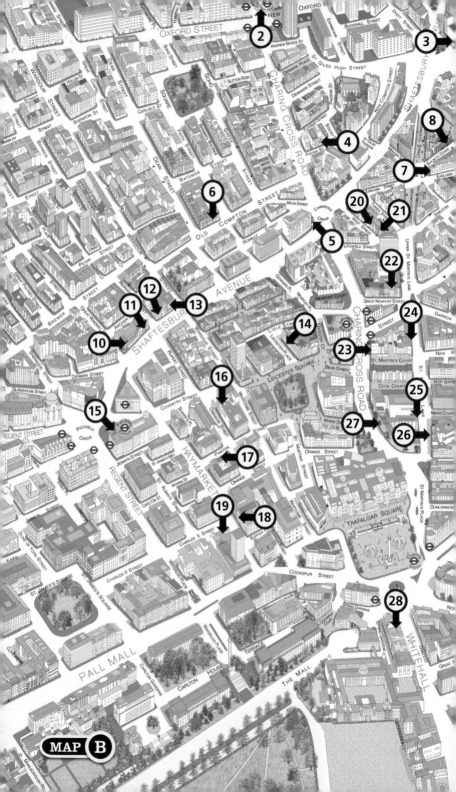

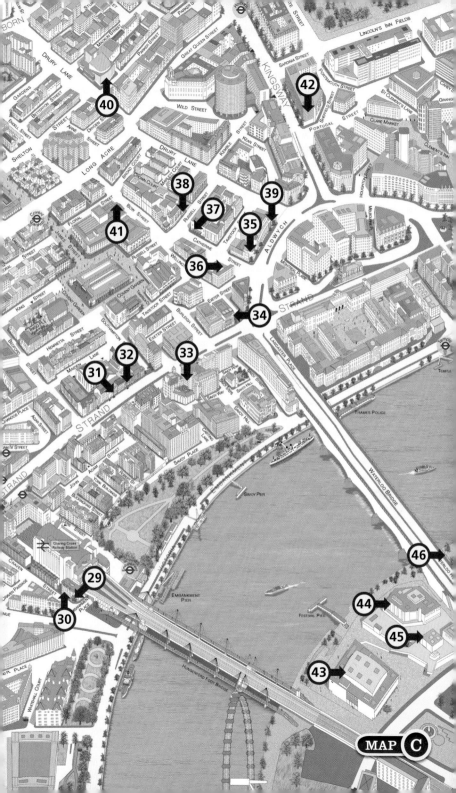

MAP **C**